A Psychoanalytic Theory of Infantile Experience

Eugenio Gaddini (1916–85) was a pioneer within the Italian psycho-analytical movement. His research into psychic conflicts in adult patients led him to realize that most archaic and primitive mental processes were close to body functions. Focusing his researches on the psychophysical syndromes of early infancy, he then sought to determine which particular functions contribute to the creation of the mind.

For this edited collection of Gaddini's papers, Dr Adam Limentani has selected those covering three main themes: imitation, which Gaddini saw as a central factor in early development; ego formation – the processes of instinctual drive arousal and the awareness of separateness from the object; and the way the body becomes meaningful to the mind through the elaboration of primitive defensive fantasies. In each paper Gaddini supports his hypotheses with ample clinical material. Dr Limentani's interpretative and explanatory introduction discusses what Gaddini and Winnicott had in common and where they differed; the points of contact and difference with Kleinian theories; Gaddini's view of imitation in the development of the mind; and his approach to psychosomatic medicine. Above all Limentani stresses Gaddini's originality and independence of thought.

For analysts unfamiliar with Gaddini's work, this book will open unexpected vistas on perennial and familiar issues to do with the organization of infantile mental life. His ideas have wide-ranging implications for the understanding of child and adult psychopathology and its therapeutic treatment.

Adam Limentani is a training and supervising analyst of the British Psycho-Analytical Society, and a Fellow of the Royal College of Psychiatry, London.

The New Library of Psychoanalysis was launched in 1987 in association with the Institute of Psycho-Analysis, London. Its purpose is to facilitate a greater and more widespread appreciation of what psychoanalysis is really about and to provide a forum for increasing mutual understanding between psychoanalysts and those working in other disciplines such as history, linguistics, literature, medicine, philosophy, psychology, and the social sciences. It is intended that the titles selected for publication in the series should deepen and develop psychoanalytic thinking and technique, contribute to psychoanalysis from outside, or contribute to other disciplines from a psychoanalytical perspective.

The Institute, together with the British Psycho-Analytical Society, runs a low-fee psychoanalytic clinic, organizes lectures and scientific events concerned with psychoanalysis, publishes the *International Journal of Psycho-Analysis* and the *International Review of Psycho-Analysis*, and runs the only training course in the UK in psychoanalysis leading to membership of the International Psychoanalytical Association – the body which preserves internationally agreed standards of training, of professional entry, and of professional ethics and practice for psychoanalysis as initiated and developed by Sigmund Freud. Distinguished members of the Institute have included Michael Balint, Wilfred Bion, Ronald Fairbairn, Anna Freud, Ernest Jones, Melanie Klein, John Rickman, and Donald Winnicott.

Volumes 1–11 in the series have been prepared under the general editorship of David Tuckett, with Ronald Britton and Eglé Laufer as associate editors. Subsequent volumes are under the general editorship of Elizabeth Bott Spillius, with Christopher Bollas, David Taylor, and Rosine Jozef Perelberg as associate editors.

IN THE SAME SERIES

NEW LIBRARY OF PSYCHOANALYSIS
16

General editor: Elizabeth Bott Spillius

A Psychoanalytic Theory of Infantile Experience

Conceptual and Clinical Reflections

E. GADDINI

Edited by
ADAM LIMENTANI

Foreword by Robert S. Wallerstein

TAVISTOCK/ROUTLEDGE
LONDON AND NEW YORK

First published in 1992
by Routledge
11 New Fetter Lane, London EC4P 4EE

Simultaneously published in the USA and Canada
by Routledge
a division of Routledge, Chapman and Hall Inc.
29 West 35th Street, New York, NY 10001

Typeset in Bembo by LaserScript, Mitcham, Surrey
Printed in Great Britain by
Mackays of Chatham PLC, Chatham, Kent

British Library Cataloguing in Publication Data
A catalogue record for this book is available from the British Library.

Library of Congress Cataloging in Publication Data
Gaddini, Eugenio.
A psychoanalytic theory of infantile experience: conceptual and
clinical reflections/E. Gaddini; edited by Adam Limentani;
foreword by R. Wallerstein.
p. cm. – (New library of psychoanalysis; 16)
Includes bibliographical references and index.
1. Cognition in infants. 2. Psychoanalysis. I. Limentani, Adam.
II. Title. III. Series.
BF720.C63G33   1992
155.42'23 – dc20   92-1035
                          CIP

ISBN 0–415–07434–7
     0–415–07435–5 (pbk)

Contents

Foreword

ROBERT S. WALLERSTEIN, MD

It has become a psychoanalytic commonplace that the past two decades have witnessed the true internationalization of psychoanalysis and its literature, with an increasing worldwide acceptance of, and accommodation to, our psychoanalytic diversity, or pluralism, as we have come to call it – a multiple pluralism, in fact, of theoretical perspectives, of linguistic and thought conventions, and of distinctive regional, cultural, social, and language emphases. A major aspect and vehicle of that process of spreading dissemination and accommodation has been both the increasing discourse across regional (or national) and theoretical boundaries through personal scientific interchanges and visits, and also the increasing translation, especially into English, of the work of prominent psychoanalytic contributors from the other major and official IPA language areas, French, German, and Spanish.

What has, however, to this point occurred far less, is the dissemination of conceptions about psychoanalytic theory and praxis from those numerous enough languages spoken in but one psychoanalytically populated country, of which Italian and the Italian psychoanalytic literature is of course the most substantial and vigorous exemplar. Psychoanalysts writing in those single nation languages who hope to relate to, and to influence, the worldwide psychoanalytic community, are caught in the dilemma of somehow appropriately dividing their psychoanalytic contributions into those articles directed to their immediate colleagues and countrymen in their own national psychoanalytic journal in their native tongue, and those articles directed to the far larger external psychoanalytic world, most often written in English and directed to the *International Journal* and the *International Review of Psycho-Analysis*.

Eugenio Gaddini was an illustrious member of that small group of Italian psychoanalysts who enthusiastically undertook this challenge.

vii

The collection of thirteen of his papers, about half re-published from a span of over two decades of the *International Journal*, and the other half, spanning the same time frame, but newly translated from Italian and now published in English for the first time, all lovingly brought together and placed into a logical ordering by his long-time close friend and colleague, Adam Limentani of London – and with a beautifully interpretative and explanatory long introduction by Limentani – attests superbly to the success with which Gaddini played out his chosen role, as the interpreter back and forth between the Italian and the worldwide psychoanalytic communities.

What is revealed by Gaddini's papers, brought together in this way from two languages, and sequenced with a logic expounded clearly by Limentani, is a truly significant corpus of cumulative contribution to our conceptions of the earliest phases of infantile mental development and the lifelong reflections of these formulations in the various arenas of child and adult psychopathology and in the issues for therapeutic technique that derive from those perspectives. Here Gaddini poses for the English-speaking, and particularly the American, audience a variety of conceptions, most of them highly original and interesting, others perhaps seemingly old-fashioned and maybe even somewhat outdated, in what has now come to be called the modern post-ego psychological era in psychoanalysis.

The ideas that may sound anachronistic today are indeed the far fewer in number, and they stem from Gaddini's firm anchoring in Freud's classical metapsychology, with his especial continuing adherence to the economic-energic-quantitative metapsychological point of view. Within this framework Gaddini formulates his own conception – and here, differently from Freud – of the temporal primacy of the aggressive drives with their primary orientation outward, over the libidinal, with their putative original orientation self-directed and inward, with their various combined vicissitudes then of successful fusion or not in the maturational and experiential unfolding of a normal or abnormal developmental process. In describing this interplay, with the libidinal always subsequent to and leaning upon the aggressive, Gaddini's formulations are novel and do pique speculative interest, however much we do or no longer subscribe to the drive-energic framework within which these formulations are cast.

For the rest – and it is indeed the great majority – Gaddini's conceptions will strike the reader unfamiliar with his work as inventive and highly original (and modern-sounding) conceptions, that invite us to fresh vistas upon perennial and familiar issues. His chosen conceptual domain is that of the organization of infantile mental life, and he grounds his ideas very clearly in, or at least links them very closely to, the theorizing of Melanie Klein – though he also gives a detailed and thoughtful critique of the reach but also the limitations, as he sees them, of Kleinian technique – Winnicott, and, to a very substantial and surprising degree, Greenacre. There is also clearly discernible a real linkage, though not made as explicit, to the developmental conceptions of Mahler, including the idea of the gradual psychic evolution, post-partum and over time, to what Gaddini calls the 'basic mental organization' (BMO) of infancy which marks (his words) the 'psychological birth' of the infant.

Within this overall matrix, then, Gaddini develops a whole series of linked conceptions and formulations, building incrementally one upon another; of imitation as a primitive process of creating perceptual identity in a first psychosensory developmental phase, and as antecedent to the next psycho-oral phase of introjection (incorporation), leading ultimately through processes of intermingling and fusion of these trends to developmentally mature identifications; of (more broadly) what he calls the body–mind continuum, with the evolution of the physiological response state through to mental symbolic activity (of 'needs' evolving to 'wishes') and concomitantly of psychophysical syndromes of a sensorial nature evolving to psychopathological syndromes of an objectual or object-relational nature (with correlated psychosomatic and psychological syndrome examples); of the progression in fantasy formation from fantasies *in* the body, to fantasies on the body, to fantasies divorced from the body; of the similar progression from loss-of-self anxiety, through the oscillations of non-integration and integration anxiety, to, ultimately, the object-related anxieties of the psychoneurotic state. Most interesting of all perhaps, during the phase of triangulation leading into the Oedipal process, the issues of what Gaddini calls 'father formation', in which he distinguishes between the initially 'extraneous father' who intrudes upon the mother–infant duo from outside and evolves, if all proceeds reasonably well, into the 'external father' of the Oedipus complex; distinguishing that psychologically from mother who is gradually differentiated by the child from the originally undifferentiated unity into the 'external' Oedipal mother – and the implications of this distinction in origin for the unfolding developmental dynamic.

And Gaddini by no means leaves all of these provocative (and speculative?) ideas on the understanding of the developmental process resting in the air for us. He does essay in several chapters to develop their implications for our understandings of child and adult psychopathology and its psychoanalytic therapeutic amelioration. He develops in this the conceptions of what he considers to be a pre-instinctual 'magical imitative transference' or 'transference of need' (as distinguished from a transference of wish or of desire) where verbal interpretations may prove completely ineffective and where recourse to the 'holding' conceptions of Winnicott (with echoes of the 'empathic immersions' of Kohut) is vigorously advocated. And at a number of points throughout the book, Gaddini further elaborates his ideas of these 'imitative transferences' (which unhappily characterize not only specific kinds of patients, but as well specific kinds of psycho-analytic candidates who seek to 'become' analysts without having to 'be' analysts or 'be analysed') as defences against object-related trans-ferences and as barriers against true internalizations and identifications, upon which, after all, all analytical processes depend.

This of course is all just a naming of Gaddini's various quite original conceptions which are laid out for us in this valuable new book. Limentani's introduction defines and spells them out eloquently and places them then as cumulative building blocks in a very distinctive view of psychoanalytic theory and praxis. For the full immersion in Gaddini's creative thinking and in his very particular contribution to the total worldwide psychoanalytic corpus, the reader will have to repair to all the chapters in this book. It is a pleasure to help introduce this, the essence of Gaddini's life *oeuvre*, in unified form, and reunited into one language, to the English-speaking psychoanalytic audience.

Acknowledgements

I am greatly indebted to Professor Renata De Benedetti Gaddini, Dr Andrea Gaddini, and Ms M. Mascagni for their help in organizing the bibliography, but particularly for providing me with a great deal of information concerning the author's thinking and conceptualizations. I can only express my admiration for the work of Mr Philip Slotkin who translated Chapters 3, 4, 6, 7, 8, 11, 12, and 13. I am very grateful to Mrs E. Spillius for her support, guidance, advice, and helpful suggestions in preparing this book. Finally, I wish to thank Miss Nancy Dunlop for her patience as well as her invaluable contribution in preparing the manuscript.

Introduction

ADAM LIMENTANI

In the course of an informal discussion with some colleagues in 1985, shortly before his unexpected death, Eugenio Gaddini was asked what was his special field of interest in psychoanalysis. His spontaneous reply was as follows:

> I must say that when I became deeply involved with psychoanalysis I was particularly interested in the primitive perceptions as described by Fenichel. At the time I understood that these were not really perceptions but rather that they were sensations. The movements from sensations to perceptions, as I saw it, led me to understand the importance of mental development in relation to the early primitive body development. I was also impressed with the extent to which the development of bodily functions conditions the mind, creating models of functioning which we later discover at the mental level. This created my interest in the study of movements from sensations to perceptions on which I am still working on the basis of the clinical material which I have accumulated. I think there is still a lot of work to be done.

Here we have a clear statement from a man who throughout his life showed a combination of scientific intuition and a tendency to put forward a hypothesis with the determination to explore it, no matter how long that might take, and no matter where it would lead. The readers of these essays can also safely expect that clinical evidence in support of such hypotheses will be forthcoming. This is in keeping with his belief that there could be no research in psychoanalysis without clinical reference, a point he stressed in his introduction to the Italian edition of *The Work of Melanie Klein* by H. Segal. There he wrote: 'In psychoanalysis research work is indistinguishable from therapeutic activity. Therapy is in itself research, and vice versa.' On another

1

occasion he referred to psychoanalysis as a process through which, from a subjective knowledge of the self, one reaches the maximum possible objective knowledge of it.

With a solid medical background behind him, he felt free to criticize those psychoanalysts who turned to psychiatry in order to find a safe base against their feelings of insecurity. He did not, however, reject biological findings, as they have been forthcoming in recent times. On the contrary, those who were close to him knew that he was trying to explore how these new findings could relate to his theories and whether and how his theories might need to be modified. To put it simply, amongst his primary concerns was an interest in the mental sense of the biological, in the way the mind comes to understand the body.

The Italian edition of his collected papers runs into over 800 pages, covering a variety of interests from metapsychology in itself, to its application to clinical work and to critical essays on art and writers. Some 200 pages comprise his original clinical notes which form the background for his theoretical discussions. His thought is original, his prose style compacted, and his theorizing is inevitably speculative, for it concerns a construction of what babies think and feel, a matter about which we have even less direct evidence than usual since babies cannot talk. Nevertheless, Gaddini's theories are of great clinical relevance for the treatment of adult patients, particularly in the understanding of psychosomatic disorders and in the identification of mechanisms involving fusion and imitation used as defences against awareness of separateness and dependence.

For this collection I have chosen the most significant papers that cover three major themes: imitation, which Gaddini considers to be a central factor in early development; the process of instinctual drive arousal, ego formation, and awareness of separateness from the object; and the way the body becomes meaningful to the mind.

Interspersed through the writings there are numerous hypotheses (sometimes described by Gaddini as 'useful fictions' rather than hypotheses) concerning the working of the infant's mind, and associated with reports of direct observations of children. Although he was not engaged in the treatment of children it is clear that he took every opportunity to observe infants. In this respect he took full advantage of the fact that he worked closely with his wife, Renata De Benedetti, a paediatrician who subsequently took up psychoanalysis. The rich exchanges arising from their close interaction have found their way into several papers written together and separately. An early investigation carried out in collaboration, 'On rumination in infants' (1959), illustrates very clearly Gaddini's capacity for combining biology and psychoanalytic theory.

2

Rumination in infants is a fairly rare condition, also known as merecysm, which can occur as early as eight weeks. It affects the alimentary system as a form of regurgitation, when previously swallowed food is re-chewed and re-swallowed. The symptom, as revealed by this investigation, shows that the infant is capable of learning and remembering during this early stage of development. In the presence of maternal failure in nurturing, the infant learns to stimulate the hard palate with one or two fingers to bring back into the mouth the milk he has just ingested. In the course of extensive observations, backed by photographic records, it was apparent that the infant was in a state of continuous tension which found temporary relief in the bodily experience of rumination, as shown by its ecstatic smile the moment the milk appeared in the mouth. The assumption is that this activity is accompanied by a fantasy in which the baby *imitates* the milk-giving activity which the mother had withdrawn from him. The regurgitation has all the characteristics of being self-protective and it occurs as a response to inadequate mothering, in itself due to emotional factors in the mother. The result of the investigation, linked with work with the mothers on the provision of adequate mothering, greatly reduced the mortality which was quite prevalent in these cases.

I have dwelt on this aspect of the author's researches at length because readers will find frequent references to it, such was the impact of these observations on his subsequent work on somatic disorders and the body–mind question. But first I shall briefly state his position *vis-à-vis* the infant who, he feels, cannot distinguish between self and non-self after nine months inside mother. For several months the infant will be unable to notice the difference between self and environment. A part of what the infant believes is his body is in reality mother's body. If a baby is hungry a breast appears, but he does not know it is not his. In fact, all that is around is a product of magical omnipotence. If all is well the present experience is not unlike intra-uterine life. The difference, though, is that learning capacity begins at birth, whereas in intra-uterine life, the development of the foetus and its behaviour are biologically pre-ordained. It follows that memory *in utero* is not necessary, so it is unlikely that we remember that time of our life.

Gaddini believed that it was pathology which was most enlightening. The appearance of skin disorders, asthma, and so on in childhood may appear to be casual, but he believed that they are pre-determined through the mental meanings assigned to physical sensations and their role in preserving the integrity of the self. Before the perception of the external world gains mental significance, external stimuli are assimilated through the physical sensations they produce, resulting in changes in the body which are noted and remembered. The earliest mental organization is still fragmentary, primarily taken up with bodily sensations and needs, especially the need to keep the fragments together by keeping them assembled within a boundary. Survival is the peremptory aim, and the non-self is appraised in the light of the subject's first experiences of being rudimentarily aware of being separate. Atopical dermatitis is likely to develop at about four to six months of age (at the time when some awareness of separation is developmentally appropriate) if the subject cannot face awareness of such separateness. The skin disturbance proclaims awareness, through contact, of the skin as the limit of the self, and expresses the feeling of mental break-up of the self through the break-up in that boundary part of the body.

His researches on the function of the skin in early development were close to those of the Kleinian analyst Esther Bick, who wrote about the disturbance in the primal skin function leading to the development of a second skin formation. There were essential differences, though, as in her conceptualization; the dependence on the object is replaced by pseudo-independence through the inappropriate use of certain mental functions for the purpose of creating a substitute for the skin container function (Bick 1968).

Gaddini's work 'On imitation' (1969), which brought him considerable acclaim, is much more comprehensive than Bick's, showing considerable perspicacity in insisting on the importance of distinguishing between imitation and identification. He thought that imitation was a basic defence and, like all defences, part of ordinary development, normally leading to identification through the integration of imitation with introjections which is essentially an oral mechanism. Frustrations, especially at the oral level, can lead to pathology like rumination, in which, as we have seen, the baby imitates the feeding function of the frustrating mother. Precocious conditions of oral frustrations cause disturbances in the psycho-oral area and, more precisely, in the introjective mechanisms. This results in the activity of imitating introjections which can substitute for true introjection. By imitating one magically becomes the external object but unhappily this will not lead to internalization. To be is not to have. What is lost can therefore be spuriously maintained, a fact that should not be ignored when analysing separation.

It should be understood that although imitation is an essential element of the structure of identification (as is introjection), it expresses a basic disposition towards the object. The avoidance of introjection by using imitation as a defence may be a way of defending oneself against the anxiety provoked by introjective conflicts. Finally, in the process of identification, imitations and introjections are fused and integrated in the service of the aims of adaptation and of the reality principle. 'Being' and 'having' are integrated, which leads to 'identity'; that is, to a true sense of being 'oneself', separate from but related to the 'other'.

The suggestion that the pathology of imitation will show us how in some instances, *perceiving* the object is experienced as *being* the object, has far-reaching implications. Some of these ideas will allow us to modify our conceptualization in the case of many sexual disorders where we often speak of 'faulty identification', disturbances of identity, and so on – whereas we should consider the presence of imitations.

This is the first chapter in this collection. In the last one, 'Changes in psychoanalytic patients', written in 1984, Gaddini extends some of his conclusions in the area of imitation to the training of psycho-analysts. There he expresses concern about the possibility that training can lead to the creation of a host of imitators rather than true psycho-analysts with their own sense of identity, a concern shared by the majority of those involved in psychoanalytic education. This chapter begins with the challenging statement that the potential relationships of patients with their therapists are mediated by the culture of the society in which they live. Patients, having been involved in psychoanalysis, soon begin to spread what they have grasped of it. Before long many people become something of an analyst. In some instances the imita-tion goes so far as to lead these people to call themselves 'psycho-analysts' as a result of a variety of training experiences when the only title that could be bestowed upon them would be that of impostors. As a result of the spreading of psychotherapy, the task of selection com-mittees across the world has become very hard, and in some instances it has led to the motto, 'Everyone can be a psychoanalyst'. This is the wisdom of unwisdom in selection, but we are warned, 'Look at what happened to Lacan's followers', who were in due course rejected by the master. The chapter contains some interesting critiques of develop-ments by Hartmann, Winnicott, and Klein when views are presented clearly without bias or animosity.

In his own metapsychological thinking, Gaddini's early papers are in some respects close to Klein, though always with his own highly original construction. Thus, for example, in the first three chapters of the present collection, published between 1969 and 1972, he regards *imitation* ('to be') and *introjection* ('to have') as simultaneous processes which gradually develop and become integrated into *'identification'*. (This process of 'identification' is similar to Klein's idea of the 'depres-sive position', though this is not a conception that Gaddini uses, and he certainly does not conceive of the earlier unintegrated period of development in terms of Klein's 'paranoid-schizoid' position.) The 'introjection' side of Gaddini's idea of dual development into 'identification' is consistent with Klein's view of there being an early rudimentary ego and early fantasies of introjection, projection, and so on. Gradually, however, Gaddini came to view imitation and 'imitative identity' as characteristic of an early phase from birth to six months (see Chapter 11) of 'non-integration' in whch sensations of contact are used magically to induce a sense of self and in which there is at first no perception, no instinctual drive, no ego, and no awareness of objects or of dependence on them. Such awareness comes about gradually through a process of '*detachment*', from the fourth to the sixth month (see especially Chapter 11). This formulation owes much to Winnicott, though its delineation, especially the emphasis on imitation and on sensations of sensual contact, are Gaddini's own.

Quite apart from changes in those who practise psychoanalysis, Gaddini draws our attention to the fact that besides the innovation of treating children, as introduced by Anna Freud and Melanie Klein, there has been a readier acceptance of characterological problems and disorders of personality in our patients. Further innovations have also been brought about by renewed interest in enquiries into early infancy by Winnicott, Greenacre, and the author himself, as well as into aggression, especially by Kleinian writers.

The issues around a psychoanalytic theory of aggression were at the centre of Gaddini's interest in the early 1970s. In 'Aggression and the pleasure principle' (1972a) and in the intriguingly titled 'Beyond the death instinct' (1972b) (Chapters 2 and 3) he reviews the concept of energy. His hypothesis at this time is that aggressive energy is present and operating in the infant from birth, qualitatively different from the libidinal energy and by nature primarily directed towards the external world. Indeed there are many points in Gaddini's writing where he uses the word 'instinctual' to mean aggressive energy primarily directed outwards on to objects. I should stress here that he thinks of libido as inward-directed. The aggressive energy can be discharged outwards by the infant organism through the striated muscular apparatus, whereas inward discharge takes place through smooth muscles, vessels, and mucous membranes. Here Gaddini reveals his disagreement with the majority of analysts on two points. First, he challenges the view that relief from tension is equal to pleasure, as some states of tension can be pleasurable, suggesting a different quality of energy at work. Second, he disagrees with the general view that aggressivity follows the libido outward. His contention here is that aggressive energy must be discharged outwardly immediately, otherwise the internal structures would suffer. Having noted some contradictions in the *pleasure principle theory*, he reminds us of a little-known letter written by Freud to Marie Bonaparte in which Freud expressed the opinion that it was the aggression that was object-related in the first instance, and not the libido. As a consequence, the libido, which Gaddini insists is basically internally orientated, is dragged out by the aggression which has been directed at an external object and is fused with it. This suggestion, quickly doubted by Freud himself, provides support for Gaddini's claim that our views concerning the early relationship between aggression and libido need to be reconsidered. In the present writer's view, there is a great deal to be commended for this novel conceptualization which would provide us with a fresh contribution to the understanding of some cases of sexual deviations associated with violence.

Gaddini is critical of the majority of psychoanalysts for not studying aggression, especially in its economic aspects, and for their frequent assumption that aggression is aroused only in response to frustration. But he is equally critical of those, especially Klein, who 'without discussion' have adopted the idea of the death instinct but who use the term 'death instinct' as if it meant 'instinct of aggression', thus in Gaddini's view confusing description with metapsychological explanation. To Gaddini, aggression is a primary instinct in its own right.

I should add that these two chapters offer interesting suggestions regarding the relationship between aggressive and libidinal energy. If the outward discharge of aggressive energy is blocked, it will be discharged internally, which would cause an immediate disruption of internal equilibrium. This disruption is halted, Gaddini assumes, by a 'compensation mechanism'; namely, by an immediate arousal of libidinal energy which counters and contains the disturbance. The compensation mechanism leads to fusion of the two instincts and to the mastering of the aggressive instinct by the evolving capacities and vicissitudes of the libidinal energy in the interests of the subject's survival. In somewhat later papers Gaddini puts forward the view that the most basic anxiety of the individual concerns anxiety about the loss of the self, a catastrophic event which tends to promote staying in a state of non-integration as a defence, a view which is of far-reaching importance to the technique of analysing adults and to ways of dealing with the negative therapeutic reaction.

In two remarkable and original papers of the mid-1970s (1974, Chapter 4, and 1976, Chapter 5) Gaddini turned his attention to a much neglected area of psychoanalytic investigation, that of the role of the father and the primal scene in the early development of the infant and child. In these papers, too, we see him moving away from the conception of the simultaneity of the 'imitative' (and also called 'psychosensory') and the 'introjective' (also called 'psycho-oral', 'oral instinctual', or sometimes just 'instinctual') modes of experiencing in early infancy, towards conceiving of them as successive phases. The father, and what Gaddini so aptly calls the *'primal scene process'*, are in part the means by which the infant moves out of his illusory world of imitative identity into the troubled world of instinctual conflicts, desire, object recognition, awareness of the parents' relationship, development of identification, and acceptance of external reality. But recognition of the father and having to recognize the parents' relationship are not only the means by which these developmental advances are achieved; they are also the product of the very advances that they help to bring about. (Gaddini's researches on the primal scene paving the way to the insurgence of Oedipal feelings heralds some of the recent work of Kleinian analysts on similar topics (see Britton *et al.* 1989).

Gaddini thinks that the child has a series of experiences of the parents' relationship and that they are elaborated in fantasy and then condensed into a special defensive construction which may make it appear as if the child had witnessed the intercourse of the parents only once. He compares the denial and condensation of the primal scene to the repression of the Oedipus complex. The mother of the primal scene is experienced as utterly different from the familiar mother of imitative identity; she is *'extraneous'* ['alien' might be a better word – Editor], a monster, sometimes with many arms and legs like a spider. The father, when he is perceived, is likely to be conceived as if he were the 'extraneous' mother – the horrible monster who attacks the child's mother of imitative identity. (Gaddini recalls Klein's descriptions of the 'combined parent figure'.) Gradually, in normal development, the mother comes to be conceived as 'external' rather than 'extraneous', and the father is accepted as a 'second object'. These developments continue into the second and third year, and Gaddini describes the later phases of them as *'the triangular phase'*.

Derivatives related to this series of perceptions and experiences are found in dreams, screen memories, behavioural symptoms, masturbation fantasies, and so on. It could be thought that the views so far presented are rather close to those proposed by Mahler about the separation–individuation phase; in reality they cover the same period but suggest a very different systematization of the first three years of life from that proposed by the American analyst.

Both these papers on the father and the primal scene (Chapters 4 and 5) are full of telling clinical examples – the case of a patient, for example, who projected on to his father not the 'extraneous' mother of the primal scene process but the idealized mother of the phase of imitative identity (Chapter 4). And there is a particularly useful description (Chapter 5) of the 'imitative transference'; that is, of patients who appear to be engaged in an object relationship with the analyst but who are actually using the relationship to establish a symbolic form of sensory contact which is meant to establish a state of imitative identity between analyst and patient which will block development towards true object relationship.

In the author's contention, which I find highly acceptable, the infant is overwhelmed by the primal scene experience, which is that of an attack on his imitative identity leading to a sense of self-mutilation. There is an experience of loss, abandonment, and disintegration due to his aggressive drives being aroused and re-directed inwardly, affecting the psychosensory area. (In this conceptualization auditory, tactile, and all other sensory stimuli are all-important during the first few months of life.) The libido, on the other hand, comes to the rescue by being stimulated and mobilized to counteract the aggressive drives.

It will be appreciated that here we are offered a new conceptualization which is helpful in understanding not only the pathology of women who regard their male partners as nothing more than a split-off aspect of mother, or men who prefer distinctly masculine women, but also the pathology met in perversions when physical contacts are sought in a casual way. The physical contact is a way of realizing an imitative identity of a primitive kind, which is helpful in evading the conflicts and anxieties involved in accepting the separateness of both oneself and the other.

I have already hinted at some areas where Gaddini stands out from the mainstream of psychoanalytic writers. It is therefore interesting to follow him on an exploration of 'Therapeutic technique in psychoanalysis: research, controversy and evolution' (1975) (Chapter 6). Here he points out how, in the case of Jung, a split seemed inevitable from quite early on in view of the personal difficulties between him and Freud. The introduction of the concept of the self has also presented psychoanalysis with a diversity of opinions which could become a threat to the unity of the movement. Similarly, the addition of child analysis could have been expected to cause severe dissensions. As Anna Freud embraced the structural theory as a legacy from Freud, she became engaged in a course of investigation and technical innovations which led to a clash with the views of Melanie Klein who had also accepted a part of Freudian doctrine, the death instinct, as a central part of her legacy. But as they both worked well within the Freudian framework, no split occurred. On the other hand, Gaddini dwells on the controversy which had been a source of profound disturbance within the British Society and goes on to show how fruitful Klein's research has been in adding to our current knowledge of the dynamics of aggressive drives and the origins of the instinctual relationship with the object. Although he believes that Kleinian conceptualization, being predominantly dynamic, renders it metapsychologically incomplete, he feels that this in no way detracts from the richness and validity of the research. He also suggests that indirectly Kleinian exploration has made a substantial contribution to the structural level too, adding to our knowledge of the early development of the ego, superego, and the earliest defence mechanisms.

Gaddini also admired the rigour and consistency of Klein's technique, though he felt that this very rigour was also a limitation. He thought that it is difficult to talk in words, difficult to make effective interpretations, especially transference interpretations, about the inchoate and some-times terrifying experiences dating from the unintegrated period of earliest infancy. And if pathology in the development from the 'whole self' to the 'individual self' has interfered with the development of the instinctual relationship – that is, with the relationship to objects and recognition of their separateness – Gaddini thinks that

> the analytic relationship must be able to operate on very deep levels remote from language, and barely if at all instinctual. Verbal inter-pretations at instinctual levels may in these cases have no meaning, whereas silence and participation may assume an important thera-peutic function.

He thought that Kleinian analysts would modify their technique to take account of the fact that the therapeutic relationship 'extends beyond the instinctual transference', and, as he notes in a postscript, was surprised to find a few months later at the 1975 Congress of the International Psychoanalytical Association in London that several Kleinian analysts had, he thought, done just that.

In 'The invention of space in psychoanalysis' (1976) (Chapter 7) Gaddini makes a first clear attempt at formulating some personal views on the formation and definition of the self *vis-à-vis* the mental structure (ego and superego) as well as the relation between the two. By using the term 'space' Gaddini points out that Freud was able to introduce into metapsychology a topographical, structural description of the mental apparatus. Thus, the space is a concept and is not real in the sense of external space. Early mental activity is fed by bodily experi-ences derived from primarily auditory, tactile, and other sensory stimuli, included under the term 'psychosensory area'. In due course, the sense of self is built on needs, at first without boundaries and timeless; Gaddini calls it the 'total self'. Slowly we reach the dramatic birth of the self, to be called the 'individual self'. This is catastrophic and mutilating to the organization of the 'total self', especially because the non-self now becomes a threat; hence the urge to survive comes into being. This urge can be dominating and capable of affecting the sense of identity, separation, and so on, if needs are not adequately met.

10

The survival urge mobilizes the instinctual cathexes; the peripheral location of the aggressive cathexes outwards and that of the libidinal cathexes, turned inwards, contribute to the forming of a boundary for the individual self. The paper is notable for the introduction of the concepts of the 'instinctuality' of the self, 'the instinctual activity of the infantile ego' in which aggression is fused with libido and turned towards an object in the outside world, which is more related to the reality principle. With the developing ego we shall now encounter manifestations of '*instinctual anxiety*' which has to be distinguished from '*loss-of-self anxiety*' which is paralysing to the ego.

Many of the experiences related to the growth of the individual self and the early activities of the ego lead to experiences oft-repeated in analysis. At first there is only anxiety related to loss of total self as it moves into becoming the individual self. Later, with the appraisal of time, another kind of anxiety linked with loss-of-self makes its appearance. I should stress here that the loss of total self is catastrophic and is seen in patients who cannot relate and who are also prone to resisting transference interpretations, giving the impression of uninvolvement. The loss-of-self anxiety, instead, is frequently seen as part of well-organized defensive structures and seems to contain a memory of something which must not be repeated. Needless to say, instinctual anxiety arises in the ego when the object is already distinct from the self. In analysis it will make its appearance through missed sessions, lateness, and so on, thus showing that patients know only too well how to withdraw into the self and away from instinctual experiences and stimuli. With the delineation of the individual self and the mobilization of instincts, loss-of-self anxiety decreases and a first mental image of the self, a circle, a circumscribed enclosed space begins to form. This is the first symbol representing the self (see Chapter 12).

In 'Notes on the mind–body question' (1980) (Chapter 8) Gaddini traces the origins of the mind–body continuum *in utero*, up to the formation of a separate self. Having established the principle that the mind is extended throughout the body, rather than being localized in the brain, he follows the path of differentiation of physiological learning from mental learning: that is, the physical model is converted into a parallel mental one (for instance, incorporation is parallel to introjection). As recent work has shown that learning in foetal life begins at about three months, it seems safe to assume that an unborn baby develops a bodily self which is in a circumscribed space. After the shock of birth, physiological functions develop. However, only memory can transform the physical models of breathing, feeding, excretion, and so forth into mental ones. In the first phase of development the individual's knowledge is based on experiences which occur alongside fantasies associated with the involvement of tactile, auditory, and to a lesser extent visual, sensations and emotions. On the other hand, for Gaddini all that is related to 'touch' constitutes a new boundary for the baby's developing self, a view well supported by his investigations into skin diseases in all ages, as I have already noted.

An important aspect of the arguments put forward here is that the first mental formation consists of fragmentary sensory experiences (the psychosensory area) related to functions which are endlessly repeated. The recognition of the body by the mind suggests acknowledgement of one's own separateness and vulnerability. In fact, during the first eighteen months of life psychophysical illnesses which translate mental disturbance into bodily terms are scheduled or dated. Rumination does not occur before eight weeks. Atopical dermatitis, as noted above, is likely to occur from four to six months, when the 'detachment' process is under way. Psychoanalytic treatment itself may be able to supply what the individual's environment did not provide during the actual period of infancy. Readers will recall, too, how some cases of dermatitis may occur in the course of an analysis when things are not going too well. Initial attachment to a transitional object tends to arise between seven and twelve months, when the process of 'detachment' and the primal scene process are, or should be, well launched. We are also reminded in this chapter of how further developments in detachment and separation occur at the same time as learning to walk, talk, and so forth, and that disturbances during this time may lead to psychophysical disturbances such as asthma, stuttering, or agoraphobia.

In the face of stress, the first mental function of non-integration may be restored and promoted as a defence, reflecting the space occupied by the fragmentary experiences of the self in relationship to the environment. No doubt psychotherapists will recognize the sense of frustration when attempting to deal with a patient who enacts the original need for self-survival and treats the analyst as a means to that end. Here the stress is on the sensorial use of the oral function, but Gaddini draws our attention to the fact that the patient regards the analyst not so much as a separate object as a source of nourishing, sensory contact, a subtle but basic distinction in terms of understanding and interpreting the transference. We all know how disturbing it is to have a patient who is unwilling to recognize the separate existence of the analyst or any external object or the external world. This is, in fact, a major factor in the presenting picture of bulimia and anorexia. It is in this chapter that we really come to appreciate the writer's value as a research worker, teacher, and therapist. A careful reading will provide us with a wealth of useful information about many patients' behaviour in psychotherapy and analysis.

A similar richness of clinical material is also to be found in the next chapter on 'Early defensive fantasies and the psychoanalytical process' (1981) (Chapter 9). A distinction is made between two kinds of fantasy. There are fantasies *in* the body which are rudimentary and proceed from body experiences in the service of defence. They lack images and are revealed through a functioning of the body activated by the mind. The psychic events associated with the rumination syndrome fall within this category. These fantasies are usually enclosed in the primitive and exclusive body–mind–body circuit and are not available for further mental elaboration. A purpose of the chapter is to show how, in the infant's mind, fantasies *in* the body are followed by fantasies *on* the body which are based on the idea of space in the developmental process and are associated with imagery. Unlike the earlier ones, these fantasies are visual and in fact they represent the first mental image of the separated self. They are usually represented in dreams, or graphically as round shapes (see Chapter 12).

A study of the fantasies in the body can contribute to a better understanding of some normal and pathological aspects of functioning of the first year of life. When they are transitory and linked with the psychophysical syndromes, they may be an expression of a fragmentary, non-integrated early organization of the self and be related to fear that this organization might go to pieces or get lost in space. This *anxiety of non-integration* is one of two main expressions of anxiety of loss-of-self, the other one being 'anxiety of integration', which is a fear that whatever change occurs in the non-integration state will lead to a final catastrophe. All therapists are very familiar with this latter type of anxiety which slows down progress. Clinically, it is essential that we should distinguish between non-integration and splitting, for splitting in Gaddini's view occurs only after an integrated state has been achieved.

The clinical examples in support of these theoretical arguments are well matched by those included in the chapter 'Acting out in the psychoanalytic session' (1982) (Chapter 10), where this troublesome symptom is regarded as a defence, usually self-oriented, magic, and omnipotent. The main aim of acting out is to regulate tensions and at times to dispose of them.

Before summarizing the contents of the next two essays, I think I should pause to examine some of the conceptual differences which separate those psychoanalysts who have been concerned with early mental developments. It will be easily recognized that a dominant feature of Gaddini's work could be described as a prelude to more advanced ego functioning. According to Klein, the breast is invested from the outset with instinctual charges. This presupposes an ego, no matter how primitive, as well as conflicts. In Gaddini's theoretical formulation, however, there is no ego immediately after birth. This has important implications as it means a postponement of phenomena attributable to introjection and projective identification, as the latter are impossible without an ego. This should not be construed as a wholesale rejection of Kleinian psychology, for Gaddini regarded it as indispensable in clinical work. He greatly admired its contribution to the study of counter-transference, aggression, and object relations, as well as for its adherence to the stringency of the setting.

Winnicott, in his seminal study on primitive and elementary activity preceding the functioning of the ego and other psychic agencies, referred to this first expression of life as *self*. His aim, of course, was to distinguish it from the ego. Greenacre and Gaddini, quite independently, proceeded in the same direction, which lends cogency to their findings. Gaddini's own observations soon led him to conceptualize the existence of a psychosensory area which has mental priority over perceptions, for perceptions are associated with structures: that is, with the existence of the ego. Imitation, which I have shown as being central to the author's thinking, is associated with sensations, whilst introjection is linked to perception. Here we notice an overlap of his conclusions with those reached by Winnicott, who claimed that there was an absence of instinctuality and conflicts in early life.

Some, if not all, of these ideas are ventilated in the chapter on 'The presymbolic activity of the infant mind' (1984) (Chapter 11), perhaps the most complete statement by Gaddini of his history of infant development. Here we are confronted by the introduction of a 'basic mental organization' (BMO), which is said to cover the period from biological to psychological birth (separateness). It is contended that the onset of mental activity is necessitated by the urge to survive. During this phase the inevitable physiological disruption acquires mental sense. The BMO serves the self as it is the result of sensory activities which dispense with unwelcome perceptions. All sense organs at first function as contact organs (visual and auditory sensations can magically abolish distance by transforming them into contact). In adult life and in analysis, as we know, sight and hearing can indeed be experienced as continuous contact and, as all therapists know, many patients will make full use of it to redefine object awareness into sensory contact. It follows that sensory experiences relating to specific functions of the body will concur to the formation of the self. The early BMO is fragmentary in nature. However, with separation some integration will occur but the self feels mutilated. The fragments that survive the mental catastrophe, as produced by recognition of separateness and as described by Bion, are kept together by the BMO. The loss-of-self anxiety described in previous chapters may oppose integration or favour it. In severe pathological states, true integration does not occur, and this accounts for the stillness sometimes found in the psycho-analytic process. This is a chapter in which we share with the author his experiences of patients who suffer from fear of integration and/or disintegration, opposing any change because of an unconscious fear that it will annihilate them, hence their preference for remaining in a non-integrated state. This state is vividly expressed by the sort of patient who is perpetually afflicted by the problem of 'I can't live with you – I can't live without you' type of anxiety. To sum up, this is what we can expect in states which precede full symbolization, the role of the BMO being in essence that of forming the first image of the bodily self.

The chapter, therefore, should be considered together with 'The mask and the circle' (1985) (Chapter 12), in which Gaddini recalls how Freud regarded the manifest dream as the mask of the latent dream content, going on to compare dream consciousness with that of waking life. The discontinuity between the two states is comparable to that of the body–mind–body continuum. Dream consciousness acts as a bridge to allow manifest access to deeper levels of fantasy life. Gaddini shows us how mental images of the body self and its primitive pathology are to be found in dreams in advanced stages of analysis. Round images appear in highly diversified forms, and patients acknowledge that the images are representations of themselves.

To justify this challenging conclusion the author points out how, in relation to the first mental learning, the circle is to be regarded as the actual origin of creative expression of the self in consciousness. This seems to happen during the second year of life when the sense of self is equal to consciousness in the ego. The circle is then a symbol invented by the child as a further expression of inventiveness already expressed in the creation of the transitional object. As he continues to grow up, the child goes on adding to the circle what he perceives of himself, mouth, eyes, limbs, and so on. The filling of the circle, of course, is done with the help of the developing ego acting between self and object. For the author the circle represents the conclusion of the dramatic process through which the individual, under the impact of anxiety of self loss, moves from the stage of the magical and omni-potent organization of non-integration to the acknowledgement of separateness and the dividing boundary between self and external environment. In keeping with this view we are once more reminded of the psychological events related to separation and recognition of vulnerability and of the psychophysical syndromes that may result from difficulties in negotiating these maturational tasks.

Before ending the chapter, however, Gaddini seizes on this opportunity to stress the fact that psychoanalysis works at the confines of the biological and that it does not oppose or invade the territory of neurophysiology; on the contrary, it proposes to extract from it what can be understood of the neurophysiological function which is at the basis of mental functions. On the other hand, he rightly insists that it does not make sense for the biologist to say that the origin of dreams is in the basic physiological processes and not in masked desires. This means that there is no structure behind the origin of dreams and its formation. Somehow I believe that Gaddini would have been delighted with current researches which show that the foetus responds to different sounds in the womb and that in the first week of life the infant can distinguish between mother's voice and that of others. One wonders too what he would have thought of the findings of Daniel Stern (1985) and others which suggest that processes of fusion and processes of self–object differentiation evolve from birth onward in tandem, rather than a phase of fusion being followed by a phase of self–object differentiation.

All psychoanalysts have in some ways been influenced by one or more teachers or colleagues whom they held in high esteem. Gaddini's deep respect and gratitude for Freud's contribution to the understanding of human nature is apparent throughout the writings presented in this volume. It is indeed a pleasure to re-read Freud under his guidance because he can be both critical and objective.

There will also be no difficulty in noticing the deep admiration for the theoretical contributions of Phyllis Greenacre, derived mainly from her writings in the field of physical determinants in the development of the sense of identity.

Reference to the work of Winnicott has been so frequent in this introduction that it is hardly necessary for me to stress the closeness that existed between these two creative thinkers regarding the intricacy of the infant's mind in areas which had been largely unexplored. It was Winnicott the paediatrician whose experiences with children could be added to the information gathered from Gaddini's collaboration with his wife, Renata De Benedetti. In this introduction I have tried to show the considerable affinity in their understanding of non-integration and integration. Gaddini's personal contribution in this area was in stressing the role of loss-of-self anxiety in individuals who cannot face separation. Here he brought together the fear of integration with the fear of autonomy and individuation. The basic overlap, though, with Winnicott's view is in the concept of non-integration as a fragmentary functional organization of the self. On the other hand, they differ in so far as Gaddini stresses the fact that disintegration presupposes some degree of integration. In my opinion there are some considerable divergences in their views on the role of illusion in early life. Winnicott believed that the self-creative process occurs in the early stages of life with an illusory quality of dependency fostered by the mother. Gaddini agrees with this but also argues that the early imitative experiences, as described in his work on imitation, are defensive in providing the baby with the opportunity of slipping back to his self-omnipotence, or, better still, giving him the means to re-establish the experience of the illusion of being at one with the object.

Another major difference concerns their ways of understanding the image of the circle which often recurs in Winnicott's writing, when he tends to use it as a potential diagram for the representation of the self since birth. If there is a break in continuity the circle divides into two circles, the psyche seduced by the intellect interrupts its relation with the soma, and we have the elements which lead to the formation of the false self, a concept which Gaddini did not use.

It is difficult to know exactly to what extent the author was influenced by Bion, although his admiration was evident in 'Paths through the creativity of Bion' (1981) and 'Ultimate Bion' (1984), not included in this collection. Undoubtedly in the last few years of his life he was more interested in the fact that Bion had worked with the earliest traces of mental life, principally derived from work with psychotics, which allowed him some comparison with his work on children. He certainly shared his fascination with the protomental, learning from experience and the analytical encounter, quite apart from seeing a close connection between Bion's views on 'the inner group' and his basic mental organization with its fragmentary multiple character and magical functioning.

In this Introduction I have attempted to stress Gaddini's independence as a psychoanalytic thinker and writer. Yet he did not believe that independence was a concept that made much sense, except in a historical and social context. He firmly believed that absolute independence is what the baby imagines the omnipotent mother has to offer at the moment of separation, as any analyst knows when the time comes to let a patient go. But growing up for this gifted analyst meant to move from total but unrecognized dependence to real dependence. In other words, it meant coming to terms with reality, particularly psychic reality. so central to his contribution. However, with that dry sense of humour so well-known to his colleagues and friends, Gaddini would also say that luckily the world is not made of reality only.

1

On imitation

This paper was first published in the *Rivista di Psicoanalisi* (1968), XIV, 3 under the title 'Sulla imitazione'. An amplified version appeared in the *International Journal of Psycho-Analysis* (1969) 50: 475–84.

This paper is a first attempt to organize some thoughts of mine on imitation, elaborated during the last ten years. What I propose to do, in the first place, is to distinguish on the metapsychological plane imitation from introjection and identification, and to show how the latter usually presupposes not only introjections but also imitations. Second, I shall try to show how certain infantile psychopathological pictures (taken from personal experience and from psychoanalytical literature) become more comprehensible if one takes into account the use of imitations in relation to the regime of gratifications and frustrations in the first period of life. Finally, I shall attempt to indicate how, in adulthood, pathological imitations may be found even in easily encountered clinical examples. I have purposely avoided developing this last part, as I intend to do so in a later paper.

When Freud (1900) introduced the concept of identification, with reference to the hysterical phenomena of psychic contagion, he stressed above all its distinction from imitation: 'Thus, identification is not simple imitation, but *assimilation* on the basis of a similar aetiological pretension; it expresses a resemblance and is derived from a common element which remains in the unconscious' (p. 145). This distinction did not imply that identification was the opposite of imitation but rather that it was a more complex phenomenon.

However, the later development of the concept of identification has not been very much concerned with imitation, but has been amplified with other complementary concepts, such as incorporation and

18

introjection (Ferenczi 1909), probably arising from the need to under-line the genetic and the dynamic aspects respectively. Unfortunately, these partial aspects have often been confused with each other, and with the concept of identification itself, giving rise to no little confusion.

Federn (1952) has objected to the concept of introjection followed by Edoardo Weiss (1960). Federn intended to clarify the confusion by eliminating the concept of introjection and substituting for it that of internalization.

Naturally, all those (even though they are not many) who have detected the presence of imitative phenomena have found themselves forced to distinguish them from what could seem, at the first glance, to be identifications. Among these few, Fenichel (1937), Ferenczi (1932a,b), Deutsch (1942), Greenacre (1958a), Greenson (1966), Stoller (1966), Ritvo and Provence (1953) and Eidelberg (1948) may be mentioned. Owing to the terminological confusions which still exist, one can still find the term 'identification' used in the place of 'imitation', and this indicates the sufficient elaboration of the concept of imitation. However, it is fairly widely agreed that imitation reveals itself as a disturbance of identification, and with the characteristics of a primitive phenomenon, which probably precedes identification in development. In this sense imitation has been recently set by Jacobson (1964) in a more decidedly metapsychological frame.

As far as the original meaning of identifications is concerned, Jacobson prefers to speak of 'early identifications' rather than of 'primary identifications'. These early identifications permit the inter-nalization of a reality, at first fragmentary and selective, in the sense of part-objects, and later of whole objects, towards which partial and selective identifications correspond to the interests of the ego; the development of identifications permits the development of other essential functions of the ego, such as reality testing, and the formation of a sense of identity and gender identity.

What precedes these 'early identifications' should, in my opinion, be indicated as 'early imitations'. The term used in this respect by Jacobson, 'primitive identifications', is in fact also used by others, but it seems to me a misleading term, since it is used to indicate phenomena which are of an imitative nature. To distinguish them from 'early identifications' may perhaps allow not only a greater clarification of both the concepts at the beginning, but perhaps also the distinction of imitation from identification in terms of processes.

Early identifications can be distinguished from imitations by the important fact that a reality, even though fragmentary, becomes intro-jected and assimilated. In this sense Jacobson uses the term 'realistic identifications'. I would like to suggest that this realistic element represents, right from the beginning, something which permits us to speak of identification proper. Early imitations, on the other hand, represent and are concerned only with unconscious fantasy. Furthermore they seem to follow a process of their own, which apparently has a distinct role in the development of the ego.

Because imitations precede identifications in the individual development, we should expect, clinically, the possibility of regressions from identification to imitation. Since imitations are concerned with unconscious omnipotent fantasies we should expect a similar regression to involve an object relationship of a more primitive type. In fact, clinical experience offers notable examples of this sort of regression with disturbances of identification of an imitative type, accompanied by fantasies of omnipotence. In my experience it is practically constant in character disturbances in general, and it may be found very frequently in male and female homosexuality, and also in fetishism and transvestism.

As far as the process of development of imitations is concerned, it seems to be distinct from, even though gradually integrated with, that of identifications. On the other hand, it seems evident that imitative activity is placed, in the course of its development, at the service of the ego functions and processes of adaptation. In this connection we should expect, besides a regression *to* imitation, a regression *within* the imitation – that is, from a more integrated imitation to one which is less integrated, or not integrated at all, in the structure of the ego; that is to say, pathological disturbances of imitation itself.

Imitation seems to be connected, originally, with perception, in the sense that primitive perception is physically imitative. At first the infant perceives by modifying his own body in relation to the stimulus. In this way, the infant does not perceive the real stimulus, but the modification of his own body. Perhaps the differentiation of the systems of perception and systems of memory has its beginning in this community of physical perception and imitation.

As we shall see, the regime of gratification and frustration to which the infant is subjected has a determining influence on the further destiny of these 'imitative perceptions' and their mnemonic traces, in the sense of their normal or pathogenic evolution. In general, a prevailingly frustrating regime tends to reinforce and make them last more than they might. The phenomenon, however, which seems to constitute the first step forward seems to take place under the sign of frustration, and is known by the term 'hallucinatory image'. Using this term we refer to the fact that, in the *absence* of the gratifying objects, and in the attempt to end the painful sensations which derive from its separation, the infant has a hallucination; that is, represents some image

20

as reality. In order to understand the meaning of separation from the object and of the subsequent representation, it should be kept in mind that, at this stage, the object is not perceived as such but as a part or an extension of the body self.

Rapaport (1951) has justly defined the hallucinatory image as 'the prototype of thought'. I would like to suggest that it can also be considered as the psychic prototype of imitation. If one bears in mind that (in the words of Freud) 'originally the mere existence of a presentation was a guarantee of the reality of what was presented (1925: 237), one can understand the meaning of this primordial psychic imitation. From now on, the biological model, 'imitating in order to perceive', changes into the parallel psychic model, in which to perceive becomes 'to be'. 'Imitating in order to perceive' becomes, that is, 'imitating in order to be'. Or rather, perceiving is still, as before, 'being', but whereas this occurred previously on a prevailingly physical level, it now does so on one which tends towards the psychic.

We do not know in what way the functional model becomes converted into a parallel psychic model, even though we can argue the economic advantage of such a conversion, but primitive psychic activity offers us more than one example of this sort. Introjection, for example, with which we shall deal shortly, is today defined as the psychic model parallel to the physical one of 'putting into the mouth', of 'incorporating' orally (Greenson 1954). We shall shortly see how some early affects may be correlated with bodily functional models. As Federn has written apropos of this,

> It will be a further task of psychoanalysis and biology to find out to what extent and detail the mental processes parallel the bodily ones, and how many somatic phenomena may and must be transposed to the mental level.
>
> (1952: 352)

Concerning the psychic protomodel of imitation – 'imitating in order to be' – it may be helpful to repeat that it installs itself not in the presence of the object but in its *absence*, and that precisely because of this, its aim seems to be that of re-establishing in a magical and omnipotent way the fusion of the self with the object.

The period immediately following consists in the active development of fantasies in which these two characteristics – no objective reference to reality and a magical restoration of the omnipotent fusion with the object – continue to constitute the essential fact. This belongs to the 'symbiotic phase' (second–fifth–sixth month) of Mahler and La Perriere (1965). These fantasies of fusion, however, can last for a long time, even beyond the pre–Oedipal period (Jacobson 1964).

21

As far as the early introjections are concerned, according to Fenichel (1945: 37) in this period 'in the unconscious all sense organs are conceived as mouth-like'. That is, the introjections also aim at the fusion of the self with the object which may come to be lacking: and this seems to be what Fenichel intends in saying that, originally, '"putting into the mouth" and "imitation for perception's sake" are one and the same' (1945).

However, these two functional models seem to determine in a distinct way, right from the beginning, that two-fold attitude taken towards an object which Freud has detected and defined: 'what one would like to be' and 'what one would like to possess'. The fact that these can be lived as one and the same thing does not mean that they are. The primitive imitative perception seems to lead to the hallucinatory image, to the fantasies of fusion through modification of one's own body, and to imitations, in the direction of the wish *to be* the object. Oral incorporation seems to lead to the fantasies of fusion through incorporation and to introjections, in the direction of *having*, of *possessing*, the object. In the narcissistic cathexis these two basic dispositions coexist, providing the reason for the fact, indicated by Freud, that in the identifications called by him primary, the relationship is both one and the other.

The early affects seem, in turn, to be modelled on the same original physical paradigms, and this seems to determine the sense of early conflicts. The early appearance of envy and rivalry (Klein 1957; Jacobson 1964) becomes in fact more comprehensible if one takes into account how near *rivalry* is to the imitative-perceptive model (the object as what one would like to be) and *envy* to the incorporating-introjective model (the object as what one would like to have). According to Jacobson, still in the first year of life, affectomotor imitations between mother and child would follow the fantasies of fusion, and in turn would be followed by imitations of the parents' emotional expressions 'induced' by them (1964).

The following step in development, however, seems to be represented by the first assimilations of imitations or introjections relative to partial or fragmentary realities. The maturational development of perceptive and mnemonic functions has certainly a determining role in this step, but other factors also intervene, connected with the characteristics of the relationship. I shall not enter here into the metapsychological problems relative to this passage. I shall limit myself to saying that the internalization of reality involves a quantitative and a qualitative modification of the object cathexes so that an external reality, gradually recognized as separate from self, and an internal part of the ego, more stable and separate from non-ego, correspond to the accumulation of the imitations and the introjections assimilated in a realistic way. Imitations and introjections converge therefore in this process, originally fragmentary and gradually more integrated, for which I would like to reserve the term 'identification'.

I should say that the distinction between imitation, introjection and identification is not found in psychoanalytical literature in the terms now described, and the reason for this, apart from the general lack of distinction between imitations and identifications, lies also in the fact that the term 'introjection' has been in turn widely fused and confused with that of identification, right from the moment when it was introduced by Ferenczi (1909). Here the confusion was justified by the fact that introjections were concerned with the oral base of identification, constantly underlined by Freud, who wrote, 'There are . . . good reasons why a child sucking at his mother's breast has become the prototype of every relation of love' (1905: 222).

However, what has complicated the development of the concept of identification seems to be the difficulty of integrating, on the conceptual plane, the evolution of the developmental area, which seems to be characterized by psychosensory activity, with that of the area which could be defined as psycho-oral. Naturally, the oral psychic area is not limited to the oral zone, just as the sensory psychic area does not exclude the oral zone. That is, if it is true that all sense organs may unconsciously be conceived as mouth-like, it is also true that the oral zone and cavity may be experienced as a sensory organ inasmuch as they are the seat of perceptions with their relative mnemonic traces. Further on, an extraordinary example will be given of imitative reactivation of the perceptions of the oral cavity, as the result of serious oral frustrations. I would like to point out here, however, that certain early conditions of oral frustration may determine disturbances of the oral psychic area – namely, of introjective mechanisms – with the result that an imitative activity of introjections may partly substitute introjective activity.

From the dynamic point of view the psycho-oral area seems to be proportionately much more exposed to the conflicts in the object relationship, while the sensory area seems to provide a possible withdrawal from the conflicts, and the exclusion of the external object which promotes them. If we refer to individual development in terms of object cathexes, identifications may be considered, in this development, as an intermediate station of crucial importance, in which the imitative phenomena of the sensory area and the introjective ones of the oral area become integrated in the service of reality and the ego processes of adaptation. In this sense, what Freud has described as secondary identification is perhaps to be considered as the only conceivable one whose appearance is to be dated right from the moment of 'early identifications' (Jacobson), or 'realistic identifications', whose development continues uninterruptedly till adulthood. What precedes I would designate as 'imitations' and 'introjections' with reference to their respective basic bodily models of perception and of oral incorporation. Imitations and introjections obey the pleasure principle, while identifications are orientated towards reality and lead, in their gradual development, to the possibility of mature object relationship, which in turn functions according to the reality principle. What Freud called 'narcissistic relationship' had originally more to do with the self than with the object, and in this sense is to be referred to the perceptive-imitative area in which the object is experienced in the service of the self; while what Freud called the 'anaclitic relationship' has more to do with the object than with the self and is to be referred to the incorporating-introjective area in which the self experiences its real dependence on the object.

Deutsch has described the 'as if' kind of identifications, which in her opinion are found in a characteristic way in the pre-Oedipal period, and which are found clinically in certain schizoid personalities which Deutsch defines as being of the 'as if' type. These patients behave as though they themselves were their love objects (1942).

There seems to be no doubt, to my mind, that Deutsch intends to refer to a markedly imitative kind of object relationship, primitive in nature, even though in the terms used by her imitation is not clearly distinguished from identification and from introjection. Deutsch seems in fact to maintain that the 'as if' phenomena are a type of 'imitative identification' based on fantasies of oral incorporation. The 'imitative identifications' of infancy are, in my opinion, 'imitations' and, compared to identifications, can at the most be considered as precursors of the latter. Consequently we are not faced, on the clinical plane, with a particular type of identification but with a regressive defence from the relationship which would involve identification. The seriousness of these patients is equal to the entity and to the extension of the imitative phenomena which substitute identifications, and to their primitive character (regression *within* the imitation). They lead to what one could correctly define as an attempt to gain a vicarious identity, magically acquired through imitation.

In a case of 'as if' character, a girl of 21, the patient tried to make up, by a striking use of imitative mechanisms, for the painful emptying of her own identity, consequent on the necessity of cutting off an essential part of herself relative to the oral area of her object relationship. Her more serious disturbances had begun in early adolescence, after her father, whom she loved very much, had abandoned the family and after a period of several months spent alone in a school in a foreign country, whose language she did not speak, so that she was able neither to understand nor to make herself understood. Through the use of markedly primitive imitative mechanisms, this patient tried to regain magically an identity, which in reality was vicarious and precarious, but which in fantasy was magically lived as her own, and which corres- ponded to fusion with idealized objects.

Federn (1952) would have preferred to reject *in toto* the concept of introjection because it confused, in his opinion, that of identification, in the sense that it led one to believe that a mental or bodily representation could be internalized by the ego, for the sole reason that it was 'thrown ("jected") within' it (introjected). He would have substituted the term 'internalization' for that of 'introjection'.

Weiss (1960) distinguishes imitation from identification, and points out that he is not referring to 'simple imitation' but to a phenomenon of 'reproduction' or 'autoplastic duplication'. The term 'autoplastic', he says, was coined by Ferenczi, to indicate 'those processes which enable an organism to acquire and modify its shape and functional parts'. The reference to the biological model of imitative perception seems obvious, and the adjective 'autoplastic' represents very closely, in this connection, what in fact is verified. But Weiss, like Federn, also considers introjection only as a badly chosen term, which confuses the concept of identification. As Weiss says,

> We must realize, however, that the metapsychological phenomenon of the extension of ego cathexis over the autoplastic duplication of the object has nothing to do with an act of throwing (or 'jecting') something within one's self. Therefore, we prefer to avoid the term 'introjection'.
>
> (1960: 35)

Weiss therefore criticizes Anna Freud who, 'like her father, does not share Federn's concept of the ego . . . for instance, she equates identification with imitation, disregarding the phenomenon of egotization, that is, inclusion within the ego feeling' (p. 35).

One cannot but agree that imitations are to be distinguished from identifications. Concerning this, the merit of having insisted on the distinction is to be given to Weiss. However, in rejecting the concept of introjection both Federn and Weiss have failed to recognize the distinction between the two basic physical models ('imitating in order to perceive' and 'putting into the mouth') precursors of the parallel psychic models ('imitating in order to be' and 'introjecting in order to put in'), and the consequent two-fold attitude towards the object. In putting them together, Weiss – albeit insisting on the distinction of

25

imitation from identification – has committed the error of assimilating introjection in imitation. Experience has in fact shown that introjection is not merely a superfluous term but a concept relative to detectable phenomena of the psycho-oral area, and it is therefore to be distinguished from imitation.

As I have mentioned above, imitations and introjections are constitutive elements of the process of identification, which aims at fusing and integrating the phenomena of the perceptive-imitative (sensory) area with those of the incorporating-introjecting (oral) area, in the function of the superior processes of the ego in the relationship with objective reality. We may be able in certain cases to recognize the various levels of development of these two areas, and also the interaction of the relative phenomena in their different stages. We should keep in mind in this respect that early identifications, with their internalization of fragmentary aspects of reality, represent in fact the first elements of the secondary process. We should furthermore keep in mind that imitations and introjections, more or less evolved, remain continuously active, independently of the fact that they represent the principal constitutive elements of identification. The latter, that is, cannot take place without the former, but on the contrary imitations and introjections can occur without leading necessarily to identification.

Experience has demonstrated that, in the study of the human mind, it is more difficult to detect and study directly what is normal, and therefore less evident, than to study the evidence of psychopathology and to move from this to the norm. The fields of study which offer us the greatest possibility of detecting and distinguishing imitations independently of identifications are, in practice, that of dreams, which represent a sort of rich psychopathology, but innocuous and circumscribed in the dream state; that of behavioural pathology, as we see it in character disturbances and perversions; and that of psychosis, a state in which the psychopathology normally to be met with in dreams has invaded, so to speak, the waking state.

What I shall now relate is the dream of an adult person, a young married woman with character disturbances. One can recognize in it a markedly primitive imitation. This patient dreamed of 'seeing' on the back part of her head (in a zone of the body, therefore, not visible in reality) a large roundish area, completely bald and more or less covered by the long hair of the front of the head, combed backwards for this purpose. 'Strange', she thought, 'they say that only men go bald, but I've gone bald too; and yet, I am a woman.' (In reality this woman wore her hair very short, like a man.)

Among the dream associations it came out in an almost casual way and as though without importance ('I'll tell you because it has come into my mind, but I don't know whether it's important') that a couple of evenings earlier she had visited her parents, whom she had not seen for some time, and had noted that her father – who was bald at the back of his head as she had been in the dream, but wore his hair short at the front – had let it grow, and had combed it back to cover the baldness. She had only briefly noticed it, and had not even mentioned it to her father, and certainly it would not have come to her mind if it had not been for the dream.

Naturally, I shall not enter into the meanings of this dream. What I want to underline is that it gives us an example of primitive imitations judging from its characteristics and from the context of the dream. This imitation in fact appeared on the basis of the memory of a perception; it represents in a hallucinatory form[1] something which is lacking in the self; it claims magically 'to be', using a part for the whole (the representation in image that is, as Freud observed, in itself a guarantee of reality); it is autoplastic in Ferenczi's sense, which is a characteristic of primitive imitation.

The following is, in contrast, an example of a primitive introjection, as it appeared in the dream of another patient. In the dream she found herself in a shop buying clothes when she suddenly discovered that the bezel of her ring was empty and that she had lost the diamond which filled it. She looked round anxiously and noticed two little girls in the open lift. One of them was showing the other a diamond: 'Look how lucky,' she was saying happily. 'I've just found it on the ground.' The dreamer intervened immediately, taking back the diamond. 'No, no', she said, 'this is mine, I lost it just now,' and as proof, she showed her empty ring. Once she had regained the stone she was seized by the worry of not knowing into which pocket to put it in order to be sure of keeping it with her. She then decided that the only safe way was to swallow it.

In the associations which followed, the dreamer added particulars on the form of the diamond. It had the form of a champagne cork. She then remembered having read that the uterus has the form of such a cork. This notion, acquired intellectually and recently, was only another indication regarding the part-object dreamt, and which was supposedly found inside the body. In turn, the bezel without the diamond represented a primitive image of the body self-conceived as empty; that is, lacking that precious content.

In contrast to the previous dream, and confirming the distinction originally made by Freud, it can be seen that the object here is not 'what one wants to be' but 'what one wants to have', or, if one prefers, *'what one wants to be through having'*, with the warning, however, that at this infantile level 'to be' and 'to have' are lived in the ambit of the only

27

reality possible: that of one's own body. In both dreams visual perception is in action while the motor apparatus, which is implied in the dream of introjection ('putting in the mouth'), does not seem to be implied in that of imitation. This does not mean that in imitations the motor apparatus is not implied, but only that this fact is a sign of the particular primitiveness of the imitation described above.

In fact, the development of the imitative process seems to influence noticeably in early infancy that of the motor activity, so that an intensification of imitative activity may enter as a determining factor in the precocity of certain motor behaviour, or of particular abilities, both motor and of the articulate language.

The intensity of the imitative process is decidedly influenced in turn by the degree of frustration of oral activities, in the sense that it increases in proportion to such frustration. With reference to this it seems necessary, however, to distinguish *frustration in an absolute sense* (due, that is to a decisive lack of oral gratifications) from *frustrations in a relative sense* (due instead to an excessive sensory stimulation, above all tactile and visual). The lack of oral gratifications is always followed by more or less serious consequences, but we should expect that frustrations of an absolute nature will lead to more regressive and damaging imitative manifestations, compared to the frustrations of a relative type. Furthermore, the precocity of the affected period of development seems to be in direct relationship to the seriousness of the consequences. In extreme cases the modification of the body self-consequent on the intensification of the imitative process may give illuminating clinical pictures.

One condition very little known to many analysts, and very serious because of its high mortality rate, but fortunately rare, is that which is known as 'merecysm' or 'rumination'. The syndrome arises in the first year of life but, in our experience, not before the third month. In a study made of six cases (a considerable number, in view of its rarity) by Gaddini de Benedetti and Gaddini (1959), in three cases the syndrome arose in the third month, in two cases in the fourth and in one in the eighth. All these children had been subjected to a regime of serious frustration of oral activities, added to the effects of traumatic weaning. In all the cases the relationship of the mother to her own child was decidedly pathological. Observation showed that rumination occurred at a variable interval after meals; in some cases immediately after, in others up to an hour and a half later. Rumination was preceded by visible tension. While, for example, the child was sucking his thumb he would stop suddenly, grip the sheet, try to put it in his mouth, then begin sucking his thumb again with feverish, anxious movements.

Rumination began with a rhythmic autostimulation of the oral cavity, obtained by introducing the thumb into it and pushing it against the back of the hard palate. The stimulation of this area was accompanied by sucking movements and by rhythmic contractions of the pharyngeal and epigastric muscles: one had the impression that the smooth musculature of the oesophagus, the cardias and the stomach was also involved. In the meantime the tongue was rhythmically projected forwards, with the central part depressed. During this stage, which could last from 15 to 20 seconds to a couple of minutes, the child had an absorbed, intense expression and showed no interest in his surroundings. At a certain moment small quantities of milk began to appear at the back of the oral cavity. The rhythm of the movements then accelerated in culminating tension, until the oral cavity was flooded with milk; this usually took a few seconds.

In these children the peremptoriness of the need to regain the fusion with the object and the intensity of the relative hallucinatory fantasies succeeded in producing modifications of the body self such as to procure a physical state of gratification similar to that which, it should be noted, had already been experienced in reality, but which had abruptly and prematurely come to an end. The fact that the syndrome was not manifest before the third month and that it was first preceded by repeated and incoercible vomiting seems to substantiate fully the view of Greenacre that

> development of defensive measures of the human organism seems to proceed in an ontogenetic fashion from early direct or reflex reactions of a purely physical nature, operating against the environment to the complex structure of psychophysical responses.
>
> (1958a: 69)

It should be added that, at least in our cases, the psychophysical answer could not be considered as casual: it was extraordinarily modelled on the physical response of vomiting. It is a fact that rumination repeats very closely the physical phenomena which occur in vomiting, except that they are in the first place actively self-induced, and not merely undergone; furthermore, they are psychically controlled and coordinated in the service of fantasy, in such way as to give rise to a physical experience imitative of that gratifying fusion which is no longer to be experienced in reality.

The syndrome of infantile rumination should therefore be defined as a psychophysical complex response (in Greenacre's sense) to a state of oral frustration of an absolute type. The first response to such a state of frustration is physical and uncontrolled (repeated vomiting). The later psychophysical response is, on the contrary, complex and organized even though primitive. It tends to put under control the physical response of vomiting and to transform it in such a way that it serves the economic aims of a more efficient defence than the merely physical one. It tends in practice to obtain a reduction of the tension aroused by the serious frustrations of the oral area and to such an end aims at regaining, through a physical, imitative reproduction, the gratification which had previously been experienced.[2]

No less extraordinary, even though, as we have said, less serious for development, are the effects following the oral frustrations which we have called *relative* – that is, due to an excessive intensification of the sensory stimuli (above all tactile and visual), and, in relation to this, a relative insufficiency of oral stimulations, in the first months of life.

We owe to Greenson (1966) the description of a case of great interest, a child whom he had the opportunity of treating analytically at the age of $5^{1}/_{2}$ years. This child, called Lance, behaved exactly like a transvestite adult, except that Lance had begun this behaviour even before he had reached the age of 1 year. At about 11 months, in fact, Lance already wanted to put on the shoes belonging to his mother and his sister (who was six years older than he was). 'He very quickly seemed to prefer above all to walk around in his mother's high-heeled shoes and wept furiously when she tried to remove them.' Since he was so small and seemed so charming, he was allowed to go on wearing them.

> Later on he was able to run up and down stairs in these shoes, to climb trees in them, ride his bicycle, etc. He gradually put on other items of clothing; blouse, stockings, purse, hats, etc., until he began to insist on dressing as a girl.
>
> (1966: 252–3)

Lance's father was on very bad terms with his wife, and Lance had hardly any contact with him. In describing the behaviour of Lance in analysis, Greenson says that Lance was hungry for identification and imitation. From the description which he gives of the child's behaviour a very intense imitative activity is evidenced, together with a very slight, not to say non-existent, capacity for identification. It was enough for Lance to watch what another person was doing in order to be capable of repeating it immediately, and well, even if he had never done it before. 'For Lance, loving was equated with becoming, with some primitive form of identification and imitation' (p. 264). Greenson says, of his relationship with his mother, that 'the tactile and visual over-exposure to his mother's body helped to confuse his gender identity' (p. 264).

Lance's mother was analysed by Stoller (1966), who reported on her in a paper complementary to that of Greenson. Stoller confirms what Greenson says. The mother allowed Lance to stay with her whenever she was nude, to a degree unusual in our culture. For the whole of the first year of life he had been seated or curled up on his mother's body like a little kangaroo in its mother's pouch.

> As he became mobile he was permitted to share her body with her as if it was his own. This was not experienced by either as hetero-sexual but was rather the same sort of unselfconscious freedom one has with one's own body.
>
> (Stoller 1966: 389)

That the hyper-imitative behaviour of Lance implied a relative lack of oral gratifications was shown by the fact that Lance was a very voracious child. 'In his first year of life,' we learn from Stoller, 'he never slept more than an hour and a half without awakening famished.' Lance wanted to have the feeding-bottle full of milk with him for the night until he was over 5 years old. In the relationship of Lance with his analyst we are struck – even though Greenson has not clarified the distinction terminologically – by the gradual arising and developing of identifications, in place of behaviour which, at the beginning of the analysis, was completely imitative.

Lance, who 'behaved with everyone as with his mother', does not seem to have had a way of developing a real sense of his own individual identity, nor of his own gender identity. His object relationship had stopped at the imitative activity obeying the need of 'imitating in order to be'. The case of Lance seems to show all the signs of a development characterized by a hypertrophy of the sensory area of development, to the detriment of the oral area.

So far we have seen an example of primitive imitation and one of primitive introjection in dreams and also two examples of pathological imitations in infancy due to the imbalance in an absolute and relative sense between oral gratifications and frustrations in the first months of life. It is to be expected that infantile psychosis should show us the most serious occurrences. Observations made by Ritvo and Provence (1953) on a group of autistic children have in fact shown that imitative activity in these children is either lacking or extremely reduced. If one keeps in mind that fact that the object relationship of the autistic psychosis is a regression to an almost exclusive relationship with inanimate objects, the important notion appears that imitative activity is originally con-cerned only with animate objects. The report of Ritvo and Provence therefore confirms that imitation is also to be considered as the earliest precursory experience of an object relationship, and that a relationship which is not reciprocal right from the beginning is inconceivable.

In our clinical work with adults, imitative activity is not always recognizable, at least not easily. This is partly due to the inveterate misuse of the concept of identification, and partly to real difficulties. To avoid confusion with identifications one should keep in mind, whenever possible, the genetic, structural and dynamic factors which we have mentioned above, and which allow a more precise definition of the phenomenon. To avoid in part the real difficulties one should keep in mind that in all the cases in which we recognize a disturbance of identity we will in all probability find pseudo-identifications of an imitative type. This is the reason why imitations are more easily met with in the wide range of character disturbances and in perversions.

Innumerable examples may be given of analytically verifiable imitation. A young man wants to marry, and this may seem an adult desire; except that, unconsciously, marriage means for him genital relationship, and this means being adult. His unconscious idea is: 'If I marry, I am an adult too, like other married people.' This young man has not identified himself with the adult, and tends to make good the lacking identification by imitation. He has partly regressed to the infantile model following which the wish to be the object is magically realized through its imitation.

The same idea of getting married may produce completely different situations. A girl, for example, who lives *more uxorio* with a married man with whom she has intercourse, is considered in her own circle as a mature person, open-minded and holding advanced views. She could in fact be so, but analysis reveals that she suffers from a deep disturbance of gender identity, so that finding herself in the role of an adult woman (according to her infantile ideas of adult woman) is unconsciously terrifying. It is later discovered that for this girl, living freely with a man has a double meaning: as far as her conscious mind and the external world are concerned, it represents proof of femininity, beyond any criticism; unconsciously, however, it holds the meaning 'being free like a man'. This unconscious meaning is betrayed in her behaviour with her partner (and with other men and women) by aspects which would usually be defined as 'male identification'. Analysis reveals that this girl's basic fantasy is that of being able to modify her own body, furnishing it in a magical, imitative and omnipotent way with the envied penis. The imitative behaviour which develops because of this fantasy means: 'If I behave in this or that way, as men do, I too am furnished with a penis.'

An example of the relationship which there may be between imitations and introjections is again a girl, another case of male pseudo-identification, in which, however, analysis reveals that the imitative activity serves to deny her feminine impulses, because the latter re-activate unconscious conflicts connected with her introjective fantasies. Here the imitative behaviour means, briefly: 'It is not true that I wish to take possession of the penis: I have already got it.' Naturally, this girl, in contrast to the previous one, has only rare and inconsistent relationships of a loving type with men, while she has frequent ones of a comradely type.[3]

These, and many other cases, may be contrasted with that of a woman of 40, who at the end of a satisfactory analysis unfortunately lost her husband. This woman, who had always maintained that she understood nothing of her husband's business, unexpectedly finds herself alone, and learns that her financial situation is worrying because her husband had recently incurred very heavy debts. Her incapacity for business is well known to certain relatives, very grasping and very expert in business affairs, who immediately try to take control of the business. This woman, who had never signed a cheque, when she has overcome the first shock, does not lose heart but faces the situation. She goes to the bank, obtains credit, deals with the creditors, gains the respect of her husband's personnel, keeps the relatives at bay, gets her driving licence, and so on. Briefly, not only does she lose nothing of what her husband had left, but within a year she finds herself firmly at the head of her business and shows that she knows how to direct her affairs with success and a sense of responsibility. We may say that in this case imitations and introjections have been integrated in a mature identification with the lost husband and placed at the service of the adaptation processes and reality aims of the ego.

Notes

1 'Seeing' serves in this case to make the imitative representation 'real'. Concerning this, note the close relationship between hallucination, imitative thought and what is called 'concrete thought'. An example of imitative type of thought is given by those patients (not psychotic) who associate almost exclusively by images, who describe saying 'I see'. Concerning this type of thought, Freud wrote:

> We learn that what becomes conscious in it is as a rule only the concrete subject matter of the thought, and that the relations between the various elements of this subject matter, which is what specially characterizes thoughts cannot be given visual expression. Thinking in pictures is, therefore, only a very incomplete form of becoming conscious. In some way, too, it stands nearer to unconscious processes than does

33

thinking in words, and it is unquestionably older than the latter both ontogenetically and phylogenetically.

(1923: 21)

2 The interest of the syndrome of rumination is also in the fact that it represents, in the light of the above description, one of the earliest psychosomatic pictures of which it is possible to delineate the genesis and the formation of the somatic symptom. The role which early imitations may play in the determination of certain somatic aspects of mental disturbance is a question which it seems to me legitimate to raise, but which is beyond the scope of this paper.

3 At this point I should like to mention the excellent contributions by Greenacre (1958b,c) on the personality of the impostor and on the relation of the impostor to the artist. The serious alteration of identifications in the impostor is equal to the degree and extension of his regression to imitations and of his deficit in the sense of identity and in reality testing. Greenacre has also shown how, in the creative activity of even very gifted artists, imposture may unexpectedly intervene, having the character of isolated episodes. Research into the role of imitation in the psychopathology of the creative process, however, has still to be carried out.

2

Aggression and the pleasure principle: towards a psychoanalytic theory of aggression

This is a modified version of a paper read at the 27th Congress of the International Psychoanalytical Association in Vienna in 1971. It was published in the *International Journal of Psycho-Analysis* (1972) 53: 191. It has appeared in the *Rivista di Psicoanalisi* (1972) XVIII, under the title 'Aggressività e principio del piacere. Verso una teoria psicoanalitica dell' aggressività'.

This work presupposes, and aims at re-evaluating, the psychoanalytic concept of energy. It is my intention to show how an examination of the contradictions Freud himself recognized in his formulation of the 'pleasure principle', together with an examination of the connections existing between ontogenetic and phylogenetic aspects in the human infant, leads to accepting as reliable the hypothesis of an aggressive energy, present and operating in the infant from the moment of birth, which is qualitatively different from the libidinal and, by nature, directed primarily towards the outside world. This energy is, however, also capable of discharging inside the infant organisms, with complex consequences. Discharge on the outside takes place through the striated muscular apparatus, and this is all the more effective, the more capable this apparatus is of coordinated muscular activity. Discharge on the inside takes place through the smooth muscles of the vessels and mucous membranes. The problem of identifying the source of this energy at the organic level is considered among the most obscure. The few suggestions given in this connection will deal with the problem *per se*, and show that perhaps it may not have any solution because of its very formulation.

Lastly, I shall attempt to show how the adoption of this dual theory of energy implies a consequent useful revision of certain aspects of psychoanalytic theory, leading to a possible solution of the contradictions of the pleasure principle, as set down by Freud, and to a further clarification of certain basic economical concepts. The discussion of these problems will necessarily be limited to the newborn period.

The term 'pleasure principle' has turned Freud's first wording, which was 'unpleasure principle' (1900), upside down. Freud himself passed successively from this first wording to that of 'pleasure-unpleasure principle', and then, for brevity's sake, to 'pleasure principle'. In the course of this change, the accent, which had originally been placed on the painful tension of the hungry infant, moved to the tendency to avoid pain (that is, unpleasure), a tendency which came to represent the basic functional model of the primitive psychic apparatus. Thus pleasure was not connected with any particular type of energy – which would have characterized it qualitatively – but with the reduction to zero of a tension corresponding to an undue accumulation of energy. The difference between pleasure and unpleasure became therefore merely a quantitative one.

Fairly quickly, however, it became clear that this view gave quite an incomplete account of the relevant phenomena. There are in fact pleasurable tensions, just as there are unpleasurable relaxations of tension. Freud then suspected that some other factor, as yet unknown, must be responsible for the difference between pleasure and unpleasure: 'Perhaps it is the rhythm, the temporal sequence of changes, rises and falls in the quantity of stimulus. We do not know' (Freud 1924: 160). His hypothesis was, that is, that a qualitative factor was affecting the quantitative phenomena. Evidently, if such a factor exists, it should be common to all the various quantitative phenomena under consideration, and in any case of such a nature that it allows a valid explanation of the connections existing between such phenomena in each case of pleasure and unpleasure. Freud could not, however, discover what the qualitative factor in question was, and although he was aware of the incompleteness of his explanation, he nevertheless continued to maintain it, perhaps because of the degree of usefulness which it had shown in accounting for the basic energic phenomena, and because he hoped that sooner or later he would be able to give a more complete explanation. Actually, Freud had given a fairly complete and convincing explanation of unpleasure, and although he could not account for pleasure in a similar way, he correctly thought that pleasure must also be amenable to a quantitative explanation.

Later on, however, thanks to the concept of homeostasis, and of optimal tension (instead of the tension = zero of the original inertia principle) unpleasure came to be considered as corresponding to a tension increasing above the optimal level, and pleasure as corresponding to the reduction of tension to the optimal level. However, this relaxation of tension = pleasure was understood as being obtained by an *external* discharge of energy, through the motor apparatus. The discharge and diffusion of energy *inside* the organism give rise to complex phenomena. While the first type of discharge is linked to the concept of *action* – a motor discharge 'designed to effect changes in the external world' – *affect* is the result of a 'motor (secretory and vaso-motor) discharge resulting in an (internal) alteration of the subject's own body without reference to the external world' (Freud 1915b: 179, footnote). It should perhaps be added that while action serves the purposes of homeostasis, affect implies a more or less controlled homeostatic alteration.

At birth, however, neither the ego nor the motor apparatus is as yet developed, and the infant is not able to obtain an efficient discharge of tension-unpleasure through purposeful, coordinated action. If, despite this serious handicap, the homeostatic balance can be maintained, this is not due to mental structure, but to the innate functioning of the muscular sucking apparatus. This apparatus, functioning as it does in a highly coordinated way, could be compared to an island, since the rest of the muscular apparatus is seriously inefficient. Although, from the biological point of view, the function of such a complex neuromotor coordination is basically nutrition, which serves the aim of the infant's survival, from the point of view of psychomotor development the sucking function can be described as the first and complete model of coordinated action. It is, however, a pre-ordained, physiological protomodel of action, and its transition to a parallel psychological model will take place along with the development of ego structure and the connected mastering of neuromuscular apparatus. As Freud indic-ated, this in turn develops along with the emergence of the reality principle.

At the beginning, however, the existence of a protomodel of action fulfils in an anticipatory way a homeostatic function; namely, the discharge through the muscles involved in sucking activity of quantities of energy whose accumulation gives rise to tension. We may suppose that, in conditions of normality, the intervention of this innate regula-tory system is triggered by a certain amount of tension (hunger), which goes beyond a specific threshold, originally very low. We may think of the external object, towards which the action is directed, as moving, so to speak, to meet the action, and of satiety as the final aim of reducing the painful tension and re-establishing homeostasis.

In this sense, the functioning of the sucking apparatus takes the place, in the earliest period of life, of the psychic regulatory mechan-isms, which do not yet exist. In fact, the uncoordinated motor dis-charges of this period are not, from the economic point of view, to be compared in efficiency with the discharge obtained through the co-ordinated action of sucking. The importance of this homeostatic function is just as essential for survival as the nutritional function. Every disturbance in the routine of feeding is also a disturbance in the function of discharge, and therefore a disturbance in the balance of energy. If the undue tension which follows cannot be discharged rapidly enough externally, through the oral coordinated activity, it will tend to discharge itself internally.

The channels of discharge within the organism are biologically pre-ordained and have been identified by Freud (see above). But the formation of affects, which uses internally discharged energy, belongs to the development of the individual, and takes place by means of a complex internal organization which the infant does not yet possess. Furthermore, the infant lacks the internal ego defences, which seem to take shape first in a psychophysical and later in a psychical form [see Chapter 1] beginning in the third month of life. This is why internal discharge is bound to cause, in the early period of life, direct and unorganized organic responses; that is, more or less serious functional disturbances at the organic level. Greenacre (1958a) seems to refer to these direct somatic responses in describing what she calls the bodily origins of the psychic defences.

This lack of psychic regulatory mechanisms for internal discharges is responsible for the fact that the infant's organism, when confronted with homeostatic alterations related to disturbances in the feeding routine, is all the more exposed and vulnerable, the more recent the child's birth. On the one hand, we may say that early psychic activity is able to develop, thanks to the predisposed biological regulation of the energic balance; on the other hand, we must consider that it develops out of the necessity of setting up new self-regulatory mechanisms. Furthermore, it develops around the nucleus or oral cavity and perioral zone perceptions (Spitz 1955), connected with the co-ordinated activity of sucking. These perceptions lead to repetitive experiences which are, under average conditions, mainly satisfying, but also, in part, inevitably painful.

The connections which Freud hypothesized between accumulation of energy, tension, and a state of pain on the one hand, and discharge, reduction of tension, and relaxation on the other, seem still now correct, when compared with clinical observations, but should we conceive of relaxation from tension as equal to pleasure or rather as equal to relief? On economical grounds, the distinction between relief and pleasure seems more than justified. It brings up a further aspect of the contradictions inherent in the pleasure principle, since the equation relief = pleasure also contrasts with the fact that pleasure may be connected with a state of tension (accumulation of energy), whereas relief is normally the result of relaxation. As such, relief may also result from relaxation of a pleasurable tension.

Once again, although the explanation of 'unpleasure' given by Freud seems largely convincing and fundamentally valid, if we are to accept it, we must consider that this explanation does not account for the phenomena which constitute pleasure. Yet, when referring to pleasure, we speak in terms of tension and discharge, we refer to energic processes of a quantitative type, as we do for unpleasure. Is there any way out of this sort of blind alley?

It seems to me that there is only one probable answer to this apparently insoluble dilemma. Since in both cases the phenomena are clearly energic, and have the same quantitative characteristics, but with a *qualitatively* different result, the most probable conclusion is that the differential element lies in the 'quality' of the energy involved in each case. In other words, the energy involved in the phenomena of unpleasure does not seem to be the same as that involved in the phenomena of pleasure.

This fact, if confirmed, would show that Freud's hypothesis of an unidentified *qualitative* element was exact. However, since we are dealing with something of considerable consequence, before we can accept it, we must try to see whether and how it fits in with the other facts we already know, whether and to what extent it further clarifies or modifies them, and what new relationships it may establish with and among other facts.

The problem which immediately emerges, and which must therefore be dealt with first, concerns the definition of the qualitative element. Which energy is involved in the phenomena of pleasure, and which in unpleasure? If we attribute the quality of pleasure primarily to libidinal energy, as what we know about libido would in all probability lead us to do, we would conclude that there is actually no pleasure which does not have something to do with the libidinal energy. Consequently, the quality of unpleasure would be connected exclusively with the other type of energy; that is, what we call aggressive energy. However primitive this energy might appear, compared to the level of individual development, the important thing is that right from the beginning it would be qualitatively aggressive. Naturally, this would also be true for libidinal energy.

This leads to a reconsideration of what has been said previously with regard to alterations of homeostasis. If what we have been saying just now is true, the painful tension which sets off discharge through the sucking apparatus would not concern either libidinal or undifferentiated energy, but rather aggressive energy. What has been so far described as characteristic of oral libido – namely, the painful tension, and the imperative need for discharge – would thus seem to be primarily an expression of aggressive energy. The existence of a physiological innate discharge system, such as described above, would seem to support this view. It is in fact aggressive energy that would seem to engage the muscular apparatus in a coordinated action aimed at modifying an internal state through modification of the external world. This is precisely what the developing psychical organization aims at achieving. Libidinal tension, on the other hand, as far as we know, is less rigid and more plastic and, inasmuch as it is a source of pleasure, it can be prolonged, even though it ultimately aims at discharge. This means that by nature its discharge is not such that it cannot be postponed.

While discharge of aggressive tension aims at the elimination of unpleasure, discharge of libidinal tension aims at increasing pleasure. This implies that, strictly speaking, the equation relief = pleasure is acceptable only as far as libidinal discharge is concerned, while aggressive discharge seems to aim primarily at relief. But if the relationship with the external world is originally set off by painful needs, and the energy involved in muscular discharge is primarily aggressive, and re-establishment of homeostasis is connected with relief, what are the original tasks of libidinal energy, and how, and to what extent, are they related to the requirements of aggressive energy? I should stress that I am purposely using the word 'task' for libidinal energy and the word 'requirement' for the aggressive energy. Not that the latter does not have tasks of its own, but, at the level of the phenomena we are considering, it expresses itself mainly in the form of requirements.

Long before he recognized the existence of aggressive energy, Freud advanced a hypothesis (1905), which he later took up again and completed (1924) and which today could turn out to be a far-sighted intuition. 'In the case of a great number of internal processes', he wrote in his *Three Essays* (1905), 'sexual excitation arises as a concomitant effect, as soon as the intensity of those processes passes beyond certain quantitative limits.' 'It may well be', he added, 'that nothing of considerable importance can occur in the organism without contributing some component to the excitation of the sexual instinct' (p. 204). And here is the completion, written in 1924 – that is, when Freud had recognized aggressive energy: 'In accordance with this, the excitation of pain and unpleasure would be bound to have the same result, too' (p. 163).

Freud's hypothesis may strengthen our hypothesis that the energy involved in pleasure is qualitatively different from that involved in pain and unpleasure. Furthermore, it permits us to answer the question we have raised as to the original tasks of libidinal energy, and as to the relationship between the latter and aggressive energy. The fact that, from the very beginning, a build-up of aggressive tension beyond a certain level gives rise to an overproduction of libidinal energy, can be described as an internal (that is, independent of the external world) physiological protomechanism aimed at re-establishing a sort of homeostatic equilibrium. This is what Freud actually had in mind: 'The occurrence of such a libidinal sympathetic excitation when there is tension due to pain and unpleasure would be an infantile physiological mechanism which ceases to operate later on' (Freud 1924: 163).

This description by Freud may perhaps be completed by adding that such a physiological mechanism ceases to operate when it is substituted by a parallel psychical mechanism. Following an expression used by Freud much later on (1937), I shall call this the 'compensation mechanism'. This internal mechanism tends to oppose the inward discharge of aggressive energy with an inward discharge of libidinal energy, and thus to compensate for the homeostatic disequilibrium. The new homeostasis thus achieved is unstable, since it is established at a level of tension different from the optimum. Especially in the first stages of life, it is noticeably more fragile and less lasting than that achieved by the external discharge of aggressive energy. Yet is is useful in coping with frequent and not too serious emergency situations such as having to bear a temporary but unavoidable postponement of the external aggressive discharge. Furthermore, this mechanism may well contribute to bringing about the processes of fusion, at a level which is still physiological.

Thus the compensation mechanism probably represents the prototype of a series of mechanisms and processes successively used to deal with aggression. As usually happens in development, the emergence of the process of fusion does not nullify the pre-existing compensation mechanism, so that the latter remains distinct in the later psychical organization, with both normal and pathological functional expressions.

However, there are still other connections which must be considered. What seems to be a contradiction between the quantitative phenomena of pleasure and unpleasure could in fact be explained by a functional contraposition between the two different energies. The 'taming' of internal discharge of aggressive energy (unpleasure) would take place, from birth onwards, by means of opposing it, and soon after fusing it, with an adequate 'quantity' of libidinal energy (pleasure). It seems legitimate to suppose that, on the average, the compensation mechanism, which depends on internal responses, comes into play every time aggressive tension reaches or approaches a certain threshold, and every time its imperative external discharge, which is totally dependent on the outside, is delayed or prevented. We may further understand how the discharge of the painful tension of hunger, through rhythmically repeated experiences of compensation and possibly of fusion between the two types of energy, gradually acquires, under average conditions, an increasing (libidinal) capacity for postponement. In other words, we can say that the compensation mechanism and the first experiences of fusion, under normal conditions, tend, through repeated experiences, to raise the threshold of tolerance to the aggressive tension of hunger, and therefore account for both the fact that the external discharge becomes gradually postponable and the concomitant increase in the capacity to bear frustration. This would lead perhaps to reconsidering the opinion that the individual capacity to bear frustrations is primarily due to constitutional factors.

Furthermore, we can better understand the concomitant progressive 'libidinization' of the oral zone. This process of libidinization seems to involve primarily the cutaneous and mucous sensory perceptions and to proceed from the inside towards the outside. The endo-perceptions of the upper digestive tract seem, that is, to precede in a functional sense the labial tactile perceptions and those of the perioral zone. This is in agreement with the idea expressed by Freud that at birth the libidinal cathexes are all internally directed, and that this situation gradually changes (Freud 1937). Finally, the possibility of tracing the mechanism of fusion back to its origin, and the notion that its primary aim is the establishment, through internal means, of a different regulation of homeostasis, seem, on the one hand, to furnish the physiological ground for the basic model of the psychic apparatus, founded, according to Freud, on the necessity of avoiding unpleasure while, on the other hand, they seem to account to some extent for the successive organization of different thresholds, by which the internal discharge of energy come to be controlled – a process closely related to affect formation (Rapaport 1953). Last but not least, the recognition of this early mechanism identified by Freud may help us to clarify further some aspects of the relationship between libido and aggression.

From what we have said so far, it can in fact be deduced that in the first weeks of life aggressive energy is much more powerful than libidinal energy, but that it is also the strongest stimulus to the production and to the initial development and differentiation of libido. Without the possibility of innate, coordinated motor discharge, the initial power of libidinal energy would in fact easily succumb, in the face of the more powerful aggressive energy. Libidinal energy is, on the other hand, capable of differentiation – that is, of developing in a qualitative sense – and seems to be intended to provide an internal

42

solution to economic problems right from the beginning, thus progressively releasing the human infant from its total dependence on the
external world.

In this sense, we would have to conclude that libido is the energy
which is destined to assume a psychical quality. Aggressive energy seems
to be to libidinal energy more or less what a natural force is to the
individual, so that the fundamental economic problem remains, for every
human being (Rapaport 1953), the necessity of mastering the force of his
aggressive energy with the evolving capacities of his libidinal energy.[1]

In contrast to libido, aggressive energy does not seem to be capable
of qualitative evolution. It seems instead to be essentially capable of
qualitative alterations connected with the quantitative variations, due
to the varying processes of fusion characteristic of libido. This leads one
to think that the so-called 'vicissitudes of aggression', which, according
to Hartmann *et al.* (1949), are altogether analogous to the vicissitudes
of libido, are only apparently 'vicissitudes' of aggression and, in reality,
the result of the capacity of the libidinal instincts to undergo vicissitudes. In other words, one of the most important results of fusion
would lie in the fact that aggression, once fused with libido, becomes
involved in the vicissitudes of the latter, and in this way made useful to
the psychical aims of the individual. On the other hand, aggression
seems to be the most powerful force behind libidinal differentiation
and development. Without fusion processes there would be, perhaps,
no reality principle.

What Freud ultimately had in mind concerning the so-called
'vicissitudes' of aggression was not far from what we have just
indicated, as is revealed in an important letter he wrote to Marie
Bonaparte – Freud (1937), quoted in Jones (1953). On the sublimation
of aggression, what he suggested was that

> 'in the regular combination of the two instincts there is a partial
> sublimation of the destructive instinct'. And on the repression of
> aggression, he wrote that it 'is the hardest part to understand. As is
> well known, it is easy to establish the presence of "latent" aggres-
> sion, but whether it is then latent through repression or in some
> other way is not clear. What usually happens is that this aggression
> is latent or repressed through some counter-compensation, i.e.
> through an erotic cathexis. And with that one approaches the theme
> of ambivalency, which is still very puzzling.'

I should stress that this is the passage which suggested the term
'compensation mechanism', which I have used in this paper.

However that may be, what I would point out is that since Freud,
very little if any progress has been made in investigations of the various

processes through which libido modifies and utilizes aggression and I am convinced that further research in this direction could greatly increase our knowledge of aggressive manifestations.

All this leads to a reassessment of a longstanding polemic with regard to libido, among those who accuse Freud of having overemphasized instinct to the detriment of the object and object relationship. Libido, it has been asserted, is object-seeking by nature. This would not in any way be confirmed by what we have seen up to now. If the energy which is discharged externally through the sucking apparatus is primarily aggressive, and if the flow of libido is primarily directed inward (initially in order to face and then to forestall and master the threat of internally directed aggressive discharge), then we are forced to conclude that it is not libido but rather aggression which is, by nature, object-seeking.

This naturally also differs from Freud's original idea that aggression is pushed outwards and channelled towards objects by narcissistic libido turned into object libido. The contrary would rather seem to be true; that is, it would seem that it is not narcissistic libido which turns aggression outwards, but, more probably, aggression which transforms narcissistic libido into object-libido and channels it towards objects. This transformation seems to occur gradually, in the earliest period of life, while the organism's economic balance is safely enough assured by biological means through the sucking apparatus.

In other words, libido cannot prevent aggression from tending towards objects but it can follow aggression towards them, and, through the manifold variants of its processes, arrive at complicated compromises between the rather 'rigid and monotonous' (Freud) aggressive tendencies and the richly variable, mouldable and adaptable tendencies of libido. Freud himself seems to have ultimately changed his mind about the original relationship between aggression and libido. 'One could imagine', he wrote in the above-cited letter, 'a pretty schematic idea of all libido being at the beginning of life directed inward, and all aggression outward, and that this gradually changes in the course of life.' Although, scrupulous as he was, he immediately added, 'But perhaps that is not correct,' it would seem, on the contrary, that he was perfectly correct, with the simple completion that what gradually changes in the course of life starts to change from the very beginning.

Perhaps the most substantial argument yet raised against the idea of the existence of an aggressive energy distinct, right from the beginning, from libidinal energy, concerns the origin of such energy. Assuming, as we do, that energy is produced at the level of the internal organs, and that this also holds true for aggressive energy, where must we look to find the aggressive equivalents of the erogenous zones – that is, bodily zones whose stimulation can produce excitation, aggressive tension and pressure for discharge – in the same way as the erogenous zones? Without presuming to furnish any exhaustive solution to this problem, I shall nevertheless advance a few considerations which seem to follow from what we have seen so far.

After the oral zones, the erogenous zones capable of building up a psychical organization under their primacy are, on careful consideration, not only zones in which the inside of the body communicates with the outside, but also seats of coordinated neuromuscular organization, made up of striated muscles, whose functioning is from birth biologically pre-ordained. The sphincters and the male and female erectile sexual organs can, in this sense, be considered, in the early phases of life, as a part of the pre-ordained biological organizations for the external discharge of aggressive energy. On the economic level, they therefore contribute to the oral homeostatic function.

From the genetic point of view, the expulsive function of the sphincters concurs with the ingestive oral function in providing the physiological protomodel of coordinated action aimed at modifying an internal situation. The fact that what passes between the subject and the external world (the substances ingested or digested) moves in a predominantly opposite direction from that followed in the oral function (towards the outside rather than towards the inside) does not make much difference as far as the protomodel of action is concerned.

If all this is true, and if it is true that, as we have seen, libidinal energy follows aggressive energy, and not vice versa, then the question arises whether an attempt to find the origin of aggressive energy in a way analogous or parallel to what we know about libidinal energy is not in fact a mistake. The real problem would instead seem to lie in how to modify our conception of the initial relationships between libido and aggression.

If we keep in mind that where libido is, here primarily aggression is, the problem would seem to be that of modifying – or better, of completing – our concept of 'erogenous zones', in the sense that they could be described as bodily zones which are intensely libidinal in so far as they are seats of concentrated aggressive energy.

Note

1 In animals this task seems to be entrusted instead to the biological organization of instinctive behaviour, in which the mechanisms or regulation of energy are pre-ordained and innate. Naturally this does not exclude the presence of libidinal energy in animals, but its development and differentiation, if they exist, may be notably limited by the presence of biologically pre-ordained regulatory mechanisms, to which, presumably, libido is also subject.

3

Beyond the death instinct: problems of psychoanalytic research on aggression

This paper was given at a meeting on Freud and Psychoanalysis in Rome in 1972 under the auspices of the Istituto della Enciclopedia Italiana, and was published in the *Enciclopedia Italiana*, Rome, in 1973. It was also given at a scientific meeting of the Centro Psicoanalitico di Roma in May 1972 and was published in the *Rivista di Psicoanalisi* (1972) XVIII under the title 'Oltre l'istinto di morte'.

Aggression ultimately confronted psychoanalysis with a challenge considerably more difficult to tackle than the one originally posed by sexuality. Freud came to recognize in aggression the characteristics of a much more powerful instinct than libido, and, over thirty years after his death, analysts' opinions are as varied and contradictory as could be, ranging from those who seem completely to accept the Freudian conception of the death instinct to those who totally reject it – and even deny that aggression is an instinct. An entire international psychoanalytical congress was recently devoted to this subject (1971). It reflected the situation of uncertainty that underlies this wide spectrum of views. The following highly authoritative judgement was expressed at this congress by Anna Freud, who stated:

> Whatever the results of earlier ventures, the last-named one did no more, obviously, than to demonstrate some of the limits of scientific group efforts of this nature. It yielded a useful survey of the relevant publications as provided by the psychoanalytic journals of the last thirty or forty years. What it failed to produce was the removal of uncertainties concerning the status of aggression in the theory of drives, or the clarification of some urgent problems, such as the part played by aggression in normal infantile development; its involvement with the various agencies in the psychic structure; its role for

46

character formation; its part in the pathogenesis of neurosis, psychosis, delinquency, the perversions, etc.

(1972: 163)

While this might seem to be a severe judgement, it is unfortunately no more than a realistic assessment of what was revealed by the Congress, and reflects the current status of psychoanalytic research on aggression. Anna Freud suggested that one of the reasons for the difficulties in this research might be precisely what the analyst knows about sexuality:

What obscures the analyst's view when he approaches the subject of aggression may be his very experiences with the vicissitudes of the sexual drive. Such findings, when displaced from the area of their origin to a new set of circumstances, inevitably create expectations, whether warranted or not. In the latter case, they take on the role of preconceived ideas which handicap an investigation.

(1972: 163)

In a recent paper presented at the Vienna Congress in 1971, I endeavoured to draw attention to a two-fold error, which is in my view fundamental, to which such a preconceived idea may in part have contributed. This error is to assume that, since aggression is to be regarded as an instinct, it must necessarily undergo vicissitudes, and that these moreover closely resemble the vicissitudes of the sexual instinct [see Chapter 2].

Anna Freud unexpectedly spoke out in support of the thesis that this concept of 'vicissitudes' of aggression remained to be demonstrated, in her conclusive, masterly paper presented at the Vienna Congress. She holds that psychoanalysts speak of aggression

as if it were a proven fact that it is the aggressive drive itself which, similar to the sexual one, undergoes consecutive qualitative transformations. Before this can be asserted with any confidence, further developmental studies of the infantile drive-mixture need to be undertaken, this time from the aspect of aggression.

(1972: 164)

I can only concur without reservation with the position taken by Anna Freud here. In my own paper referred to above, I had drawn attention to Freud's own uncertainty towards the end of his life about the existence of vicissitudes of aggression [see Chapter 2].

The fact is that the error of believing in the 'vicissitudes' of the aggressive drives and of deeming them similar in all respects to those of the sexual drives has persisted to the present day, and still prevails in the majority of analysts. Since it can now be definitely asserted that this error by itself has practically prevented us from investigating the nature and characteristics of the aggressive instinct, we are bound to wonder how it could ever have been able to persist for so long. We may recall the following sorrowful words written by Freud at the age of 74:

> I can no longer understand how we can have overlooked the ubiquity of non-erotic aggressivity and destructiveness and can have failed to give it its due place in our interpretation of life.
>
> (1930: 120)

Freud's error had been to regard aggression solely as a component of the sexual instinct, and it had for a long time prevented him from distinguishing it as a separate instinct. The subsequent error of the analysts is extremely reminiscent of the situation in an analytic treatment when a patient appears to accept a significant interpretation willingly but in the unconscious part of the ego quickly adjusts his defences to the new position, so that not only does nothing change within him but also the interpretation itself is placed in the service of the defences. In fact, advances in knowledge always meet with resistances and defences that are deeply rooted in human beings, and the ones we call 'errors' are often manifestations of this. The majority of analysts have – in general, for good reasons – discarded Freud's conception of the life and death instincts and have readily accepted what, after Freud's work, it was no longer possible not to accept – namely, the fact that aggression was to be regarded as an instinct, separate from the sexual instinct. Immediately afterwards, however, taking the view that, as such, aggression had vicissitudes similar to that of libido, they implicitly re-established the confusion between aggression and libido, which Freud had succeeded in overcoming after so much time and with so much effort. The idea of a differentiation of libido and aggression from the common matrix of an undifferentiated energy may also have contributed to this error.

The question cannot be merely one of terminology. After twenty-five years of constant research, Freud rightly defined instincts as 'at once the most important and the most obscure element of psychological research' (1920: 34). Psychoanalysis is based on the study of the psychical derivatives of the instinct, and its path has hitherto been indissolubly linked to the progress of its psychological knowledge of the instincts. If the undeniable distance we have travelled since Freud has not brought any substantial enrichment of our metapsychological knowledge about the aggressive instinct, the conclusion must be that we have grown more in strength than in stature. This would be understandable, considering that psychoanalysis, having originally developed mainly from the work of one man, grew quickly in stature in its early stages.

Yet it must be pointed out that, taking a diametrically opposite position, a minority of analysts have adopted without discussion, not so much the new Freudian theory of the life instinct (Eros) and the death instinct, as the death instinct in itself as the theoretical foundation of the dynamics of aggression, observable in child analysis in particular. This minority has amassed an impressive body of clinical documentation on how aggression operates from the very beginnings of individual life – and has furthermore shown how aggression is especially destructive in the early days and weeks of life. Yet there is nothing in the important work of these analysts to confirm or invalidate Freud's conception of the death instinct, except as regards the innate character of aggression in its most destructive aspects. Hence, if the term 'death instinct' were changed to 'instinct of aggression', this would make no difference to these analysts' discoveries. But the fact that they never put the problem to themselves in these terms indicates how and why all this group's work, however much it may have added to our knowledge of the dynamic phenomena of aggression, has contributed very little more to our metapsychological knowledge of aggression as an instinct. One is reminded in this connection of Freud's reply to Abraham's letter commenting on the first draft of 'Mourning and melancholia' (1915–17a) – a reply that seems to me to be surprisingly relevant to the present situation:

Your comments on melancholia I found very valuable. I have unhesitatingly incorporated in my essay what I found useful. The most valuable point was your remark about the oral phase of the libido; the connection you had made between mourning and melan-cholia is also mentioned. Your request for criticism was easy to fulfil; I was very pleased with everything you wrote. I will only lay stress on two points: that you do not emphasize enough the essential part of my hypothesis, i.e. the topographical consideration in it, the regression of the libido and the abandoning of the unconscious cathexis, and that instead you put sadism and anal-erotism in the foreground as the final explanation. Although you are correct in that, you pass by the real explanation. Anal-erotism, castration complexes, etc., are ubiquitous sources of excitation which must have their share in *every* clinical picture. One time this is made from them, another time that. Naturally we have the task of ascertaining what is made from them, but the explanation of the disorder can only be found in the mechanism – considered dynamically, topo-graphically and economically.

(Freud's letter, in Jones 1953: 329)

The current situation could be summarized in metapsychological terms as follows. We now know a great deal about aggression from the dynamic point of view; much less from the structural point of view; and even less – very little, in fact – from the economic point of view. That little, which is practically what Freud discovered, is and remains, however, of the greatest importance, giving us sound reasons to believe that aggression is probably an instinct, qualitatively different from the sexual instinct, and that there are therefore two different kinds of energy in the psychical apparatus.

However, neither the term 'instinct of aggression' nor the current term 'death instinct' corresponds to any actual metapsychological knowledge of aggression as an instinct. We read, for example, that 'the vicissitudes of aggression resemble those of sexuality to such a degree that the assumption of a constant driving power comparable to that of libido seems appropriate' (Hartmann *et al*. 1949).

Here, the metapsychological foundation of the concept of an 'instinct of aggression' does not seem to have been demonstrated any more convincingly than the supposed and undemonstrated similarity of vicissitudes to libido.

Again, neither the term 'instinct of aggression' nor the term 'death instinct' has much to do with Freud's conception of the life and death instincts, which have hitherto served rather as simple supports for the dynamic, and in part structural, exploration of aggression. Because so little account has been taken of the economic aspects, a gap has opened up between these and the dynamic and structural aspects, so that, more than thirty years after Freud's death, we are still unable to speak of aggression in terms of instinct.

The question concerns the appropriateness of, and the forms to be taken by, research in psychoanalysis. For instance, we have too often heard it repeated that in psychoanalysis therapy is also research. This may be true, as long as we do not believe that the research inherent in therapeutic aims is the same as research with a scientific object. Scientific research must have a purpose which does not only not exactly coincide but may conflict with the therapeutic purpose; and it calls for a necessarily different method. Again, in view of the degree and type of involvement of the analyst in the therapeutic relationship, psychoanalytic research inevitably demands an effort of – and appropriate capacity for – objectification that has no counterpart in other types of scientific research. These are only a few of the reasons why the transition from therapy to research is neither simple nor easy for an analyst. In addition, with the developments accruing from technique and dynamic acquisitions, it has long been possible for the analyst to conduct a good therapeutic psychoanalysis, and this may combine to adverse effect with the difficulty inherent in the transition to research – quite apart from the concomitant trend towards professionalism which this fact may have encouraged.

At this point it is worth repeating what Freud himself had to say about the relationship between therapy and research:

> One of the claims of psycho-analysis to distinction is, no doubt, that in its execution research and treatment coincide; nevertheless, after a certain point, the technique required for the one opposes that required for the other. It is not a good thing to work on a case scientifically while treatment is still proceeding – to piece together its structure, to try to foretell its further progress, and to get a picture from time to time of the current state of affairs, as scientific interest would demand. Cases which are devoted from the first to scientific purposes and are treated accordingly suffer in their outcome; while the most successful cases are those in which one proceeds, as it were, without any purpose in view, allows oneself to be taken by surprise by any new turn in them, and always meets them with an open mind, free from any presuppositions. The correct behaviour for an analyst lies in swinging over according to need from the one mental attitude to the other, in avoiding speculation or brooding over cases while they are in analysis, and in submitting the material obtained to a synthetic process of thought only after the analysis is concluded. The distinction between the two attitudes would be meaningless if we already possessed all the knowledge (or at least the essential knowledge) about the psychology of the unconscious and about the structure of the neuroses that we can obtain from psychoanalytic work. At present we are still far from that goal and we ought not to cut ourselves off from the possibility of testing what we have already learnt and of extending our knowledge further.
>
> (1912: 114)

Precisely sixty years on from the penning of these instructive words, we may say that we have perhaps accomplished much more than Freud, in his modesty, then expected. Whereas on the one hand awareness of what we do not yet know has increased and become more specific, on the other hand, paradoxically, what we have acquired puts us more at risk than at the time when Freud wrote the words, cutting 'ourselves off from the possibility of . . . extending our knowledge further'. Although Freud, who was always inclined to undertake research, posed the ethical problem of research against therapy, we, oddly enough, may now have to confront the opposite ethical problem: that of therapy against research.

This, of course, is in no way to detract from the major psycho-analytic purpose of therapy, the original purpose that was the starting

51

point of Freud's own research in his day. However, psychoanalysis has now gone so far in its investigation of the human mind that it cannot in any way be identified simply with psychoanalytic therapy. The psychoanalytic edifice is in fact so constructed that doctrine and therapy are indissolubly interdependent. It is impossible to conceive of any extension of metapsychological knowledge not based on clinical experience, or of any therapeutic psychoanalysis without the assumption of and constant testing against metapsychology. It should therefore be clear that any further extension of knowledge accruing from research cannot but give rise to a further development of therapeutic psychoanalysis. This might suffice as justification of the ethical problem, in the terms in which it appears to be specifically posed by the current situation. However, it is in any case self-evident that the investigation of human mental activity is important enough fully to justify by itself the ethical problem of therapy against research.

Of course, it cannot be said that sufficient research in psychoanalysis has not hitherto been conducted, or that this research is of inadequate quality. The foregoing considerations suggest that the problem is different and is a matter of completeness rather than of qualitative or quantitative adequacy. With regard to the requirement of metapsychology, our research has in general so far lacked completeness.

This may be explained as follows. A phenomenon may be correctly evaluated dynamically, genetically, and also structurally, but if it is not also appropriately evaluated in economic terms, two risks arise. First, we may merely have described the phenomenon correctly but not succeeded in explaining it. Second – and this is much more harmful for the purposes of research – we may fail to realize this and assume that the correct description is the explanation. This is the 'error' that Freud was concerned to point out to Abraham in the letter quoted earlier, but which has persisted since Freud's day into our own time, albeit with exceptions. This explains the lack of development of the economic viewpoint in metapsychology, giving rise to the gap referred to earlier, and leads us to conclude that quantitative evaluation of the observed phenomena represents the ultimate objective, and at the same time the one most difficult of achievement, of psychoanalytic research.

This is borne out by the very history of metapsychology. Freud had understood very early on that quantitative phenomena underlay mental activity when he wrote:

In mental functions something is to be distinguished – a quota of affect or sum of excitation – which possesses all the characteristics of a quantity (though we have no means of measuring it), which is capable of increase, diminution, displacement and discharge, and which is spread over the memory-traces of ideas somewhat as an electric charge is spread over the surface of a body.

(1894: 60)

However, over twenty years were to pass before Freud succeeded in formulating the economic point of view. This formulation in fact came last in his constitution of metapsychology:

Up till now [Freud then wrote], it [psychoanalysis] has differed from that psychology [the descriptive psychology of consciousness] mainly by reason of its *dynamic* view of mental processes; now in addition it seems to take account of psychical *topography* as well, and to indicate in respect of any given mental act within what system or between what systems it takes place. On account of this attempt too, it has been given the name of 'depth-psychology'. We shall hear that it can be further enriched by taking yet another point of view into account.

(1915b: 173)

This was precisely the economic point of view. It is obviously no accident that Freud was only then able to write his astonishing series of great metapsychological works (1915b). Nor is it any wonder that Abraham at the same time was still making the mistake of confusing a correct dynamic description of phenomena with an explanation of these phenomena. What should surprise us is that this tendency has obstinately and unyieldingly persisted to the present day, even though all analysts have been perfectly conscious of what is meant by the metapsychological presentation of a phenomenon.

However, rather than being surprised, we should become aware of this tendency and realize that, because of it, we have so far failed to lay the foundations of a psychoanalytic theory of aggression. While, as we have seen, research in general calls for effort on the part of the analyst, research on the economic level seems to demand an even greater effort – as if the resistances increased disproportionately in response to it. Some analysts have recently gone so far as to propose the elimination of the concept of energy; this would, of course, free us once and for all from the economic point of view. I do not deny that the idea of eliminating what is a source of frustration may sometimes appear to be an instance of obeying the reality sense, but we ultimately find that it is as a rule in fact more a matter of obedience to the demands of the pleasure principle. Such an idea becomes a dangerous pitfall in scientific research because it may more or less finally take us away from the reality aims pursued by research. Before dispensing with the fact, discovered by Freud and abundantly borne out by experience, of the quantitative foundation of both normal and pathological mental phenomena, we should first be in a position to show that it is untrue. In addition, before assuming that quantitative criteria do not allow us to extend our knowledge further, we should ask ourselves how on earth this might be possible, considering that they have allowed us to learn everything we know so far. The fact of the matter is that in metapsychology the economic viewpoint since Freud has developed little if at all, for the simple reason that it has been neglected and not sufficiently investigated.

There must plainly be intrinsic difficulties in the very investigation of the economic aspects. One difficulty is certainly the need to deal with quantities which we have no way of measuring. However, the economic concepts of psychoanalysis allow us to study the various types of quantitative modification observed and to understand their functions in the sphere of mental processes. This is what Freud did with the sexual instincts, and it is what we are used to.

What is perhaps a greater difficulty has to do with the fact that the quantitative processes are very close to biological processes, if they are not actual borderline processes, whose prototype is the process to which the psychoanalytic concept of instinct relates. However, we need only think of the still mysterious relations between somatic pathology and psychopathology. The researching analyst cannot overlook the biological root of the process, but is bound to seek the phenomena derived from it in the psychological field and to investigate them by metapsychological criteria. 'Psychoanalysts never forget', wrote Freud, 'that the mental is based on the organic, although their work can only carry them as far as this basis and not beyond it' (1910b: 214).

It is interesting to note that Freud must have understood this necessity precisely while he was writing his 'Project for a scientific psychology' (1895). This is evident from his decision, so momentous for psychoanalysis, to put this important work away in a drawer for ever when its ink was barely dry. True scientific psychology could not but be 'psychological' – that is, a psychology able to recognize psychical functioning as an integral part of the functional continuum of the organism, and at the same time to recognize psychical activity in that continuum as a distinct function whose post-natal development attains such high and complex levels of differentiation as to call for an appropriately conceived method of investigation, which must needs be psychological in nature. As we know, it took twenty years for this method – metapsychology – to be perfected and tested. On the basis of experience, we can now say that our progressive difficulty in moving from the investigation of the dynamic aspects to that of the topographical aspects and the all-important investigation of the economic aspects reflects the sequence in time of these stages as gradually developed by Freud. The difficulty therefore lies in the nature of the economic phenomena. The dynamic aspects are obviously much more approachable on the psychological level than the quantitative aspects, which are by nature so close to the biological level.

However, the study of the instincts makes an investigation of the quantitative processes essential. The validity of the metapsychological method is demonstrated in this sense – if indeed such a demonstration were necessary – precisely by the present situation of psychoanalytic research on aggression. Having failed to pursue the enquiry on the economic level, we find ourselves unable to say anything convincing about aggression as an instinct, even if we are more or less fully conversant with the dynamic and structural aspects. As a result, we do not yet possess a satisfactory theory of the instincts. Freud was always keenly aware of the importance for psychoanalysis of constructing a convincing theory of the instincts. The complex twists and turns of the path followed by him in arriving at an appropriate systematization of human instincts should greatly help each of us when we embark on further research into aggression. Since a theory of instincts which Freud could take as a basis did not exist, his first classification clearly derived from biology: the instincts of preservation of the individual on the one hand and those of preservation of the species on the other. The latter, understood by the term 'sexual instincts', immediately came under his scrutiny. For want of anything better, the others for a long time remained the 'self-preservative instincts', about which Freud knew very little. Suddenly, in 1910a, in a short paper that was relatively insignificant for him, he referred to them as 'ego instincts'. He did not abandon the previous term but began to use the two interchangeably. A few months later, however, in the Schreber case history (1911), came the first mention of the discovery of narcissism, a discovery that gave him access to the unknown area he called the 'ego', which, however, would eventually call into question precisely the 'ego instincts' he had just defined.

Narcissism was a stage in the early infantile development of libido falling between the stages of autoerotism and object libido. Before turning to an external object, the individual 'takes himself, his own body, as his love-object'. This meant that initially the ego was cathected with libido. How then were the libidinal instincts to be distinguished from the self-preservative instincts in the ego? 'Narcissism', Freud replied, was 'the libidinal complement of egoism' (1917: 223). The former antithesis between sexual instincts and ego instincts is now supplanted by a new antithesis, between ego libido and object libido.

However, the problem did not escape Freud's notice at this point: two different types of instincts – that is, two different types of energy – would then coexist in the ego. Freud was assailed by doubt and by the idea that it might perhaps be possible to eliminate the concept of the preservative instincts (the heritage of biology) with their relative energy and simply replace them by narcissistic and object libido. But he rejected this idea, on the grounds that the antithesis of ego libido and object libido 'is an unavoidable corollary to an original hypothesis which distinguished between sexual instincts and ego–instincts' (1914: 76). Finally, however, he was compelled to admit that this original hypothesis was not in fact based on psychological evidence but was fundamentally a biological hypothesis: 'But I shall be consistent enough to drop this hypothesis if psychoanalytic work should itself produce some other, more serviceable hypothesis about the instincts' (1914: 79).

This 'consistency' of Freud's is, we can see, another reference to his constant need to distinguish psychoanalytic from biological thought. However, it is also a sign of the methodological rigour of his research on the economic level. The problem was to gain a better understanding of the so-called 'ego instincts' and the type of energy used by them. It is precisely in the Schreber case history (1911) and in his paper on narcissism (1914) that Freud introduces a new term, in addition to the term 'ego instincts'. This *third* term is 'interest', or 'ego interest', or 'ego interest in general'. The term does not appear to have made much headway either in Freud's thought or in psychoanalytic thought in general. Rather than actually defining something, it was an expression of the difficulty of defining the non-libidinal instincts of the ego and their relations with the libidinal ones. This difficulty begins with the introduction of the concept of narcissism and gradually becomes more acute, until the radical revision of the theory of instincts featuring in *Beyond the Pleasure Principle* (1920).

In his paper on narcissism, following a suggestion of Ferenczi, Freud observes that a person tormented by a physical disease 'withdraws *libidinal* interest from his love-objects'. Immediately afterwards he remarks: 'Here libido and ego-interest share the same fate and are once more indistinguishable from each other' (1914: 82).

On the other hand, since the term 'interest' stands for 'ego instincts', it also signifies instincts of preservation, which are distinct and separate from, and opposed to, the libidinal instincts. This is the form in which 'interest' tends to appear in 'Instincts and their vicissitudes' (1915a). The same opposition is confirmed a year later in the *Introductory Lectures on Psycho-Analysis* (Lecture XVI): 'We termed the cathexes of energy which the ego directs towards the objects of its sexual desires "libido";

all the others, which are sent out by the self-preservative instincts, we termed "interest"' (1916–17: 414).

In *Beyond the Pleasure Principle* (1920), however, Freud declares that the 'narcissistic libido was of course also a manifestation of the force of the sexual instinct' and that 'it had necessarily to be identified with the "self-preservative instincts"' (p. 52).

It seems to me that these apparent contradictions can be resolved if it is remembered that, besides the polarity of *sexual instincts/ego instincts*, Freud now introduced the polarity of *ego/object*. He distinguished narcissistic libido (of the ego) from object libido (the libidinal cathexes turned towards the outside). It is these latter that are opposed to the homologous *object* cathexes of the 'ego instincts' or self-preservative instincts or 'interest'. The libidinal cathexes of the ego (narcissistic cathexes) on the other hand, 'share the same fate' as the *egoistic* cathexes of the ego instincts (self-preservation, interest), with which they must 'be identified'. In other words, there is not opposition but complementarity between egoism and narcissism. 'Narcissism', Freud says, 'is the libidinal complement to egoism. When we speak of egoism, we have in view only the individual's *advantage*; when we talk of narcissism we are also taking his libidinal satisfaction into account' (1916–17: 471).

But, however necessary this clarification, it adds nothing to any special meaning of the term 'interest' used at that time by Freud. From this point of view, it seems evident to me that the term is perfectly interchangeable with the terms 'ego instincts' and 'preservative instincts'. But since terms are never just words in Freud, we may be certain that 'interest' is not a pleonasm. As we know, Freud was not satisfied with the theory of instincts he was using, considering it to be too biological and insufficiently based on psychological knowledge. With regard to the sexual instincts, the term 'libido' had been very useful to him, having had the connotation of the 'energy of the sexual instincts' and having thus allowed him to undertake the entire psychological study in economic and dynamic terms of the development and manifestations of the sexual instincts. This was to lead him to formulate a 'libido theory'.

In the matter of the self-preservative instincts, he was aware that he knew very little on the psychological level. A new, less biological term was needed to correspond more closely to what he was looking for: a type of energy different from sexual energy, which he could investigate in a similar way to his successful enquiry into sexual energy. The introduction of the term 'ego instincts' (1910), apparently out of the blue and very discreetly, was an attempt in this direction. He did not use it to replace the term 'self-preservative instincts' but placed it alongside this term, as if to try it out. The term 'interest' followed shortly afterwards, and was to coexist with the other two, which remained useful. Compared with 'ego instincts', however, there is no doubt that it expresses the biological meaning of 'self-preservative instinct' on a much more psychological level. In this sense, these terms appear as manifest signs of the internal dynamics of Freud's thought, as, from 1910 on, he gradually moved towards the conquest of the fortified citadel of the ego. The study on narcissism (1914) was the first decisive step in this direction; the campaign was to culminate in *The Ego and the Id* (1923).

However, this objective also involves a gradual approach to the aggressive instinct. From the biological 'self-preservative instinct', Freud cautiously moves on to 'ego instincts', and thence to 'interest', which may be egoistic or narcissistic, or egoistic and object-related and anti-libidinal. It is this last position of the ego which gradually leads on to aggression and the death instinct.

The suspicion of an aggressive energy that had nothing to do with libido is latent in those years and emerges for the first time, significantly, in 1915 – that is, the year when the libido theory could be said to have been finally completed. At this point, in 'Instincts and their vicissitudes', Freud becomes aware of the love/hate polarity. At first, he still seems to be looking for a legitimate way of maintaining his positions. He remarks that love and hate are not properly 'instincts' but affects and 'attitudes' of the ego as a whole (1915a). However, he then enters into the study of the love/hate polarity and distinguishes its various meanings, referable to the stage of primary narcissism. He gradually comes to realize that hate directed towards the object 'can . . . be intensified to the point of an aggressive inclination against the object – and intention to destroy it' (1915a). Whereas love ultimately becomes attached to sexual objects as a source of pleasure, hate obviously remains connected with the ego instincts and tends to attack objects as sources of unpleasure (*Unlust*).

> The relation of *unpleasure* seems to be the sole decisive one. The ego hates, abhors and pursues with intent to destroy all objects which are a source of unpleasurable feeling for it, without taking into account whether they mean a frustration of sexual satisfaction or of the satisfaction of self-preservative needs. Indeed, it may be asserted that the true prototypes of the relation of hate are derived not from sexual life, but from the ego's struggle to preserve and maintain itself [p. 138]. Hate, as a relation to objects, is older than love. It derives from the narcissistic ego's primordial repudiation of the external world with its outpouring of stimuli. As an expression of the

reaction of unpleasure evoked by objects, it always remains in an intimate relation with the self-preservative instincts; so that sexual and ego-instincts can readily develop an antithesis which repeats that of love and hate.

(1915a: 139)

From this description we can already catalogue a number of characteristics of a possible aggressive instinct, which, however, still lacks the possibility of being so named. It resides in the ego, as early as at the time of narcissistic libido; from the ego it is directed towards objects, no less than object libido; it has to do with sensations or feelings of unpleasure, while the libido has to do with sensations or feeling of pleasure; it is not a component of the sexual instinct, as was formerly believed; on the contrary, it may be in conflict with the sexual instinct; and finally, it is older than the libidinal instinct. The passage quoted above also gives rise to the following comments.

With the advent of the structural theory, the instinct, which has become the death instinct, will, like the libidinal instincts, be situated in the id. With regard to the priority of hate over love, this temporal relationship, displaced on to the death instinct and libido, will subsequently be confirmed. Should we ever succeed in conceiving of a metapsychologically acceptable aggressive instinct without resorting to the life and death instincts, I believe that we should have to take into account this indication of the priority of the aggressive instinct, which seems to be borne out by certain facts [Chapter 2]. Finally, it appears from the passage quoted above that Freud considered aggression to be merely a response to frustrations, of whatever kind. However, it should be remembered that this is Freud's first position concerning non-libidinal aggressive manifestations, which he regarded as affects and not as instinct. The majority of analysts today still maintain that aggression is an instinct but is primarily a response to frustration. It seems to me that these two propositions are contradictory. If it were possible for them to coexist, we should probably have to reformulate the metapsychological definition of an instinct. In my opinion, the response can be defined as a manifestation of the instinct, but this does not identify it with the instinct. I therefore venture to suggest that the relation between aggression and frustration remains to be defined in the economic sense.

We see that Freud ultimately conceived aggression as differing from libido only from the point of view of object cathexes. His experience of the First World War may well have played a part in inducing him to recognize destructive aggression. But throughout all the years of his work, Freud's latent problem with aggression was more concerned with the mystery of aggression turned against the self. Apart from the experience of the war in the evolution we have observed in the theory of instincts, however, the obscure area of the ego as the seat of an energy different from erotic energy gradually came to be seen as the seat of an aggressive energy. With the structural theory and the division of the psychical apparatus into the three agencies of id, ego, and superego, the ego and the id are defined in their relations, and all the terms previously used to define the ego (which is now no longer an instinctual agency but, on the contrary, regains its position as a repressing agency, which may come into conflict with the id) no longer have a *raison d'être*. The concept of the superego enables Freud to understand that the main problem of aggression in man is its internal administration. In this sense, 'The economic problem of masochism' (1924) remains Freud's greatest attempt, and the indispensable starting point, for any further research on aggression. The concept of the death instinct dramatically underlines the point about the internal administration of aggressive energy, and many facts of clinical observation confirm that the psychical capacity to produce internal self-regulating mechanisms of aggression in which the libido is strongly involved is a prerogative of Man. Unfortunately, however, there is no possibility of clinical verification of the entire cellular theory of the life and death instincts. Although Freud had been able early on to lock away his biologically based 'Project for a scientific psychology' in a drawer and move on to a scientific psychology based on a psychological method, making this into a kind of disciplinary rule to which he had always strictly adhered, at the end, like a latter-day Orpheus, he turned round at the fateful moment to take another look at the lost biology.

Fifty years on from that moment, all we can say is that, from Freud's last theory of the instincts, the almost unanimous conviction, based not so much on his theory as on the discoveries due to his research in economic terms, that aggression is an instinct, has remained with us and grown stronger. Only if we become able to prove it can we go beyond the death instinct.

4

Formation of the father and the primal scene

Read at a scientific meeting of the Centro Psicoanalitico, Rome, in January 1974 under the title 'Formazione del padre e scena primaria', this paper was published in the *Rivista di Psicoanalisi* (February 1977) XXIII and in *Revista de Psicoanalisi* (Argentinian Psychoanalytic Association) (1979), under the title 'Formación del padre y scena primaria'.

It is perhaps inappropriate to say that the father is a second object in infantile development. A better definition would at least need to take account of the fact that this second object, for the first time in infancy, assumes the form of a love object to be acquired. Unlike the mother (or the breast), which the child initially experiences as self and only gradually learns to distinguish from himself and see as 'external' (not extraneous) to the self, the second object appears to the child from the beginning as 'extraneous' (and hence as external) to the self. This new fact has many important consequences. The child reacts or responds to this experience, which is in many respects disturbing, in ways which involve substantial changes in the primitive relationship with the mother and the child's image of himself. Through the triangular situation, these also promote a decisive development of the object relationship. This paper as far as possible investigates the complicated process whereby the child gradually comes to form and acquire a first love object located outside the space of his primitive relationship with the mother.

Introduction

The father appears very early in the psychical life of the child, around the second half of the first year, or a little earlier. This is one reason why investigation of the early stages of the child's relationship with the father is not easy. Another reason is that the very nature of the child's experiences during this period gives rise to powerful, primitive defences, which tend constantly to circumscribe and limit the effect of those experiences on the contexts of other, both earlier and later, experiences. This means that clinically we seldom have evidence that can be related to the father in this period, and even when we do, it tends to appear in the form of derivatives.

On the other hand, there is no doubt that, however justified the charge that psychoanalytic research tends to concentrate too exclusively on the child–mother relationship and to neglect the relationships with the father, the phenomena of the relationship with the mother really are of overwhelming importance in the first months of life and remain paramount throughout the first year.

The appearance of the father, for its part, cannot be regarded as a single event. From the moment when it begins, it occupies a prolonged period, during which maturational processes of fundamental importance take place. According to Greenacre (1973),

> at least in the first half of the first year, auditory, kinesthetic, and tactile responsiveness may be equal to or more important than vision. Within a few weeks after birth, focusing of vision occurs and is first directed toward the mother's face. . . . This soon begins to cooperate with hearing, which elicits reactions to stimuli not immediately at hand. . . . But there is a gradual increase in the pressure to *see*. . . . During the second year there is a definite increase in the vulnerability to genital stimulation

and the child passes through 'a period of momentous maturational change'. The child has learnt to walk and talk, so that his 'range of stimulation and reactivity' is increased. 'Heightened bodily invigoration is evident and frequently associated with the appearance of infantile masturbation. There is a sensitivity to both general and genital excitation' (Greenacre 1973: 14–15).

While these fundamental maturational processes are taking place, no less fundamental processes are unfolding in the mental life of the child, on the object-relation level. In attempting to describe these processes, I shall inevitably have to return to some earlier concepts of mind which featured in previous publications, albeit in different contexts.

The basic organization of the object relation

In discussing (1969) the early vicissitudes of the relationship with the object, I distinguished between two areas of mental experience, corresponding to a two-fold primitive attitude towards the object, defining them as the *psychosensory* (or sensory psychic) and the *psycho-oral* (or oral psychic) areas respectively. The first, and more ancient, has its source in primitive perception through the soma, while the second is connected with the gradual perceptual recognition of stimuli external to the self, as through oral activity. Whereas the psychosensory experiences tend to avoid recognition of the object as 'other than self', expressing a disposition to 'be' the object, the psycho-oral experiences confront the child with the object in a more pressing and real manner, giving rise to wishes, conflicts, frustrations, instinctual anxiety, and so on, and basically expressing a tendency to 'have' or possess the object. As I then added, 'naturally, the oral psychic area is not limited to the oral zone, just as the sensory psychic area does not exclude the oral zone' [see Chapter 1].

The activity of the psychosensory area develops in accordance with a functional model – 'imitation in order to be' – which is the psychical equivalent of the biological model of primitive perception ('imitation in order to perceive') and leads to the hallucinatory image, to fantasies of fusion by way of magical identity with the object and to imitations, in the direction of 'being' the object, and hence of *not* acknowledging it as external and separate. The activity of the psycho-oral area, on the other hand, develops on the basis of the functional model of intro-jection – which is the psychical equivalent of the biological model of incorporation – and leads to fantasies of fusion through the taking of the object into one's own self, in the direction of 'possessing' the object, involving the gradual recognition of the object as external to the self and the need to confront real dependence on the object.

From the point of view of the primitive structure and of the interaction of the two areas, we can imagine the psychosensory area as being in a central position and the psycho-oral area on the periphery. In terms of the famous image of the amoeba, the psycho-oral area is well represented by the pseudopodia, which make sorties into the outside world with a phagocytary aim, while the body of the amoeba stands for the central narcissistic organization, in which psychosensory activity predominates. The image of the amoeba also serves to demon-strate what is effectively the primordial primacy in the narcissistic organization of the central body – which in the child has its origins in the pre-natal period – and shows how its pseudopodic activity is in fact exercised in relation to an external environment, which can take shape from birth on. In other words, the pseudopodia constitute the difference between the post-natal situation and that of the foetus, and express the mental experiences associated with oral activity.[1]

Imitative identity

Psychoanalysis has concentrated particularly on these psycho-oral experiences in the early relation to the mother and on their significance in terms of individual personality development. The same cannot be said of the phenomena in the early relation to the mother which derive from the activity of the psychosensory area. Yet these phenomena, although more tacit and less noticeable, constitute the foundation of mental functioning at the beginning of life and draw great strength and continuity from the fact that they are directly and deeply rooted in somatic functioning. Their main role seems to be the maintenance within the self of a homoeostatic equilibrium, which, however, is constantly and increasingly called into question by the vital needs which impel the child to relate to the environment.

It is these needs which give rise to mental experiences in the psycho-oral area, backed by instinctual pressures. Whenever the primitive drives do not find immediate satisfaction (which can only come from the outside world), the internal tension quickly begins to threaten homoeostatic stability. The infantile self's first elementary defence is, again in terms of Freud's amoeba image, to withdraw the pseudopodia – that is, to retreat into the psychosensory area – while the second is to create autonomously in this area a substitutive experience, modelled on that of the instinctual satisfaction that is lacking, but which the child has already experienced on other occasions.

In this way, the infantile self gives up the object, withdrawing cathexes from it, and implicitly annihilates it by itself becoming the object capable of gratification. I have suggested that imitation can be defined as the mechanism of psychosensory activity whereby the infantile self achieves a magical identity with the object [see Chapter 1]. The imitative mechanism – and consequently the imitative identity – does not call for any organized psychical structure; on the contrary, it is the expression of elementary mental phenomena, concerning which Freud commented that 'originally the mere existence of a presentation was a guarantee of the reality of what was presented' (Freud 1925: 237). In this sense, the hallucinatory image is to be regarded as a prototype of imitation, as well as of imitative identity.

Basic economic aspects

The aim of imitation is presumably to reinforce the integrity of the self, threatened by unsatisfied instinctual tensions, and to do so in a way we define as 'magical'. The elementary mechanism is that described by

Freud for dreams, and in particular children's dreams, in which wish
fulfilment and need satisfaction are obviously one and the same thing.
It is perhaps worth pointing out that dreaming can be described as the
most manifest and observable expression of the activity of the psychosensory area of the mind, which thus persists throughout the life of
each individual. This activity is rendered latent in the waking state by
the predominance of the psycho-oral area. The latter's activity is,
however, suspended during sleep. External perceptions and the relation
to the outside world cease, while the continuous basic functioning of
the psychosensory area comes to the fore again. This area of mental
functioning includes the internal perceptions, proprioceptions, and the
identity relations of imitations, even the most primitive ones. Much of
this complex activity is intended to translate and elaborate the experiences of the waking state, experienced in the psycho-oral area, according to the internal needs of the self.

In discussing aggression [see Chapter 2] I have alluded to one of
Freud's last hypotheses, expressed only in private (Freud 1937, quoted
in Jones) but nevertheless extremely convincing, that at birth the
libidinal cathexes are all turned inwards and the aggressive ones outwards, this situation subsequently being reversed. This hypothesis
provides us with a plausible representation of the economic situation at
the beginning of life, which we can then compare with clinical
experience.

This hypothesis thus makes it easier for us to accept a vitally
important fact, for which we have in fact had clinical evidence for a
long time. The instinctual drives which present themselves in the first
weeks of life as brooking no delay, and which thus tend towards
immediate satisfaction, are aggressive in nature, contrary to long-
established belief, and not a primitive type of libido or as yet undifferentiated energy [see Chapter 2]. In addition, these drives are quantitatively predominant in an absolute sense. Since they prove to be
strongly destructive, it is difficult to say to what extent this character is
attributable to their alleged primitiveness and to what extent to their
absolute quantitative prevalence. However, they are originally aggressive – that is, not erotic – and directed towards the outside world (from
which alone, moreover, they can receive satisfaction). On the basis of
the foregoing, we may add the obvious point that these drives are the
ones that prevail in the pseudopodia of the amoeba image – that is, in
the psycho-oral area of early mental functioning.

The libidinal cathexes, on the other hand, are massively concentrated in the self and turned inwards during this period, with the
aim of actively maintaining and protecting the stability of the self
(homoeostatic equilibrium). These cathexes form the basis of the

functioning of the psychosensory area. The non-erotic instinctual tensions disturb the internal equilibrium, and if they increase beyond a certain threshold, which is presumably very low in the first weeks of life, they begin to threaten the stability and integrity of the self. Very soon – that is, as soon as sufficient mnemonic traces have been laid down – even short delays in the satisfaction of the non-erotic drives give rise not only to immediate withdrawal from the psycho-oral area but also to the primitive imitative fantasy which we call the 'hallucinatory image'. In functional terms, it may be said that the activity of the psychosensory area now begins to succeed by psychical means, however elementary, in temporarily raising the internal threshold of non-delayability of the drive [see Chapter 2].

But it would be wrong to assume that, because a psychical phenomenon is elementary, it must on that account be simple. It should be noted first of all that, as a product of the area of psychosensory activity, the hallucinatory image is attributable to the work of libidinal cathexes. Second, since the hallucinatory fantasy is modelled on the representation of the internal situation of gratification *already experienced on other occasions*, we must assume that the mnemonic traces relating to the bodily gratification situation have been previously cathected with libido in the psychosensory area. This means that when the self is confronted with an internal economic situation in which unsatisfied aggressive drives – that is, ones which cannot achieve discharge to the outside – threaten to spill over into the psychosensory area, thereby seriously jeopardizing internal stability, it is able to counterpose 'significant' libidinal cathexes capable of changing the situation of frustration into the specifically opposite one of gratification. It may be wondered whether this mechanism of *selective libidinal counterposition* does not play a fundamental part in the determinism of the energetic fusion processes which remove from the psychosensory area gradually increasing quantities of libido, selectively fused with the aggressive drives, in the direction of the object. Again, I believe that the idea that the fusion is selective from the outset may help us to understand how libido through the fusion processes at the same time facilitates a process of differentiation. At least two characteristics of this last process could be described: the first, that it includes selective libidinal cathexes; and the second, that this selectivity allows the use of relatively small quantities of libido to confront proportionately much larger quantities of aggressive cathexes.

Be that as it may, having regard to the original economic conditions and considering how gradually the fusion processes and the process of libido differentiation get under way, the aggressive drives are undeniably present in the first weeks of life and consequently play a part in the child's early relationship with the mother. It therefore seems to me necessary to distinguish sharply between the aggressive instinctual drives – which are primary, are set in motion by situations of need on the part of the organism and are directed from the beginning towards an object, their main aim being to incorporate that object – and the aggressive 'responses' to frustration, which are secondary to the non-satisfaction of the drives, which may be manifested in different ways and whose form of manifestation also depends on the degree of frustration suffered along the scale of gratification–frustration. This distinction obviously does not concern the nature of the primary drives and of the secondary responses, which is the same, but their significance in individual psychical life and the differences in their internal administration in the relationship with the self and the object.

So far I have been attempting to describe this relationship, together with some essential phenomena of early mental functioning. To sum up, the salient points in this description concern the two-fold primitive attitude of the self towards the object, the corresponding organization of basic mental functioning (the psychosensory and psycho-oral areas), the origin and functioning of each of the mental areas, their mutual relations, and the economic and dynamic significance of their functioning. I have also discussed the respective relations of functional priority of internal libidinal and aggressive cathexes and of external aggressive and libidinal cathexes, and distinguished instinctual aggressive drives from aggressive responses. Finally, I have proposed a hypothesis on the metapsychology of the hallucinatory image whereby certain aspects of the fusion processes and of the process of libido differentiation could be clarified.

The mental organization hitherto described allows the child to move on cautiously from complete identification with the mother's breast towards a distinction of the object from self and of self from the object, and towards close physical and mental contact with the object. Under normal conditions, changes usually take place in the self and in the relation to the object during the course of these progressive oscillations. The timing of the father's appearance does not, of course, depend on the father but on the level of visual and aural perceptions attained by the child, allowing him to respond to a certain extent to remote stimuli connected with the father's presence.

The primal scene: clinical aspects

To this period of infantile life usually belong a particular type of experiences which have a great deal to do with the presence of the father and are capable of generating extremely dramatic responses in the child. I mean the experiences which, since Freud first described them in his account of the Wolf Man (1918), we have subsumed under the name of the 'primal scene'. Ever since, we have continued to use this term to mean simply the perception by the child of the parental intercourse, thereby uselessly carrying on an argument begun by Freud as to whether the child actually experienced the primal scene or merely fantasized it. However, more useful information has been forthcoming about the sexual theories of children, which are strongly influenced in the individual child by his or her own primal scene experiences.

It is widely believed that the derivatives of the primal scene encountered in adults are always pathological. However, this opinion is changing. According to a recent, authoritative statement (Greenacre 1973), the primal scene is a ubiquitous experience. Other authors have also lately suggested that the primal scene is an experience that forms part of normal development (Bradley 1967; Edelheit 1974). I too have expressed such a view, at the International Psychoanalytical Association Paris Congress (1974), giving my reasons for holding it, which are closely bound up with the process of acquisition of a second object.

We are confronted in clinical work with derivatives of the primal scene far more often than we think. I would say that there is no analysis in which some aspects of the ways in which the primal scene was experienced do not sooner or later emerge. I shall confine myself to a few remarks on the subject.

The derivatives may be of various kinds. Greenacre (1973) gives us an exemplary enumeration: 'dreams, screen memories, behaviour and symptoms of later life, and especially . . . the fantasies associated with masturbation'. It may be added that certain experiences in the transference are sometimes recognizable as primal-scene derivatives. The patient of a candidate in supervision was suddenly assailed by anxiety during the session at the sound of the analyst's chair creaking. He later confessed that the idea had occurred to him that the analyst was masturbating. The associations aroused memories in the patient which could clearly be referred to aural experiences of the primal scene.

The derivatives may be more or less obvious or cryptic. We must sometimes content ourselves with supposing that certain elements may be related to the primal scene and wait for subsequent confirmation. On other occasions, the derivatives appear as *non*-derivatives – that is, as direct memories. These are screen memories, which usually refer to much later periods than those of the actual primal-scene experiences, which the screen memory keeps unconscious (Greenacre 1973).

The derivatives may be expressed by symptoms. A woman patient with character disturbances suffered from a single phobia which dated back to her childhood, a phobia of pigeons. The analysis brought back memories which clearly derived from primal-scene experiences and from which it was possible to reconstruct the formation of the phobia. It was discovered in this way that the window of her bedroom when she was a child looked out on to a courtyard, one of whose walls was of natural rock. This natural rock was full of dark folds and recesses, in which a number of pigeons lived. As a little girl, the patient used to see them coming out and going in, disappearing into the dark cracks in the rock, and this made her very afraid. She recalled with horror the little pigeon, hatched in the rock, which she used to see coming out. Early in the morning, she was often woken up by the guttural call of the pigeons, which terrified her. The bedroom adjoined that of her parents, and the patient was the eldest of four siblings, the first of whom had been born when the patient was less than 3 years old. The phobia clearly derived from a displacement outside her room and her house of what she had had occasion to see and hear in the house, on the other side of the door that led to the parents' bedroom. Later, dreams and other memories made it possible to reconstruct the primal-scene experiences sufficiently exactly. One specific memory was of the sight of the father's genitals, to which the patient had been frequently exposed as a child, as he used to move about the house in his pyjama jacket without trousers. But she had also seen the mother's genitals at an early age.

The screen memories can sometimes be surprisingly early. In one case, however, the memory proved to be the result of a defensive organization that was definitely later in origin than the time to which it appeared to refer, yet the memory provided extremely precise timings. The patient declared that he could recall – very clearly – his own baptism. In the memory he was very small, lying in a festively bedecked cradle, around which there were adults looking at him. The patient knew he had been baptized at the age of 6 months, and realized that his memory might be incorrect. Yet the memory was so vivid and realistic that he himself was surprised by it. In fact, the patient had a brother, born when he was 15 months old, and the scene of the memory concerned the brother's birth, which he had blotted out by putting himself in his place. At 6 months he had indeed been baptized, but that age also in all probability coincided with his experience of the primal scene, which took place, if the information is accurate, exactly 9 months before the brother was born. In the scene of the memory, the adults around him were looking at him, just as it had fallen to him at that time to look at the adults. Of course, the pseudo-memory might have related to the brother's baptism rather than his birth and thus have dated back to when the patient was just over 1½ years old. It does not matter very much. At any rate, although the patient knew so well the age at which he himself had been baptized, he had no idea how old the brother was at the time of *his* baptism.

Dreams sometimes include fragments of memories which would remain incomprehensible if they could not be fleshed out by consciousness. A female patient dreamed that she was very small, 2 or 3 years old, and was running along an avenue that led to a square. That was the entire dream. However, the patient said she knew the location very well: a house where, when she was a little girl as in the dream, there had been a celebration for the wedding of an aunt, her mother's sister. In trying to remember when this had been, she said after some thought that she must have been 2 years old or slightly more, as she remembered well that her sister had not yet been born (she was born when the patient was 2 years and 9 months old). 'In any case', she added, 'I have memories of when I was under 2 years old.' She then said that she remembered the new house, into which they must have moved at that time. In this house, she recalled the room in which she had slept by herself, next to her parents' bedroom, and her fears, as a result of which the parents had left the door to their bedroom open. One room in the house had no floor. She remembered her satisfaction when the floor was laid. In the next session she told how, visiting her mother, it had occurred to her to ask her about that time of her childhood, to see whether her memories were correct. The mother had confirmed everything point by point, but to her surprise had told her that at the time of the celebration of her aunt's marriage, her younger sister was already 2 or 3 months old. Somewhat disconcerted by this, she had then been compelled to admit that at the time of that wedding she had been 3 years old and not 2, as she had confidently believed.

It is merely necessary to substitute the parental intercourse for the aunt's wedding, which was a displacement, to have an immediate explanation of why the patient was disconcerted. The mother's testimony had so to speak dismantled the only error, but a significant one, that could be detected in the screen memories which the patient had retained from an early period of her life, when she had had particularly momentous experiences. Moving house had disrupted her internal stability. The anxiety about the empty, unfinished room was concealed behind the memory of the satisfaction of seeing the floor laid. She had been put to sleep in a new, unfamiliar room. A situation already so potentially pathogenic had perhaps contributed substantially to the traumatic effect on this patient of the primal-scene experiences of that time, which had been facilitated by the open door of the parents' bedroom. The succeeding months also saw the mother's pregnancy (of which the patient had no memory at all) and finally the sister's birth, which had taken place at home. She did remember the birth. She said she had experienced it as an illness on the part of the mother. Her father had hoisted her piggyback on to his shoulders and taken her into the room where the mother was in bed. 'Do you like your little sister?' She could not see her. They pointed her out to her, all wrapped up in a brown cloth, and brought her close to the patient. She had seemed 'monstrous' to her. This was a case in which the primal scene had seriously affected the subsequent development of the patient.

The primal scene and the transition to two objects

My point, however, is that in general, and also in the examples given above, we can reach the primal-scene as a single experience in the course of our clinical activity without insuperable difficulties. We find, too, that this experience is often somehow bound up with procreation. This fits in with the fact that primal-scene experiences are also connected with infantile theories about the birth of children, but does not explain why this connection is made at such an early age, and always leaves open the possibility that the single experience, reconstructed through the derivatives, might not have been the only primal-scene experience but the one used by the boy or girl for unconscious purposes. Again, the father in these derivatives is implicit but is not, so to speak, mentioned. Finally, we learn from many patients that primal-scene experiences occupy quite a long period, and one of vital importance to development, extending from the age of 4 to 6 months until the second half of the third year. I do not believe we can continue to regard the primal-scene experience as a single and sporadic fact and go on wondering whether it is genuine or a product of fantasy. It seems to me that there is sufficient evidence to conclude that the phenomena which we group together under the heading of the primal scene cannot be separated from the vicissitudes of the object relationship in a particular phase of development.

More particularly, I feel that these phenomena should be seen as indicative of a crucial phase of development; namely, the phase of transition from the first object relation to the formation of a second object, distinct from the mother and from the self. This phase seems substantially to coincide with the period of the primal scene and approximately with the entire period which Mahler (1968) calls the phase of separation–individuation. The phenomena which constitute and characterize it may appear to us through their pathological expressions as if they were all located in one and the same plane, rather like the stars in the sky. However, as in the case of the stars, they may be situated at different levels and may represent different stages in a prolonged process.

From this point of view, some of the ambiguities pointed out by many authors in relation to the different forms in which the object appears to the child in the primal scene assume the significance of vicissitudes of the object relation during the 'primal-scene process', as I would prefer to call it on the basis of what I have said so far. During the course of this process, the gradual recognition of a second object appears to be experienced by the child as an unexpected and bewildering series of changes in the only object that he knows, the mother. At one end of this series may be the hugely enlarged image of the mother, practically doubled in volume and in number of limbs (I encountered a pathological expression of this primitive stage of the primal scene in a case of spider phobia); while at the other end the mother appears as finally split into two separate entities. But at this point, something fundamental in the primitive relationship with the mother has also ceased to exist. Between these two extremes, a variable number of intermediate images and every kind of combination may be experienced. The 'combined parent figure' described by M. Klein may in this sense include a whole range within the series rather than corresponding to a single image.

The diversity of these noteworthy experiences in my view accounts for the intensity of the child's responses. In order to imagine what the experience of the primal scene can arouse in a child aged about 6 months, it must be considered that the unrecognizable mother corresponds for the child to a kind of mutilation of the self, and to an aggression from *outside* against his relation of imitative identity. It must also be borne in mind that the powerful aggressive instinctual cathexes to which these sensations may give rise have no possibility of discharge other than in fantasy, and that rage, impotence and anxiety can raise the aggressive tension to the limiting threshold of tolerability by the self. Finally, such a situation is perceived as an internal danger and gives rise to fresh anxiety, whose components of loss and abandonment, and those of disintegration (from the flowing back of aggressive cathexes into the psychosensory area), can certainly not be distinguished by the child. It is these economic foundations which lend force and substance to the well-known mechanisms of defence connected with the fantasies of psycho-oral mental activity (introjections, projections, reintrojections, and combinations of these), as well as mechanisms that belong to the sphere of psychosensory activity. In this last group, the *mechanism of compensation* [see Chapter 2] assumes particular importance in the primal-scene process. This consists in the massive opposition of libidinal cathexes to the prevailing aggressive instinctual cathexes, which, having no possibility of effective discharge to the outside, threaten to disrupt the internal stability of the self.

Freud was the first to identify and describe this mechanism (1905 and 1924), even if he did not define it with a particular term; his original idea was that when the intensity of processes capable of causing painful and distressing tension 'passes beyond certain quantitative limits', 'sexual excitation arises as a concomitant effect' (1924: 163). Freud was referring in his description to a *physiological* functional model, which he for the time being considered to be limited to childhood, becoming lost during the course of growth (Freud 1924). Later, however (Freud 1937), he held that there was a psychical mechanism whereby libidinal cathexes were massively opposed to aggressive cathexes with the aim of making the latter latent. In my view, this mechanism is clearly definable as the equivalent and parallel psychical model of the physiological functional model described earlier. Like all basic mechanisms, the processes which constitute its foundation are quantitative in nature. Nor does it call for selective libidinal cathexes.

I find that the transition from the physiological functional model to the psychical defensive model takes place during the second year of life, under the powerful stimulation of the primal scene and impelled by the need to achieve mental mastery of the physiological model so that it can be used actively, with defensive intent, against the internal danger deriving from the powerful aggressive instinctual tensions. The 'appearance of infantile masturbation' and the particular 'sensitivity to both general and genital excitation' (Greenacre 1973) observed in the second year of life in this sense appear as the most significant manifestations of this transition. The compensation mechanism normally persists into adult life, with the important function of controlling or preventing access to consciousness and to the executive apparatus of aggressive cathexes felt to be dangerous by the ego. Towards the end of his life, Freud in fact showed that he considered the idea of a 'repression' of aggression to be improbable. 'What usually happens is that this aggression is latent or repressed through some counter compensation, i.e. through an erotic cathexis' (Freud 1937). Freud suggests, too, that the mechanism of compensation might also have something to do with 'the theme of ambivalency, which is still very puzzling' (Freud 1937).

When the mechanism of compensation becomes established in pathological form – as occurs when the primal-scene process attains traumatic intensity – the subsequent development of the libido and of object relations is severely affected. Excesses of immature libidinal cathexes, from pathology of the mechanism of compensation due to the primal scene, are usually encountered in the perversions – specifically, fetishism and the sadistic and masochistic perversions – in symptoms such as compulsive masturbation and in certain no less compulsive forms of promiscuous and/or polymorphously perverse sexual acting out. There is an infinite variety of pathological defence mechanisms. Greenacre (1973) has recently given us an excellent description of a particular form of disavowal, symbolized as a wall, and derived from the traumatic character of the primal scene.

My point, however, is that the second object never appears as such on the child's mental horizon. It arises from the mother by way of a prolonged and varied sequence of bodily transformations which are more like those of meiosis than of human birth. Any real pregnancy of the mother, experienced over a period of many months during this phase of development, is perceived as actual evidence of a seemingly irreversible bodily change in the first object. It is no coincidence that the mother's long pregnancy during this period and the resulting bodily changes are usually completely repressed. The same fate may in such cases befall subsequent pregnancies of the mother, even when they occurred at ages usually more accessible to memory – for instance, during latency.

However, it should be remembered that for the child the primal-scene process overall represents the first and essential experience of the mother's overwhelming procreative ability. On the one hand, this accounts for the legendary celebration of this event, which tends to find expression in myths, religions, and artistic productions (Bradley 1967; Edelheit 1974), while, on the other hand, it accounts for children's interest in birth, an interest which appears so early in childhood.

In my view, this explains why the association between the primal scene and birth (the mother's procreativity) is established very early in infantile life, and why the birth of a younger sibling in the first years of life – that is, during the period over which the primal-scene process extends – may assume the character of a traumatic event, or, at any rate, one capable of giving rise to extraordinarily intense responses. After all, this event is experienced as a real and observable consequence of the most disturbing components of the primal scene. In our clinical work with adult patients, we often find a close association between still detectable components of the primal scene and *that* particular birth of a brother or sister which took place in the first years of life. It is not unusual for us to be able to determine the exact time in infantile life to which the detectable primal-scene components relate, and it is then found that the interval between that time and the birth of the younger sibling corresponds surprisingly well to the period of the mother's pregnancy. Some examples of this have been given in this paper.

However, it seems to me obvious that what we succeed in reconstructing clinically is only what the patient has constructed within himself over the course of time. In this construction, which is made at a later date and is retrospective, the experiences of the birth of the younger brother or sister are related to a condensate of what has been experienced throughout the primal-scene process. This is probably why the primal scene appears to us clinically as a single event and, characteristically, as an event which arouses doubts about its actual reality. The doubt is legitimate, but only to the extent that it is a matter not of a single event but of a construction, and not of a single real event but of a condensate of diverse experiences extending over a prolonged period. During the course of these experiences, I would say that the monstrous mother of the primal scene appears to the child as *extraneous* before she appears as *external*. 'Extraneous' means unknown, mysterious, horrible, threatening, and attacking. These are the aspects of the 'non-self'. The 'extraneous mother' is totally different and does not correspond to anything with which the child is familiar. Only gradually does she become more 'external' and less extraneous ('other than self'). This transition, which takes place by way of repeated night-time and daytime experiences, is certainly facilitated by the progress of the perceptual capacities during daytime waking periods.

On the other hand, it is quite likely that the fear-inducing effects of fantastic nocturnal distortions of perception do not always correspond with actual scenes of parental intercourse. Once the child has had such experiences, the recurrence of the situation when they took place may itself become a ground for anxiety. The dark thus becomes a source of anxiety, and a prolonged fear of the dark in infancy, and sometimes also in adulthood, should suggest to us that the primal-scene process has been traumatic. Similarly, the moment of falling asleep may come to induce anxiety and give rise to sleep disturbances. The triggering stimuli in the dark or half-dark may be of various kinds: visual stimuli, such as the size and difference in shape of the mother, covered and outstretched, or the shapes of the parents seen as combined by the bedcover or the child's particular viewpoint (Greenacre 1973); aural stimuli, such as snoring or heavy or otherwise noisy breathing, groans or other sounds emitted by each of the parents during dreaming; or the very fact that the mother, although there, is present in those different and mysterious ways and is completely separate from the child (that is, sleeping). My point is that the child, as a result of recurring partial stimuli of this kind, repeats and multiplies in fantasy the experience of the primal scene, in whole or in part, and this gives rise to a kind of background continuity of the experience, which may be gradually varied, modified, and elaborated by the child in the course of time. However, what the child undergoes without any possibility of modification or attenuation are the actual primal-scene experiences. The earlier these take place in the life of the child, the more overwhelming their intensity will be. And if their frequency is excessive, the child will be unable to assimilate them adequately in fantasy, so that the primal-scene process may become traumatic for that reason alone.

In my view, some well-known anxieties of children in the part of the first year of life which corresponds to an early phase of the primal-scene process have not been appropriately connected with this experience. I have already referred to fear of the dark. Here I should like to mention the so-called 'fear of the stranger' and the anxiety arising at the moment of falling asleep.

The former is directed towards any human form different from the mother – namely, that is reminiscent of the 'extraneous mother'. In other words, a human form that presents itself to the child from *outside* at this stage cannot but be experienced by him as *extraneous*, and must therefore arouse anxiety, as it is immediately equated with the 'extraneous mother'. This is how the second object, the father, is experienced (the father actually being the first object which so to speak intrudes from the outside into the relationship of imitative identity with the mother), in the first perceptions the child has of him in his waking states. From his initial position as an 'extraneous mother' who arouses anxiety, the father gradually comes to be distinguished perceptually and accepted as a dichotomous aspect of the 'external mother'. It is at this point that the process of differentiation of the father from the mother can begin.

However, we know that in the dreams of our adult patients 'a stranger' or 'an unknown man' may still stand for the father, and we must bear in mind that in this case the reference is to a very remote father, who represents the extraneous mother. But that is not all. An 'extraneous' and mysterious part – which on that account arouses anxiety and terror – remains for a long time concealed behind other 'external' aspects of the father and mother, giving rise to more or less fearful latent fantasies in infancy and sometimes in adult life.

Anxiety at the moment of falling asleep, for its part, is also earlier than fear of strangers. The child comes to 'invent' a transitional object (Winnicott 1951b) principally because of this anxiety, with the aim of reducing it. Unlike the anxiety-arousing stranger, who is imposed from the outside and becomes defensively emblematic of the future phobic object, the transitional object is one that is characteristically *inanimate*, which the child *actively* finds and selects in the external world, mainly on the basis of tactile perceptions (R. Gaddini 1974), with the aim of reducing the anxiety that precedes falling asleep. The transitional object in fact represents the first successful active defence achieved, with developmental significance, by the infantile ego against the anxiety of loss of the self of the imitative identity caused by the primal-scene process. That is to say, the relationship of imitative identity with the mother's breast, to which the primal scene has put an end, is magically reconstituted by way of the tactile sensation of contact with an inanimate object. Characteristically, as against the fear-inducing and unrecognizable *changes* of the mother of the primal scene, the transitional object must be *always the same* and *always to hand*, if the anxiety is not to break out again.

The transitional object is the end result, which is not always achieved, of a difficult process characterized by desperate attempts to keep the relationship of imitative identity alive. These attempts give rise to so-called 'precursors' of the transitional object (Gaddini and Gaddini 1974), which do not in any way reach the outside world and are characterized by preservation of a physical contact, either with the subject's own body or with the mother's. The transitional object, however, is characterized by contact with something that is neither the one nor the other, and is therefore no longer an attempt to preserve the imitative identity as such, but only to represent it in symbolic form. But, as pointed out by Winnicott (1951b), the transitional object is not yet an external object. We may add that it is not an *extraneous* object, in the sense defined above, either. It not only lacks the latter's capacity to arouse anxiety but also has as its main purpose the prevention or reduction of anxiety. In this sense it is the antithesis of the extraneous object, but as a symbol it may re-elicit it and reawaken anxiety if it is changed – that is to say, if it is no longer the same. As a symbol, the transitional object is located precisely in an intermediate area between the self and the external world – an area for the identification and description of which Winnicott must take the credit.

At any rate, once a second external object has come into being, the child may be driven first of all to displace on to the new representation of the mother the conflictual aspects involving her loss, in an attempt to re-establish and perpetuate with the mother the relationship of imitative identity interrupted by the primal scene. On the other occasions, conversely, the child may invest the new representation with what has been lost in the first one, in an attempt to re-establish with it a conflict-free relationship of imitative identity. There are then two possibilities; either this first massive displacement may allow the child to work through the loss of the relationship of imitative identity with the primary object more easily and gradually, at the same time instituting the delicate and complicated processes of development that lead to the symbolization and acceptance of this loss and to the creation of a transitional object in Winnicott's (1951b) sense; or it may be used for the establishment of pathological defences, whose aim by their nature is to confirm the permanence of the relationship with the primary object and to a greater or lesser extent therefore adversely to influence the formative processes of the subsequent stages of development and the structure of the adult personality.

However, a new process may now commence, involving a gradual differentiation of the object recently distinguished in reality, but unconsciously not yet separable from the first object, into a second person, whose sexual identity and ways of treating the child and responding to it do not correspond and cannot be confused with what is known of the mother. All this first involves a new phase of the conflict of dependence, in which the omnipotence of imitative identity must come to terms with the demands of reality, and subsequently the conflicts of the phallic phase and Oedipal situations, for which the primal-scene process in fact paves the way.

The fundamental difficulty of the process of acquisition of the second object lies in the loss it entails of the primitive relationship of imitative identity. The relationship is inherently powerful, but its strength increases further in direct proportion to its degree of pathology, whether excessive or insufficient, perhaps ultimately more or less severely obstructing the acquisition of the second object and the concomitant change in the relationship with the mother.

Again, the strength of the instinctual components, which is characteristic of this new phase of development of the object relationship, threatens to disrupt the internal stability of the self. The introjective mechanisms of psycho-oral functioning, in particular, continuously expose the self to the dramatic internal situations aroused by conflicts against anxiety. The reinforcement and exhausting perfectionism of the imitative relationship constitute the basic defence of the infantile ego: the ego aims by their use to replace the conflictual dynamic concerning possession of the object, and thereby to eliminate the real object and, with it, all conflict.

With this alternation of introjections and imitations, processes whereby the former are integrated with the latter gradually come to be established and develop during the course of childhood, reaching their conclusion only in the genital phase – that is, in adolescence.

Integration of the imitations with the introjections gives rise to the formation of *identifications*, which, unlike their two components (imitations and introjections), allow the ego gradually to internalize the object in stable and permanent form [see Chapter 1]. The identifications allow the infantile ego to internalize aspects of the reality of the object which are at first fragmentary and later more complex and integrated and selectively partial (Jacobson 1964). The transition from the *extraneous* to the *external* mother would not be possible without the commencement of infantile identifications. The acquisition of the second object, in the sense of differentiation from the mother, and the concomitant revision of the first relationship with the mother, would not be possible without the evolution of the processes of identification. These processes are structuring for the ego, so that adult identity remains indissolubly bound up with the evolution of identifications; in the same way, the first infantile identity was indissolubly and exclusively bound up with the imitative mechanisms. In any disturbance of adult identity, we must therefore expect some degree of prevalence at clinical level of imitations instead of identifications, and some degree of confusion of the self with the object, the reality of which depends absolutely on the degree of achievement of adult identity.

It follows from the foregoing that the acquisition of the second object − that is, the process whereby it is differentiated from the relationship of imitative identity with the mother − is of crucial importance to the evolution of the processes of identification, to the formation of adult identity, and ultimately to the achievement of sufficient maturity of the object relationship.

Aspects and problems of therapy

For all these reasons, we are justified in saying that the acquisition of the second object may become the fundamental task of the therapeutic process. I have come to see that the entire therapeutic process is principally a matter of this task in the vast majority of cases. Since the acquisition of a second object is probably achieved normally only to a certain extent, and because it is influenced by, and in turn influences, other processes essential to the structuring of individual personality, it should come as no surprise that the therapeutic process focuses on it, so important is it in our patients' pathology. In reality, as is often the case with the obvious, the process of acquisition of the second object is so much in the limelight in all its manifold aspects during the unfolding of the therapeutic process that it may simply escape our attention.

However, other factors may, of course, also contribute to this unfortunate possibility. The very fact that the father is experienced primarily as a dichotomous aspect of the mother and may subsequently be fixed for all time in the situation dictated by this origin may greatly blur the field of observation. In reality, since the acquisition of the second object is precisely what has not occurred as it should have, we should, for example, be more aware that, very often, what assumes the form of male figures in dreams or memories, and what is experienced as a relationship with men in adult life, has less to do with the infantile relationship with the father as a second object than with a split-off and displaced part of the infantile relationship with the extraneous mother and with the mother of imitative identity.

The real personalities of the father and mother may decisively influence what part of the infantile relationship with the mother is split off and displaced and what part remains with the mother. If the extraneous mother is split off and displaced, the patient may emphasize the conflictual relationship with the father, and only the analysis will be capable of showing the patient that the father as an object has not been separated from the mother except for defensive purposes and that he was never sufficiently differentiated as such. This was the case with a severely agoraphobic woman patient who had had to submit all her life to a father who behaved towards her like a sadistic and paralysing lover.

The agoraphobia arose after she married an extremely gentle and protective man, who had to accompany her to the analytic sessions and take her home from them for many years. The situation was similar in the case of a homosexual with pronounced masochistic characteristics, who had been constantly scorned by a sadistic father, who used to hit him on the mouth when he was a child and take him himself to the toilet, where he stimulated the child's anus with a finger in an attempt to overcome his constipation. This patient remembered that, as a child, he had spent many hours crouching at the feet of his mother, whom he recalled as gentle and submissive and with whom he had never felt himself to be in conflict. When he grew up, he had married a girl at the latter's initiative, re-establishing the infantile relationship of identity with the mother. Because the relationships were of this kind, both the agoraphobic patient's marriage and that of the homosexual patient could pass as happy and successful.

Cases in which the split-off and displaced part of the infantile relationship with the mother concerns the imitative identity may be particularly complex. In distinguishing the clinical aspects deriving from this powerful defence from those due to splitting and displacement of the extraneous mother, we must bear in mind that *physical contact* is the method of choice for achieving imitative identity, whose aim is withdrawal from the conflicts and anxiety associated with the object area. It may be added that the imitative identity originally relates to the bodily self and that it is the product of primitive libidinal cathexes – that is, ones turned towards the interior of the self (Freud 1937). When used as a defence, it is therefore often to be found embedded in sexual manifestations of adult life in deceptive ways – that is, disguised as a genital love relationship. We have known for a long time that a genital sexual relationship is not always equivalent to the genital level. In these cases, however, the sexual relationship may come to be experienced as the situation of physical contact capable of temporarily re-establishing the imitative identity. That is why it has to be repeated. It would in my opinion be a mistake, when treating such patients, to interpret this kind of repetitive sexual behaviour as an acting out of the transference, rather than as imitative sexual behaviour.

A woman of 25, who looked no older than 20–21 and was about to marry, decided to break off her engagement and embark on an analytic treatment. In response to the increasing tension of the early stages of the analytical relationship, this patient began to act out sexually on a larger and larger scale. This was her way of reacting to the growing anxiety aroused by the analytical relationship – a reaction which, understood correctly, could provide useful information on the patient's structure and on the extent to which imitative mechanisms pre-dominated in her instead of identification.

Particular mention should be made of the imitative type of trans-ference, whereby the patient aims to avoid the commitment of the relationship for fear of the instinctual components. The patient in these cases tries to *be* the analyst and to use the session, like sexual relation-ships, as a contact situation, to secure magically the basic imitative identity. The analyst, however, may have the impression that such a patient is participating satisfactorily in the relationship. The patient after all seems to understand the interpretations well, brings dreams, arrives punctually, associates, and, as in a sexual relationship, may perform completely and satisfactorily in the session and appear as the ideal patient. *If* he or she has four sessions, he or she may ask to have five, and this too may sometimes appear as a wish to do the best possible thing. In actual fact, the magically reconstitutive contact with the analyst constructs little if anything, and the patient's 'participation' is merely the result of his or her 'need for contact'. There is perhaps no defence which uses the analysis against the analysis more than this one. The strength of this defence is on a par with its fraudulent essence. In considering this strength, it should be borne in mind that the imitative identity is opposed to the structuring processes of adult identity not as some defence mechanism or other but as a fundamental alternative

81

which can, by the use of imitations, assume the guise of many important aspects of the adult relationship with reality, and appear as adult identity. A decisive point here is that the prevalence of imitations instead of identifications is accompanied by a kind of tachypsychism, a capacity for rapid learning and special technical abilities. Imitators may thus be more intelligent than the average (as measured by tests) and well or very well educated. Their academic performance may be excellent. These patients also quickly learn psychoanalysis, by contact, but unfortunately tend to use it too in the service of their imitative identity.

Outside the analysis, when we manage to discover this, they behave like genuine analysts, speaking in the same way and using the same inflexions as their analyst. In the most serious cases, the patient may even imitate the analyst in the analytical situation itself, without being at all aware of it.

I should, however, like to point out that, where the analysis takes a favourable course, some degree of imitative transference is usually present and should not in itself be regarded as pathological. Identifications could not come into being without imitations. As it happens, just as occurs in normal development (and particularly in adolescence), imitations may, in analysis too, precede the structuring of identifications, as an indispensable preliminary stage.

Note

1 In Winnicott's last work, *Playing and Reality* (1971), it seems to me that he too was substantially referring to this primitive two-fold disposition towards the object, which he understood as 'the female element' and 'the male element', both of which were present in each individual. In his description of the way in which the female element relates to the object, he says, for example, that 'the pure female element relates to the breast (or to the mother) in the sense of *the baby becoming the breast (or mother), in the sense that the object is the subject*'. He adds: 'I can see no instinct drive in this' (p. 79). This seems to me to correspond completely with what I have defined as the psychosensory aspect of the relation with the object, not excluding the addition about the instinct drive. On this last point I had previously written that the sensory area seems to provide for a possible withdrawal from conflicts and for the exclusion of the external object that gives rise to them [see Chapter 1]. A similar concordance can be found in the way the male element (the psycho-oral area, in my definition) relates to the object. In Winnicott's words: 'object-relating backed by instinct drive belongs to the male element in the personality uncontaminated by the female element'.

5

On father formation in early child development

Presented at a round table discussion on 'The Role of Family Life in Child Development' at the 29th Congress of the International Psychoanalytical Association, London, July 1975, this paper was published under the title 'Discussion of the role of family life in child development' with a subtitle, 'On father formation in child development', in the *International Journal of Psycho-Analysis* (1976) 57: 397–401.

After reading the papers by Maurice Friend (1976) and Horst-Eberhard Richter (1976), I found myself thinking of the word 'familiar' and of its being associated with the idea of family as something one is supposed to be well acquainted with. This is certainly not so for the growing child, for whom the task of becoming familiar with his family's structure and life is certainly immense. The unsolved mysteries and riddles of early life may later turn into psychopathology, and sometimes into creative research and expression. Once indeed they gave rise to no less than psychoanalysis itself.

I shall take this opportunity to make an attempt to approach what is for the child (and partly still for us, too) one of the basic mysteries: namely, the father. I refer to the psychological role of the father in early child development.

While, on the sociological side, the role of the father has undergone striking changes in this century – at least in our culture – his psychological role, in my view, does not seem to have changed, and possibly is not going to change in the foreseeable future. I am obviously not referring to the many ways in which his role may be distorted, rather than changed, within different family situations, but to what the father basically means to the growing child and, before then, to the child's mother.

In fact, from the very moment a woman knows that she is expecting a baby, her relation to herself and to her husband changes. She becomes more self-centred, less concerned with her husband as her lover, and shows a greater need of tender affection. She wants to share her 'primary maternal preoccupation', as Winnicott (1957) has described it, with him, and she needs to be relieved and protected from external preoccupations. Her relation to the baby growing inside, the way she experiences the gradual changes in her body, her expectations concerning the actual delivery and the baby's appearance, are certainly influenced by her husband's attitude towards her. All this is just to say that the father's role, as well as the mother's, begins to exist before the child is born, although the father cannot help being left out from the mother–child bodily coexistence. His influence on the child to be born lies in his capacity to influence the mother's attitude towards the baby inside her body.

Of course, the relationship between mother and father soon becomes tremendously important to the born child but, for a period of at least some months after birth, the father will still have a mediated relation to the child, through the mother–child relationship.

Many things do happen, however, in this early period of child development, and I shall only refer to Winnicott's (1961) work to emphasize his opinion that developmental experiences of this early period do not necessarily imply instinctual drives, mechanisms, or conflicts. In an earlier paper [see Chapter 1] I expressed the same opinion, although my approach was different. I was then describing early imitation as a basic defence, the aim of which was to allow the child to withdraw from the instinctual experience into an area of the mind in which he could re-establish his self-omnipotence (or, one may say, re-establish in fantasy the experience of 'illusion').

What I want to say is that between the early experiences of illusion and self-creativeness (Winnicott 1951b), and the subsequent engagement in the instinctual (oral) experiences, there seems to be an intermediate period of time during which the child oscillates, so to speak, in and out of his self. When he is 'out', he is facing instinctual experiences and when he is 'in', he withdraws. In this way he is magically able to wipe out instinctual external stimuli when they become too painful. When he withdraws, he is able to hallucinate a bodily experience which satisfies him and which, although created omnipotently in fantasy by himself to compensate for an unsatisfactory one, is an imitative attempt to repeat a kind of satisfaction which he in fact has previously experienced. The difference from Winnicott's (1951b) 'illusion' is that illusion was an actual experience of the self, while imitation is a later defence which aims at re-establishing the experience of illusion. In other words, one can say that imitation is a defence shaped on the experience of illusion.

Imitation, then, cannot be separated from fantasy formation and fantasy cannot be separated from bodily experience. In this early period, however, instinctual oral experiences gradually develop, together with oral mechanisms, mainly introjections (and projections). Introjections are being imitated to the extent that they are passively and helplessly endured. Early introjects, in fact, may really be 'introjected' *into* the child, rather than being *introjected by* the child (P. Greenacre, personal communication), through the mouth, or the eyes, or the ears, or the skin; and then, while on the level of instinctual drives and mechanisms, he can actively project into the object what was experienced as an intrusion into his self, on the level of the self he may actively withdraw and re-experience in fantasy a satisfactory experience of oral incorporation. This interplay soon becomes very complex, and that, in my opinion, is responsible for the developing processes of identification, which are an essential part of the integrational process.

Anxiety, of course, is soon at the centre of this interplay. Dependence on the external object exposes the child to the loss of self-omnipotence. It is the object, then, that acquires the most powerful and threatening omnipotence. This anxiety is mainly self-centred, and seems mainly concerned with self-loss. Retreat into the mental area which serves the self is able to restore its omnipotence and the feeling of being, which then allows the child to expose him/herself again to the instinctual scene. On the other hand, object dependence exposes the child to the fear that the object is not stable enough, that it can be lost, and that the self will not survive. Having to trust an object may imply a different fear of losing oneself. Then retreat into the mental area which serves the self may help to prevent the experience of object loss. In other words, instinctual anxiety may only gradually be distinguished from the anxiety of self-loss – and thus faced accordingly – and only in so far as the basic self is stable enough to be able to go through this process. Otherwise, when anxiety of self-loss is overwhelmingly prevailing, instinctual and object-relationship development will be consequently impaired.

It was necessary to discuss these matters first in order to understand when and how the father comes to exist. He enters the scene at some time during this early instinctual development. But he does not enter as something given. Descriptively, we may consider him as a second object, although he would be more properly described as the first object which comes to the child from the external world. To the child, however, it is somewhat different. The mother as an object comes from within the child, and the moment she begins to appear as something different from the child's self a long process starts, at the end of which mother becomes 'external', but split into two figures. In other words, while mother comes from the child's self, father comes from mother, as a split part of her. This long process is a threatening one to the child, but it is an essential one in early instinctual and object-relationship development. In the fantasy of our adult patients, it can be detected in significant ways through what comes to be expressed as primal-scene material. Further, primal scene and the actual birth of some sibling in that period of life may be found to be unconsciously linked.

I came to the conviction that what we call primal scene is actually a derivative of a series of early experiences of the parents' relationship between themselves. These experiences have been elaborated in fantasy life in the course of years and then condensed into a special defensive construction, which may appear to us as if the child had once witnessed intercourse between the parents. I am convinced that the primal scene is in general really and repeatedly experienced by the child, although in different ways, but not infrequently the way we detect it may reveal also some details of the long story of how the father came to the fore. We may happen to know, for instance, that the most threatening aspect of that experience concerned the mother, who was suddenly different and no longer part of the child's self. Some unexpected perceptions of the mother were then impinged upon the child from the outside, and forcedly '*introjected*' *into* the child. For this very reason, but also because of the actual situation in which he experienced it (Greenacre 1973), and because of the developmental sensorial capacities of the child at the time, his perceptions could not help being grossly distorted. What these perceptions refer to is what I would describe from the child's point of view as an '*extraneous*' mother. The different shapes that this 'extraneous' mother can take are terrifying, and express also the series of attempts by the child to interpret them [see Chapter 4].

I have also stressed how father appears as a duplication of mother, not yet a second object. Although both parents appear as 'external', the child has gone through a different kind of experience with each of them. Father, in fact, has come to exist *only as an external figure*, and only at the point when *mother has become external*. In this sense one can say that father is to the child the first external object.

However, once the primal-scene process approaches this stage – that is, at about 6 or 7 months – the child develops a strong need to wipe out all the bewildering experiences which went along with it. Denial organizes itself at this point of the process, and it becomes the first and the most powerful defence against the early experiences of the primal scene. In terms of defence-specificity, one could say that denial is to the primal scene what, later on, repression is to the Oedipus complex.

When this early phase of the process is experienced in a traumatic way – which may happen for a number of reasons, among which there may be a new pregnancy of the mother in that early period, or too much exposure of the child to the actual experience of the primal scene – then denial may acquire such power that it becomes a pathogenic defence. Greenacre (1973) has given an excellent account of this kind of denial of the primal scene, which may be represented in dreams and in associations as a wall.

More usually however, while denial is being organized, it may influence the child's attitude towards the father in a way which is different from that which it does towards the mother. While the external mother comes to be sought as a source of self-reassurance, and to be used essentially as a valuable support in the need for denying the 'extraneous' mother, the father is closely linked, in the child's mind, with the experience of the latter, and is at first rejected, as he closely represents all that the child intends to deny. This sharp distinction between mother and father could be described as an inner split, which parallels the splitting of the object. It is not a long-lasting distinction, but it lasts long enough, and is sharp enough, to allow the child to establish a reliable organization of the mechanism of denial. During this period the father appears to the child as a 'stranger', and is able to arouse in the child that kind of anxiety which is soon manifestly extended to anybody who comes from without (that is, is external to) the child–mother self-assuring link. With reference to what Freud (1926) said, I would consider this an early instance of signal anxiety, which aims at preventing the child from re-experiencing the primal-scene catastrophic anxiety of self-loss.

Once it is established, however, denial enables the child to face in a less fearful way what may be considered as the second stage of the primal-scene process. The increasing improvement in perceptions, mainly visual and auditory, and the increasing capacity to master motor activities, are among the special characteristics of this phase. Time does not allow me to enter into all its intricacies; thus I shall limit myself to a few comments.

This phase prolongs itself until the third year of life and could be objectively described as the triangular phase of the process. I should like to point out, however, that a triangular relationship is not estab-lished by the simple fact that the child is able to see two *separate* persons. At the beginning the child is not yet able to distinguish them as *different* from each other and from himself. A long process of father differential is now starting, and it will be an essential task of this second phase of the primal-scene process. Further, it will essentially contribute to the child's differentiation of the mother as well, as a love object, from the father and from himself. Renewed experiences of the primal scene, which may actually be repeating themselves during this period, play a major role in the differentiating process. Actually, one may say that a triangular relationship will be gradually forming itself only in so far as the process of father differentiation can develop. This differentiation, in fact, requires an increasing involvement of the child into an instinctual kind of relationship, and an increasing capacity to face dependence on a love object. The interplay between imitative mechanisms and oral instinctual ones (mainly introjections) gradually turns into their mutual integration, a necessary step to further the development of identifications [see Chapter 1]: the latter, in turn, allow the child's ego to develop object relationship and identity formation. All this paves the way for the turmoils of the triangular situation of the phallic–Oedipal stage.

An indefinable number of factors can interfere with the many delicate and closely interwoven processes along the way. Of course, this phase of the primal-scene process is heavily influenced by the way in which the previous one was experienced. Apropos of this I have already mentioned pathogenic denial, and I shall conclude with a short description of another crucial occurrence, which follows from a traumatic experience of the early phase of the primal-scene process. What may happen is that, once mother splits into two external figures, the child may no longer be able to re-establish a self-assuring kind of relationship with the mother, and to displace on to the father his fear of renewing the terrifying experience of the 'extraneous' mother. This fear is still centred upon the mother, whom the child can no longer trust. What then is displaced on to the father is the child's need of a soothing and nursing mother.

Such an inverted situation at the beginning of the triangular phase is, in my experience, an ominous one for future development. Above all, instinctual development will be seriously impaired. Although the fear of the father as a stranger is soon overcome, this fear of mother may last for ever, and the father may forever be expected to be that part of mother which would save the child from the danger of self-loss. Mother, on the other hand, becomes the major source of this danger, which is mainly linked with aggressive destructive drives. Instinctual development may thus be prevented both on the mother's side and on the father's. Last but not least, the process of father differentiation may be so much impaired that he may never be able to become the father.

An illustration of this fateful inverted situation in the relationship to parents in early life may be found in the dream of a severely agoraphobic patient in his late fifties, after several years of treatment. The dream is as follows.

I was in a room with a very little child, whom I had to care for and to protect from possible danger. I had been given this task by my mother and father, who had gone out. The child was in fact taking much of my attention: he was repeatedly attempting to walk, but each time he fell down after a few steps, and each time I picked him up. In spite of my attention, at one point the child was able to approach a big cupboard, and before I realized it, he had managed to open one of its doors and was badly hit on the mouth. I could immediately see a deep wound in his mouth, which was bleeding awfully. I felt desperate, I did not know what to do, but I knew that something had to be done quickly, otherwise the child was going to die. Just then, my mother and father appeared. As soon as I saw them, in terrible anguish I put the child into my father's arms, asking him to do something quickly, to save the child. Mother was standing by silently, and father didn't seem to share my fear at all. I woke up from this dream in deep anxiety.

The father's response to this request of the child will depend essentially on his personality structure and on his capacity to relate to the child. Although a father should, as we have seen, always be able, at least temporarily, to be like a mother to the child, in these cases he may be asked to give up his paternal role indefinitely. There are fathers who are strikingly able to assume the mother's role for ever, and others who are not. Between these, there is a great variety of possible father responses. Whatever it may be, father response will contribute essentially to the different ways in which the described pathological occurrence will influence further development and the final pathological structure of the child in adult life.

6

Therapeutic technique in psychoanalysis: research, controversies and evolution

Published in *La psicoterapia di oggi*, G. Tedeschi (ed.), Rome: Il Pensiero Scientifico, 1975, under the title 'Ricerca, controversie e evoluzione della tecnica terapeutica in psicoanalisi'.

In Freudian psychoanalysis, the clinical data represent the source of experience on which the truly scientific part of the theory constantly draws. This constant confrontation with clinical experience compels the theory to undergo continuous processes of transformation, revision, definition, and re-formulation of its basic concepts, as with any evolving science. This development of scientific knowledge in turn imposes continuous transformation, adjustments, and improvements on therapeutic technique. Before the 1920s, a counterphobic attitude achieved during a treatment might have been mistaken for the cure of a phobia. Nowadays, however, if an apparently new phobia, which was in fact previously concealed by a counterphobic attitude, were to arise during the treatment, we would not consider that the patient had taken a turn for the worse. On the other hand, the clinical evaluation of such a change, in one sense or the other, would today call for a consideration of the dynamic, structural, genetic, and economic processes involved, and this consideration would have to conform to our present-day knowledge.

However, it would be wrong to regard psychoanalytic theory simply as a unitary and integrated whole that is gradually evolving. This it is only to a certain extent, inasmuch as the theory is in effect the result of currents and tendencies in research that are so diverse as to appear sometimes irreconcilable, but which are nevertheless an intrinsic part of the evolution of psychoanalytic theory as well as of technique. During the history of the psychoanalytic movement, there have been controversies which arose principally out of differences in trends of research. In the days when the theoretical structure of psychoanalysis was still frail and undeveloped, the fear that it could somehow thereby be damaged was readily understandable. Such controversies could therefore more easily give rise to splits within the movement.

The first and without doubt the most important of these splits was represented by the secession of Jung. More than sixty years after this split, it has remained perhaps the only one that is still deeply felt by both sides, but now, with calmer counsels prevailing, we can see that it was unavoidable. Jung's field of research, although stimulated by psychoanalysis, in fact needed a wider space than Freud's area of concern at the time, into which it would not fit, so much so that it could only develop in an autonomous sphere of its own. The 'self' is a concept which has only recently been introduced into psychoanalytic therapy, and not without bitter resentments and controversies, so that it at first remained, as it were, an alien concept. It subsequently came to be used much more widely, to the extent of gaining complete acceptance. Today, although a universally agreed definition is still lacking, there is no doubt that the 'self' has become a concept of fundamental importance in psychoanalytic research, allowing it to extend and delve into hitherto totally or relatively unexplored basic areas of the mind. The point, however, is that, by virtue of the latest developments in psychoanalysis, the psychoanalysts' stubborn antipathy to Jung – à la Glover – has gradually softened, Jung's work coming to be valued more highly and more objectively. One of the most prominent recent workers in the field of psychoanalytic research, D.W. Winnicott, even wrote (1964):

> In a way Jung and Freud turn out to be complementary; they are like the obverse and reverse of a coin; we can see when we know Jung, as we can now do, why it was not possible for him and Freud to come to terms with each other in those early years of the century, those early years in which Freud was struggling to establish a science that could gradually expand, and Jung was starting off 'knowing', but handicapped by his own need to search for a self with which to know.

Winnicott went as far as to warn the psychoanalysts:

> Jung was a being, a real person, one who happened to live in Freud's time and who inevitably met Freud. The impact of their meeting provides material for serious study, and the manner of their parting is no less interesting to the student of human nature. Psychoanalysts can choose to line up with Freud, and to measure Jung against him,

91

or they can look at Jung and look at Freud and allow the two to meet and to go together and to separate. In the latter case they must know their Jung.

(1964: 450)

I have dwelt on the split between Jung and Freud because it is the most conspicuous historical example of all the disagreements in research that have led to splits during the process of the growth and consolidation of psychoanalysis. Later, of course, other divergences in research also led to serious dissension in the psychoanalytic movement, within whose ranks, however, they were contained without giving rise to splits. An example from the past is the controversy aroused by Alexander in Chicago, while another, which has been raging for some decades and still persists, was kindled by the research of Melanie Klein. These controversies have undeniably seriously perturbed the psychoanalytic movement by reawakening the old fears for the stability of the young science, which was again felt to be in danger. The Kleinian school in particular — the so-called 'English school' — for a long time seemed to represent, and for some analysts still does represent, a 'crack' in the psychoanalytic movement, a *de facto* if not a formal split.

Clearly, however, there must have been reasons inherent in the psychoanalytic movement why an actual split did not take place; and clearly, even if there has been a crack, it must be something different from an actual split involving separation. In this sense, if Winnicott was able to see Jung's research as 'complementary' to Freud's, there is all the more reason for us today, over forty years on, to be able to regard the research of Melanie Klein and her school as an essential, not to say indispensable, 'component' of the psychoanalytic movement.

A glance back at the main lines of psychoanalytic research may help to show the truth of this statement. Freud devoted the first twenty years of his research to studying the libidinal drives and at the same time constructing a psychoanalytic methodology. This methodology formed the scientific basis of metapsychological research. The libidinal theory and the metapsychological methodology were completed in 1915. It was only after this time that Freud began to see aggression as a different type of energy from libidinal energy. The theoretical formulation of the death instinct dates from 1920 (*Beyond the Pleasure Principle*) and necessarily called for a complete re-formulation of the theory of instincts. All this revolutionized the concepts applicable to the mental apparatus. The re-formulation of the latter in structural terms dates from 1923 (*The Ego and the Id*), while the last great metapsychological paper on aggression was written in 1924 ('The economic problem of masochism'). As we know, the theory of the death instinct baffled the great majority of analysts, who, however, readily accepted the structural theory. Among the few analysts who had no doubts about the existence of the death instinct, only Melanie Klein was able to use this concept as a fundamental postulate for her own research.

Child psychoanalysis now began, its protagonists being Anna Freud and Melanie Klein. The latter, however, must take the credit for the discovery that children too form a transference in the therapeutic relationship and for the substitution of play for free association. Anna Freud and Melanie Klein, as we know, soon found themselves in opposing camps. Of the two main legacies of Freud's research, the structural theory and the theory of the death instinct, Anna Freud received the former and Melanie Klein the latter. Of course, in the eyes of the majority, tradition, faithfulness to Freud, and, in a word, psychoanalysis, were represented by Anna Freud. The most authoritative theoretician in this majority after Freud's death was to be Heinz Hartmann. But, from a historical point of view, Melanie Klein was alone in venturing fearlessly into what was then the most advanced field of psychoanalytic research, a field which Freud did not reach until late in his life and was therefore able to do no more than open up: the study of man's aggressive drives. On the basis of this study, Melanie Klein became convinced that an object relationship existed from the very beginnings of extra-uterine life, and she charted the vicissitudes of the mental representation of the object in the early days and weeks of life. In this way, but in disagreement with established opinion, she was able to demonstrate the pre-genital origins of the Oedipal relationship and of the superego. She showed the importance of introjection and projection as basic mechanisms in the early relation to the object. Melanie Klein therefore dènied that there could be an objectless phase in infantile development.

This is not to say that the opposing, majority camp neglected the study of the aggressive drives. The fact is that, whereas Melanie Klein and her followers never questioned the death instinct, which was the very foundation of their research, this concept failed to stand up to the consistent criticism to which it was subjected by the psychoanalysts – criticism that was supported and reinforced by the reservations of non-psychoanalytic scientific disciplines. However, this destructive criticism was not accompanied by appropriate research activity aimed at supplying a metapsychologically more convincing substitute for the theory of the death instinct. An 'instinct of aggression' was somewhat hastily cobbled together in its place, its vicissitudes being conceived, but never demonstrated, as coinciding completely with those of the libido. This incorrect initial approach was thus greatly to hamper the deep investigation of the aggressive drives.

However, the majority camp did make considerable progress in the study of individual personality, and in particular the psychoanalytic study of the ego, on the basis of Freud's structural theory. It is uncertain to what extent Freud himself unintentionally encouraged this direction of research. It is certainly true that his daughter, Anna Freud, published *The Ego and the Mechanism of Defence* in 1936 and that he was very interested in it. We also owe a great deal to Heinz Hartmann for his work on the ego and to Ernst Kris for his studies of the preconscious and of creativity.

However, the innovation in the structural theory concerning the ego was precisely that this agency was regarded as a complex system whose functions were not only conscious and preconscious but also extended into the unconscious. My point is that the majority camp's contributions to knowledge of the ego were more concerned with its structure, its functions, the organization of internal defences, its relations with the id and the superego, and its extraordinary activity at preconscious level, less attention being paid to the problems of the early formation of the ego. The Kleinian school's contributions, on the other hand, related primarily to the very earliest phases of ego functioning, the early stages of superego formation, and the character and vicissitudes of the primitive instinctual derivatives in the object relation. This does not mean that the majority camp ignored the problems of early ego functioning. We need only recall the admirable contributions of E. Glover, W. Hoffer, P. Greenacre, Hartmann himself and others who cannot be mentioned for reasons of space. The difference was that for them these matters constituted only a part of the research, whereas they represented its essence for the Kleinians; the majority group's research took the structural theory as its starting point, while that of the Kleinians was the death instinct.

The foregoing, although necessarily concise, will, I hope, suffice to give an idea of reasons why the Kleinians could not leave the psychoanalytic movement. They rightly considered themselves to be descended from Freud and Abraham and to be continuing a line or research mapped out by them. Unlike Jung, they were therefore legitimate members of the psychoanalytic movement begun by Freud. This historical review also shows more clearly why Kleinian research today appears as one of the two essential components of post-Freudian psychoanalytic research – namely, research on aggression and object relations – the other being research on structure and intersystemic and intrasystemic relations.

Therapeutic technique in psychoanalysis has been influenced in different ways by these prevailing trends and by the growth of psychoanalytic knowledge. To avoid confusion, I shall confine my discussion of technique to two basic aspects: interpretation and the therapeutic relationship. Note, however, that this is not an arbitrary choice: the vast majority of the problems that have arisen in the theory of technique and in therapeutic practice over the years, and hence also the refinements and improvements to the latter, can indeed be traced back to interpretation and the therapeutic relationship.

From the very earliest model of the analytic situation, interpretation has been the specific therapeutic instrument of psychoanalysis. By virtue of interpretation, what had hitherto remained unconscious in the patient was supposed to become conscious, and, since making the unconscious conscious was considered to be in itself therapeutic, interpretation quickly came to be accepted as the specific therapeutic instrument of psychoanalysis. In this first model, interpretations were exclusively of content, and the analyst's position in the relationship was taken to be similar to that of a mirror, whose function was to reflect back to the patient's conscious mind what he was unconsciously projecting on to it. However, from the time of this first model, it was implicit in the idea of making the unconscious conscious that therapy involved a modification of the patient's structure, a structure which had its origins in the first description of the mental apparatus. But the conception of the therapeutic relationship corresponded to the scientific model dear to Freud's time, in which the analyst assumed the position of an attentive but detached observer and the patient was the object of his observation.

As we know, this conception did not last long. Freud's first vexed statement about the counter-transference (1910a) and his first memorable description of the analyst's attitude towards the patient's unconscious (1912) show how, already in those first years of the century, the idea of the analyst-as-mirror, cold and detached, was quickly giving way to a more conscious realization that the analyst was necessarily involved in and a party to the relationship between himself and the patient. The analyst's personality thus came to be a legitimate object of concern. Freud's first idea was that it was not possible to be an analyst without a capacity for self-analysis. Since such a capacity was not readily verifiable and also did not offer a sufficient guarantee, it became obvious that the analyst himself should previously undergo psychoanalytic treatment. This eventually led to the institutionalization of training, which, of course, involves not only the candidate-analyst's personal analytic treatment and theoretical courses and seminars but also the treatment of a few patients by him under the supervision of expert analysts.

The supervision in particular was to prove a valuable source of information on the various manifestations of the counter-transference.

This opened up a new and wide-ranging field of research, which not only ultimately broadened and transformed the concept of the counter-transference but also contributed inestimably to our knowledge of the therapeutic relationship and to the analyst's part in the unfolding of the therapeutic process. As a result, the extraordinary complexity of this process became considerably more intelligible. It is evident how much this contributed to the modification and improvement of therapeutic technique.

There is no doubt that the contribution of the Kleinian school to research on the counter-tranference and its consequences has been fundamental. This has to do with the Kleinian conviction of the importance of the object relation from the very beginning of life. For this reason, the study of the transference and the counter-transference has always been very important in Kleinian research. In addition, the Kleinians characteristically give priority to the clinical aspect.

To understand the repercussions of Kleinian research on therapeutic technique, it should be remembered that its investigations extended to a still largely unexplored area (the instinctual drives in the earliest object relation, studied in babies and in psychotics), where the individual structure described by Freud did not yet exist or was only embryonic, and where theorization in truly metapsychological terms proved to be exceedingly difficult. Again, the existence of the death instinct was taken for granted by Melanie Klein, although no enquiry into this concept in particular had ever been made. The study of the aggressive drives did not therefore lead to the economic investigation of instinctual energy and its vicissitudes – such as Freud would have undertaken, and did undertake until 1924 ('The economic problem of masochism') – but concerned principally the other aspects of the drives, as observable in clinical practice. I should add that although Kleinian research has conspicuously enriched our knowledge of the dynamics of the aggressive drives in relation to the object from the earliest days of life, the relative lack of attention to the economic aspects has meant that it has made little contribution – and this also applies to majority, non-Kleinian, psychoanalysis – to our still inadequate knowledge of the energy we call aggressive and its vicissitudes. The Kleinian concep-tualization thus came to be based principally on the dynamic aspects and was therefore open to criticism from the metapsychological point of view on the grounds of incompleteness. For the reasons mentioned, it lacked the structural and the economic parameter. However, this in no way detracted from the validity of this conceptualization on the operational level, which was then also that of clinical verification. This explains the Kleinians' privileged valuation of the analytic situation and everything pertaining to it. Hence the particular importance assigned to technique.

In this sense, Melanie Klein may be said to have accomplished her revolution within the strictest orthodoxy. While the psychoanalytic setting in general is considered by outsiders to be extremely rigorous, the Kleinian setting appears equally rigorous to other psychoanalysts. The rigour of the formal aspects is paralleled by the no less rigorous and systematic use of interpretation – so much so that the interpretations seem to be inflicted on the patient rather than supplied to him, within a relationship that normally operates on deep, but sometimes merely remote, levels of development. The interpretations are usually of content, and concern principally unconscious fantasies relating to oral and anal wishes and conflicts, experienced through such mechanisms as introjection, projection, and projective identification and with introjected part-objects, defined as 'internal objects'. Since the interpretations are considered the more effective the more they are transferential, all the material brought by the patient is as a rule considered and interpreted by the analyst as transference material.

Of course, I have no intention here of entering into the many problems, let alone the many controversies, aroused by Kleinian technique, but wish merely to identify some of its fundamental points, which may help us to understand the ways in which this technique has come to contribute to the evolution of psychoanalytic technique in general. Some of the points I have discussed – the particular rigour of the setting, the high valuation placed on interpretation as a therapeutic instrument, and the privileged use of transference interpretation – may at first sight appear not to be new at all but simply to be emphasized and insisted upon as compared with non-Kleinian psychoanalytic technique. In fact, these quantitative differences have also been used polemically by both sides and may have also served the Kleinian analysts as proof that they certainly could not be accused of failing to observe the rules; yet, plainly, had there not been substantially qualitative differences within these quantitative ones, they would not have disturbed anyone. On the other hand, it would be quite wrong to maintain that the 'severe orthodoxy' of the Kleinians was nothing other than a tactical move intended to endorse what was in practice a substance that lacked orthodoxy.

The Kleinians' emphasis on interpretation can in fact be related to at least two undeniably important factors. The first of these is, so to speak, intrinsic and has to do with the fact that Kleinian research has coincided with a period when interpretation was in general given pride of place, as it was regarded as the specific therapeutic instrument of psychoanalysis. The second factor is more intrinsic to research and therapy and concerns the need to translate a world of fantasies and, in general, a mental activity which largely antedate language, into a verbal form that can be articulated in language. The possibility of decoding pre-verbal thought and re-coding it in verbal symbols may in itself have a valid economic reason – which will therefore be useful in the therapeutic process – namely, reduction of the original cathexes and consequent greater accessibility of the content. Even if this economic reason probably applies to interpretation in general, it has assumed particular relevance in Kleinian interpretation, not only because of the type of unconscious contents and mental mechanisms revealed by Kleinian analysis, which were still largely unknown in psychoanalysis, but also, and in particular, because the interpretation was borne primarily on the transference – that is to say, *on the analytical relationship*. In other words, the transference interpretation virtually coincided with the need to make intelligible the experiences of the analytical relationship *at the moment when they were taking place*. Again, all analysts agreed that transference interpretation was in itself more directly comprehensible to the patient, itself becoming an experience, and that it therefore attained a maximum of therapeutic efficacy (Strachey's mutative interpretations). However, in maintaining that every interpretation must be a transference interpretation, the Kleinian analysts went far beyond this, in practice denying that any other type of interpretation could have therapeutic value. This approach also led them to interpret with a continuity unmatched by other analysts.

Kleinian technique and theory thus displayed, more than strict orthodoxy, a degree of absoluteness, from which other analysts shied away. It is this that has given the Kleinian school great strength, but here too lies its limit. While Kleinian research conferred on psychoanalytic technique a more meaningful sense of the therapeutic function of the relationship in the analytical situation, the whole of psychoanalysis was in any case tending in this direction, although by different routes. Regarding interpretation, the other analysts had learned to diversify and calibrate it, calculate its timing and forms, and above all to refrain from it, precisely as a function of the relationship and its vicissitudes. They had come to recognize how the patient could sometimes progress not so much because of the interpretations given as of those not given, and how certain silences experienced together with the patient could be worth more than any accurate interpretation. In consequence of these and other facts and of studies of the countertransference, the relationship came to be seen as an actual therapeutic instrument, the analyst being regarded as an essential component of the therapy, not so much, or not only, by virtue of his ability to give

98

effective interpretations as for his capacity to be in the relationship in the necessary ways and on the necessary levels.

Admittedly, all this did not lead to absoluteness; nor, unfortunately, did it lead to clarity. The Kleinians, however, did have the strength and consistency of clear and distinct ideas, compared with which the empirical achievements of the other psychoanalysts often appeared mutually contradictory or inconsistent. Yet this does not mean that the truth was all on the one side and that the other side was all wrong, or the other way round. In the non-Kleinian camp, some contradictions arose out of errors in approach which we are only now coming to recognize. An example is the idea of an aggressive instinct different from libido but identical with it in its vicissitudes. Another is the idea of aggression defined first as 'instinct' but then conceived exclusively as 'response'. Similar errors of approach could also lead to inconsistencies on the technical level. Other contradictions, however, were only apparent, attributable to the fact that, as in any science, the observations referred to actual data, but data which were partial and fragmentary, which could have been integrated in the light of late knowledge. In my opinion, such contradictions included the observations – as it happens, entirely accurate – of the therapeutic efficacy of a correct interpretation (and sometimes also, as Glover showed, of a wrong interpretation) and the no less accurate observations of the equal or even greater efficacy of non-interpretation or the total inefficacy of many technically correct interpretations.

Now if this contradiction was not experienced in the Kleinian camp, the reason was the absolute consistency of a system in which the interpretation, with the characteristics mentioned above, did not allow of any further doubts. This, however, is the point where absolute consistency can cease to be a strength and become a limitation. The problem of interpretation was clearly not an end in itself, and still less a narrowly technical problem. The observations on therapeutic silence were to be supported both validly and unexpectedly in new research on the earliest aspects of the object relationship. From the studies in the United States of P. Greenacre on the somatic origin of the first psychical defences and of M. Mahler on the process of separation-individuation, to the powerful research of D.W. Winnicott in the United Kingdom on the facilitating or non-facilitating role of the environment in early development and on the child's early auto-nomous processes in object relations, as well as my own study in Italy of the first imitative processes and their relation to the identificatory processes and the coming into being of the object relationship, an abundant crop of new data came to fill the gap of what was once known as the 'objectless phase'.

The existence of this phase had been rightly denied by Melanie Klein, whose research had revealed the remoteness of the object relation and the – predominantly aggressive – conflicts involved in this relation. However, in the Kleinian theory, the primitive part-object, the breast, is an external given, which the child 'internalizes' by the operation of oral mechanisms such as introjection, projection, and projective identification. Post-Kleinian research has highlighted a complicated and painful process of distinction of the self from the object, with which the self is at first fused and confused. In this process the contribution of the environment (mother, breast) is fundamental, but what is most important is that this *precedes the instinctual relationship with the object* and is then for a long time combined in complex ways with the instinctual relationship, helping to temper the anxiety to which it gives rise. Where the process of 'creation of the self' (Winnicott) is somehow disturbed, the result is a pathology of the self which will interfere more or less severely with the development of the instinctual relationship and hence with the identificatory processes and the formation of the subject's own identity. In such cases, the analytical relationship must be able to operate on very deep levels, remote from language, and barely if at all instinctual. Verbal interpretation at instinc-tual levels may in these cases have no meaning, whereas silence and participation may assume an important therapeutic function. Winnicott wrote in one of his last works:

> it is only in recent years that I have become able to wait and wait for the natural evolution of the transference arising out of the patient's growing trust in the psychoanalytic technique and setting, and to avoid breaking up this natural process by making interpretations. It appals me to think of how much deep change I have prevented or delayed in patients *in a certain classification category* by my personal need to interpret.

(1971: 152)

This recent research has led to a further deepening of our knowledge about narcissistic pathology, as well as, in particular, extending and deepening our knowledge of object development. Its contribution to therapeutic technique is therefore very far-reaching. The same thera-peutic process now appears in a new light, and not only in narcissistic patients. In practice, every disturbance of the object relationship entails the deployment of defences rooted in an altered basic narcissistic structure; this is true much more frequently than had hitherto been understood. If we can strengthen the narcissistic foundation in its most elementary aspects of object need, we can confront the instinctual wishes and conflicts in the object relation and in particular the associated anxiety. The more difficult it is to abandon the elementary position of need in the object relation, the more serious is the instinctual anxiety. But the more serious the basic narcissistic wound, the more difficult it is to abandon this position. For at this level, the anxiety is bound up not so much with the conflicts and aggressive instinctual cathexes as with the danger of disintegration of self. If this disintegration anxiety is not appropriately overcome, distinction and primary separation of self from object is impossible, still less the appropriate development of the instinctual relationship with an object separate from self.

The therapeutic task is complex and subtle and sometimes very frustrating for the analyst. The patient does not reveal his relationship of need in the transference except in very indirect ways which are difficult to recognize. Since the analyst tends principally to recognize the instinctual transference, and the analytical situation is implicitly intended to promote a relationship, the patient may, for example, deploy primitive imitative mechanisms in the transference whereby the instinctual anxiety is held in check and the analytical relationship is reduced to a kind of life-giving contact similar to the pre-conflictual, magical, and omnipotent contact with the primary object. If the analyst is not careful, he may easily fail to recognize this defence, which may, however, undermine the entire therapeutic process; he may continue to interpret in instinctual terms a transference which the patient is unconsciously living in imitative, magical terms. The result is that the analysis apparently progresses, the analyst is satisfied, and so too is the patient, especially at the deepest level, where he is sure that the analysis will not give rise to the slightest change in structure. The reason why many analyses prove 'interminable' or fail is that the analytic treatment aims too exclusively to interpret the instinctual dynamics with the object.

My point, however, is that the imitative transference, the transference of life-giving contact but which is not structuring, becomes all the more redoubtable a defence the less it is recognized. Moreover, the knowledge that it exists is not sufficient for its recognition. The aspects in which it may manifest itself indirectly are legion. What can be said is that, just as we have come to understand that in the instinctual transference the interpretation counts not for itself but in the framework of the relationship, so in the magical imitative transference what matters most is the analyst's ability to be 'involvable' in the relationship at the level required by the patient. Responding in the appropriate ways to the relationship of magical contact in which the patient puts himself means extending the therapy to the needs of a self that were not sufficiently met at the relevant time.

At this point I should like to mention some other changes that have taken place in our conception of the transference and the counter-transference. Concerning the former, while the concept of the transference as a substitute for memory (repeating instead of remembering) remains valid, we have now come to recognize that in the 'repeated' relationship the patient may find himself living *for the first time* experiences which were lacking in the primitive relationship. As for the counter-transference, I have already mentioned that our knowledge of it has grown and deepened in parallel with our knowledge of the object relationship. Experience has shown that the relationship of need in which the patient may put himself quite often arouses negative responses in the analyst, and this explains why the analyst may find it more difficult to recognize the transference of need than the instinctual transference. Again, I have found in supervision that highly gifted young analysts, capable of appropriately meeting the patient's elementary reconstitutive needs, may appear suddenly disconcerted and, unusually, unable to see or understand what is happening in the analytical situation, at the point when the patient, by virtue of the work done with the analyst, begins to show signs of an instinctual transference. In the counter-transference, according to our present knowledge, it may happen that the analyst himself lives the internal situation of the patient, which is equivalent to perceiving it. In the cases mentioned above, the analyst seemed to be perceiving and himself living the residual separation (disintegration) anxiety that the patient was profoundly experiencing at the point when he was looking out from the position of the relationship of need towards the instinctual relationship.

So far I have sought to show how psychoanalytic technique has evolved closely in step with the progress of theoretical knowledge and how this progress for a time was achieved by way of splits and controversies, the noisiest of which corresponded to new and important trends in research, to which the evolution itself of psychoanalysis gave rise. I dwelt particularly on the Kleinian controversy, to show how fruitful Melanie Klein's research has been for our current knowledge of the dynamics of the aggressive drives in the early days and weeks of life and of the origins of the instinctual relationship with the object. If the Kleinian conceptualizations have been predominantly dynamic and therefore metapsychologically incomplete, this in no way detracts from the validity of the research. Apart from meeting a need due to the incompleteness for the time being of the metapsychology, Kleinian research may today be said actually to have made a substantial contribution on the structural level too, adding to our knowledge of the early development of the ego and superego and the earliest defence mechanisms.

I also noted that the Kleinian conceptualization tended to create a consistent and absolute system and that this might ultimately constitute a limitation detrimental to the evolution of the system. Obviously, one reason for this absoluteness has been the need for out-and-out defence with a view to protecting the research from the continuous attacks to which it has been subjected.

Post-Kleinian research has not in fact shown any serious discrepancy with Melanie Klein's views, but has on the contrary set in motion a process of integration of Kleinian and general psychoanalytic research. Again, our current knowledge of the early object relation does not contradict the Kleinian conception but extends it into an area un-explored by Kleinian research. It is, of course, difficult to predict the future. All that can be said is that, if the incipient process of integration continues, the Kleinian analysts too, in the same way as the other analysts, will modify the technique hitherto used, taking account of the fact that the therapeutic relationship extends beyond the instinctual transference.

Postscript

The prediction in the last lines of this paper very quickly proved to be accurate, namely, on the occasion of the 29th Congress of the International Psychoanalytical Association, held in London from 20 to 25 July 1975; that is, after only three months, considering that my paper was sent to the publisher at the end of April. At the International Congress, and in particular at the traditional Pre-Congress held two days earlier by the British Psycho-Analytical Society (at which the British analysts usually discuss clinical material with foreign colleagues), authoritative Kleinian analysts such as Herbert Rosenfeld, Esther Bick, Betty Joseph, and Sidney Klein did indeed show that they were modifying, as I wrote above, 'the technique hitherto used, taking account of the fact that the therapeutic relationship extends beyond the instinctual transference'. This capacity of the Kleinian authors for evolution immediately becomes a crucial factor in accelerating the process of integration of the different psychoanalytic currents in Europe. However, this process cannot extend to the United States in the same ways and with the same timing, as Kleinian research has never been recognized there and structuralistic positions have so far been upheld and defended in that country as the only ones compatible with Freud's psychoanalysis.

The invention of space in psychoanalysis

Unpublished, this is an elaboration of a paper presented to the 3rd Congress of the Italian Psychoanalytic Society, Venice, May 1976.

The psychoanalytic invention of space

As we know, psychoanalysis has the distinction of having described the mental apparatus in spatial terms for the first time. This description ultimately made it possible to place the study of mental activity on the level of a natural science and to remove it from the realm of the philosophical and moral sciences. However, it should be clear that when we refer in this description to the 'space' of the mental apparatus, we are merely using a concept, just as when we refer to the id, the ego, and the superego, the functional systems which make up the structure, conceived in spatial terms, within which mental phenomena are held to take place. That is to say, internal space is not real in the sense in which we say external space is real; but it is not a *hypothesis* either, in the normal scientific sense of this term. Methodologically, the psycho-analytic use of the spatial dimension in fact seems to correspond very closely to what Vaihinger (1924), the philosopher of the 'as if', defines as a *fiction* in scientific thought.

According to Vaihinger (1924), a *hypothesis*

refers continuously to reality [. . .], is subject to verification of its *reality* and aspires to the latter – that is, its aim is to be demonstrated as the *true, actual, concrete* expression of a concrete datum. A hypo-thesis aims to establish without exception something *real*; even if we are not absolutely certain that the datum, assumed hypothetically, is indeed preliminary, we nevertheless hope that this might one day be demonstrable.

A *fiction*, however,

> does not by any means end with the expression of something or other that is real but a something *whereby account can be taken of reality*.

Unlike a hypothesis

> a fiction [. . .] in science has only one practical purpose, since it does not at all give rise to *genuine knowledge* [. . .]. A hypothesis may eliminate contradictions observed in reality, whereas a fiction *generates logical contradictions* [. . .]. A hypothesis *aims to discover, while a fiction aims to find* [. . .]. To the extent that fictions are scientific instruments of thought without which high-level formation of thought itself is impossible, it may be said that fictions are *invented* [. . .]. The counterpart of the verification of a hypothesis is the *justification* of a fiction [. . .]. A fiction must be *justified* by the service it renders to empirical science [. . .]. Fictions which are not *justified* – *i.e., which cannot be justified as useful and necessary* – must therefore be eliminated, like unverified hypotheses [. . .]. Just as the formation of hypotheses is both justified and indispensable as an instrument of scientific research, so too is the making of fictions.
>
> (1924: 90ff)

As Vaihinger (1924) points out,

> an interesting necessity [. . .] is not to allow oneself to be confused by the contradictions of the fiction with the reality of experience and by those of the fiction in itself, and not to allow oneself to be trapped in the so-called riddle of the world, which flows from these contradictions.
>
> (p. 95)

The contradiction between time and space, as I shall try to show later, is precisely a kind of riddle of the world.

To sum up, according to Vaihinger's (1924) definition, a fiction is deemed first of all to be 'invented'; second, it must be borne in mind that, unlike a hypothesis, it gives rise to 'logical contradictions'; and, third, it has to be 'justified by the service it renders'. Before discussing the 'invention' of space as a fiction, I should like to point out that an obvious 'logical contradiction' to which the fiction of space has given rise in psychoanalysis is the way in which mental phenomena have been and still are described: on the one hand in terms of topography and intersystemic and intrasystemic relations, and on the other in process terms. In the first case the connections are spatial, while in the second they are temporal. However, this logical contradiction, to which some have drawn attention and which has aroused polemics

105

among psychoanalysts themselves, in fact in no way detracts from the practical utility of the spatial description of the mental apparatus and hence from the scientific *justification* of this description.

In considering the fact that a fiction may be said to be *invented*, it therefore seems to me to be advantageous to distinguish two aspects, corresponding to two different moments. The first, as we have seen, is the practical aspect of the invention: the fiction serves in order to find. This also constitutes its general methodological justification. The second aspect is that the fiction is in turn invented *preliminarily*.

We are perhaps helped here by the Latin etymon, which is the same for 'invent' and 'find': *invenire*. But while *invenire* in the sense of 'find' relates to the first aspect (the practical effect of the fiction of space), *invenire* in the sense of 'invent' concerns a preliminary mental operation, which can be defined as an invention, in a creative sense, of space itself. In other words, this invention presupposes a mental significatum of space which makes it possible.

This distinction between *invenire*-finding and *invenire*-inventing may help us to understand the noteworthy fact that Freud concerned himself hardly at all with internal space as a significatum but simply used the category of space in his topographic, and later structural description of the mental apparatus. This enabled him to *find* and describe mental phenomena in scientific terms for the first time, to locate them spatially in the various systems of the structure, and to find and describe the dynamics and economics of these phenomena within the sphere of the relations between the different systems and within each system. For a long time after Freud, psychoanalysts throughout the world simply continued in the same way, and to great advantage, to use his topographic hypothesis and his structural theory – in other words, his *spatial fiction* – without manifesting any obvious specific interest in space as an experience of the internal world. In order for psychoanalysis to be able to make the mental invention of space an object of its research, the knowledge derived from the 'finds' obtained by virtue of its spatial fiction had to become sufficient to make this possible. This means that – as we can say today – it had to be possible, as did in fact occur, for the research to be extended to the point of encompassing the earliest stages of mental activity, in which the idea of space arises and begins to evolve and take on meaning, and with it, form and dimension. However, this means that the study of the idea of space eventually became the study of an experience taking the form of a process during the course of the mental development of the human individual. In other words, as a precondition for the commencement of the study of the mental invention of space, the use of the dimension of time first had to become possible.

106

We shall have occasion shortly to discuss the relation between time and space in individual development. But before proceeding further, it seems to me necessary, in the light of the foregoing, to consider briefly the relationship that psychoanalysis, a theory based on a spatial fiction, has come to have with the dimension of time.

The psychoanalytic acquisition of time

Although there is no mention in Freud's metapsychology of the function of time in mental phenomena understood in spatial terms, Freud and psychoanalysis have nevertheless made use of it: the study of mental phenomena in process terms has from the outset constituted a distinctive and indispensable aspect of psychoanalytic research. One need only think of the theories of symptom formation and libido development and of the fundamental idea of infantile origins of adult pathology. Yet the *theoretical* recognition – by which I mean the scientific awareness – of the importance of time (the *genetic* viewpoint) was attained only at a later stage. As we know, the dynamic and topographic viewpoints were the first to be formulated meta-psychologically, and it was only much later that Freud (1915a) completed his formulation with the economic viewpoint. However, it should be noted that the latter in spatial terms related to the most *elementary* level of mental activity, at the boundary of the biological, but that, for the same reason, it also concerned the *remotest* level of mental development in temporal terms. In my view, it was no accident that we find here the first discrepancy between the awareness of the economic problem on the theoretical level, sanctioned by Freud's formulation of the economic viewpoint, and the use of the economic function in the study of mental phenomena, which, for its part, dates back to the very origins of Freud's research (1895). My point is that, without the appropriate use of the dynamic and topographic viewpoints in research, it would not have been possible for Freud to arrive at a satisfactory formulation of the economic viewpoint.

This is even more true of the second and more extensive discrepancy, concerning on the one hand the use and on the other hand the theoretical awareness of time. Such is the discrepancy that the addition to metapsychology of the genetic viewpoint is in itself post-Freudian, but in systematic and rigorous research such as that initiated and pursued by Freud, the sequence of the arguments brought to bear cannot but result from the very development of the research. This accounts for the fact that Freud was unable to accept an 'instinct of aggression', which Adler considered he had discovered in 1908 but himself withdrew not long after. As stated above, the economic point of view allowed psychoanalysis to investigate the remotest, as well as the most elementary, mental phenomena, and this also made it possible to understand and study them appropriately in terms of process.

My point is that, apart from Freud's intimate knowledge of the function of time in the mental apparatus, the development of his research inevitably meant that the genetic viewpoint could only have been formulated after and at an appropriate distance from the formulation of the economic point of view.

It is, I suppose, clear that this necessary sequence of meta-psychological viewpoints has to do only with Freud's methodological invention of space: a fruitful investigation of the invention of space as a mental process could develop only after and at an appropriate distance from the formulation of the genetic point of view. But Freud's lifetime was not long enough for this.

The mental invention of space

The attempt on which I shall now embark is not an easy one. Following the research of, in particular, D.W. Winnicott and W. Bion, it can, I think, be fairly confidently asserted that the psychoanalytic investigation of the mental process of space substantially coincides with the investigation of the earliest mental organization of the self. Hence, while concentrating on the evolution of the process of space in the infant mind, I shall not be able to avoid grappling with the problems of the formation of the earliest organization of the self and the changes undergone by this organization. However, I do not wish to go into these complex and wide-ranging matters except to consider the limited aspects that are relevant to this paper.

Primary mental activity

Primary mental activity is fed essentially by bodily experiences, and the mental representation of the baby's own body, which is absent at birth, is laboriously acquired through the baby's gradual experience of it. In functional terms, own-body experiences seem to precede those of the external world and hence to predominate over the latter. Since external stimuli are perceived only through the reactions and modifications they induce in the bodily state – that is, through the baby's own body – primitive perception is physically imitative; in other words, its functioning conforms to the biological model of 'imitation in order to perceive'. The infant's reflexes, which have been comprehensively described in neurophysiological terms, seem to be in the service of this type of perception, with aims directly connected with survival. Examples are the rooting reflex (the head rotation reflex) and Moro's reflex (immediate response to the feeling of being dropped). Sander (1977), in the United States, has recently for the first time studied, described and documented in detail the neonate's bodily movements in response to the sound of the mother's voice.

I have described elsewhere the transition from this biological model, via the prototype of the hallucinatory image, to the parallel mental operation of the first *psychical imitations*, according to the functional model of 'imitation in order to be'. 'We do not know', I then wrote, 'how the physical functional model is converted into a parallel psychical model, but primitive mental activity offers us more than one example of this kind' [see Chapter 1]. In the light of subsequent experience, I have become more and more convinced that the mental reproduction of biological functional models is to be regarded as one of the fundamental principles of early psychical functioning.

A second principle, which follows directly from the first, could be formulated as follows: *the functional models of experiences already had (therefore 'known'), are actively and repeatedly reproduced when the infantile mind is confronted with the imposition of different functional models involving 'unknown' experiences.* This second regulating principle of basic mental functioning may account, on the one hand, for the rapid structuring of defences such as regression and, on the other, for the imperceptible but very early arising of the dimension of time which (intervening between an experience and its reactivation) implies memory.

The second regulating principle, whereby unknown experience is warded off by the reactivation of known experience, tends to oppose the different, which is implicit in any change. However, it is precisely change which gives rise to process and also, because constitutive of a before and an after, to the gradual acquisition of time.

Yet the early coming into being of time does not correspond to an early awareness of time as a dimension. By comparison, the awareness of space seems to arise decidedly earlier, even if it in turn implies a series of preliminary processes during the course of which the meaning of space gradually becomes organized. That is to say, each individual's space in the mental sense – at least in terms of when at a certain point this space attains the threshold of consciousness – seems to have its origins in the sphere of the baby–breast relationship.

The space of things

Of course, in this very early phase, the baby expresses not so much wishes as needs, and the ego which caters to these needs is the mother's. The needs arise from a bodily self which, usually by way of repeated and adequate satisfactions and a smaller number of frustrations, gradually acquires an initial sense of itself, which we may imagine as a kind of primitive space. This very early space is strongly marked by biological (bodily) functioning and is not properly an internal space, because it arises in the baby–breast sphere, but it is experienced by the baby as a first totality of self. Again, of course, the bodily experiences of this 'phase of need' are of a predominantly sensory nature, considering that the perceptual activities related primarily to the bodily self and the modifications of its state. Oral activity is so to speak at the centre of the baby–breast sphere, but, as the only neuromotor activity already coordinated at birth, it is governed primarily by the needs of the self, with predominantly sensory and feeding functions, and *not yet* by the drives. In other words, the nascent mental area of the self is a space without structure, without a boundary of its own, without form and without time. It has in common with cosmic space the preclusion of the possibility of conceiving of the existence of any other space, of something beyond its own totality.

This primitive space is one that is expanding. It tends to develop and consolidate itself. In the absence of structure and of the possibility of conceiving of a non–self (which would immediately become a different-from-self), the primitive total self is magic and omnipotent. Everything that comes from outside to satisfy its needs is experienced as magically produced by the self, and contributes to confirming and consolidating its omnipotence. Within the sphere of the total space created by itself, the self continuously creates itself.

Outside such an experience, however, this infantile universe is objectively describable as a small composite universe – the baby–mother (breast) sphere – immersed in the larger universe of the surrounding environment. In other words, the external world is present from the outset with its physical dimensions of space and time and its expectations, by virtue of which the infantile universe can be fed in its omnipotent expansion or confronted to different extents by restrictive stimulus situations. The baby's actual body is objectively real and dimensioned, and its objective functioning may be experienced as alien to the total experience of the self whenever one of its needs is not appropriately met in the external environment.

The lack of structure and of effective organized defences makes this infantile universe extremely vulnerable and restrictive experiences (frustrations) extremely dangerous. For this reason, the degree in which these are administered, as compared with the experiences of satisfaction, is of crucial importance to the self-creative process of the self. Essentially, the baby at this stage – and often the patient in the analytical situation – needs to be fed and held. The fact that the baby cannot hold itself with its spinal column even in a sitting position and cannot hold up its head with the cervical spinal column, corresponds literally on the mental level with the need to be properly held in addition to being fed. Some patients do indeed exhibit acute painful syndromes of the vertebral column when, in my experience, the analyst fails adequately to meet the patient's need to be 'held'. In a young female borderline patient, an acute attack of this kind occurred a few sessions before the separation of the summer holidays. In another case, however, a painful syndrome of the cervical spinal column accompanied a prolonged negative therapeutic reaction for a time. Sometimes, when the connections do not become manifest, we should ask ourselves in what respect or way we have failed to meet the patient's elementary needs.

While the baby is growing and consolidating itself physically, the space of the baby–mother sphere takes on consistency and expands, and the baby experiences it as the space of the self and as a sense of self. The 'reality' of this space in the infantile experience coincides with the 'concreteness' of bodily functioning. Peripheral stimuli, whether tactile, visual, or auditory, and deep stimuli, especially those originating in the oral cavity and the digestive tract, give rise to movement responses or modifications of the internal state, which, in the form of sensations, lend concreteness to the baby's experiences.

This space of the baby–mother sphere, which is objectively a common space but subjectively its own, fed and filled in this sense by bodily experiences, could be defined as the 'space of things'. Its experience not only precedes the dimension of time but is itself a space *sui generis*, which is pre-dimensional. There is no place in this space for symbolic operations. Since they remain strongly rooted in somatic functioning, the experiences remain 'things', in the sense used by Freud (1923), and do not yet have the possibility of becoming symbols.

With the gradual commencement of functioning of the mnemonic systems, things become the memory of things, but this is not sufficient to give rise to symbols, or even to furnish the sense of time. Memory makes them essentially 'known', but the known things remain things.

It would be more correct to say that, at this stage, 'known' is not equivalent to 'retained in the memory' but simply to 'part of self', and that these 'parts of self' have their origins in concrete 'experiences of self' – that is, bodily, and hence 'real', experiences. Freud (1925: 237) characteristically observed that 'originally the mere existence of a presentation was a guarantee of the reality of what was presented', and, while this is the case, it is because originally each presentation is equivalent to a repeated – but not 'remembered' – concrete, and hence real, experience of self. This means that originally memory serves not to temporalize but only to make present in the here and now, and that this making present is experienced by the self as an active creation of self. In this sense, the mnemonic traces may be said to contribute essentially to the magic and omnipotent functioning of the self, and especially to its magic control of bodily functioning and its omnipotent expansive tendency. If there are no factors to alter its course, the process which gradually leads to the creation of the symbol seems to get under way concomitantly with the first obscure perceptions that something, in the space of the total self, escapes the omnipotent control of the self.

The space of the individual self

I cannot here go too closely into the steps of the evolutionary process which lead from this 'space of things' of the total self to the next stage. Suffice it to recall that these are perhaps the most painful and difficult steps in the entire process of individual development. They involve the shattering of the organization of the *total self* and, we may say, the dramatic *birth* – experienced as a catastrophic and mutilating collapse – of a self I would call *individual*. Because of the way this happens, the conditions of the individual self at the beginning can be described as terribly fragile and precarious. The omnipotence with which it was endowed as a total self is now in effect swallowed up by a gigantic, monstrous, and all-enveloping non-self, by which the newborn individual self feels evacuated and peremptorily threatened with total annihilation. The only force available to the individual self in such a desperate situation is its own biological urge to survive.

This survival urge seems to be the original stimulus for the mobilization of the instinctual cathexes. The effects of this instinctual mobilization and of its location in the space of the self are in my opinion of fundamental importance to the immediate situation and have incalculable implications for subsequent development: the peripheral location of the aggressive cathexes, turned outwards, and of the libidinal cathexes, turned inwards, contributes essentially to the formation in the self of the sense of a *boundary*, in its two-fold aspect as a containing and protective barrier towards the inside and as an interface with and defence against the outside. Instinctual mobilization,

112

associated with the sense of the subject's own boundary, also tends substantially to mitigate the painful state of depletion of the self, giving rise to a new kind of omnipotence, *instinctual omnipotence*, which is qualitatively different from that of the illusion (in Winnicott's sense) experienced in the sphere of the total self: for this new omnipotence is not simply experienced but actively pursued and nourished in the service of the needs of the self, foremost among which is the need to survive.

Finally, the peripheral disposition of the aggressive instinctual cathexes, turned outwards, and of the libidinal ones, turned inwards, is responsible at the outset for the differentiation of an *instinctual* and a *sensory* area in early mental activity. Whereas sensory activity is bound up with the internal functioning of the self and is essentially libidinal in nature, with aims which are seemingly not so much instinctual as primarily economic, instinctual mental activity is connected with the development of the peripheral area of the self in its relations with the outside world. Unlike sensory mental activity, instinctual mental activity is originally essentially aggressive in nature, even if, as Freud had occasion to say, 'things change'. The changes are induced by the initiation of processes of fusion of libidinal with aggressive cathexes, into which I shall not go further here as I have discussed them elsewhere. However, I should like to take this opportunity of putting forward a hypothesis which I consider to be borne out by clinical evidence and which concerns on the one hand libido and on the other aggression.

A hypothesis and a distinction

The hypothesis derives directly from the description given above of the individual self and from that description's account of the disposition of the energetic cathexes that characterize it. I must say first that I have already in a previous paper [see Chapter 2] expressed the view that it is primarily the aggressive cathexes which 'seek' the object, and not the libidinal cathexes, which, for their part, are 'entrained' towards the object by the processes of fusion with the aggressive cathexes. The hypothesis is that libido is not originally a properly instinctual energy – if, as I believe, we associate with the concept of instinct, or drive, that of action and relationship with the separate object – but that it *becomes* so by way of the processes of fusion with the aggressive cathexes, whose nature is primarily and exclusively instinctual. In other words, what in the past was defined as 'narcissistic libido' is in this hypothesis the libido which serves for the maintenance and functioning of the self

113

and which has no need to be instinctual for this purpose; on the other hand, what used to be defined as 'object libido' would be nothing other than libido *instinctualized* by the way of the processes of fusion with the properly instinctual – namely, aggressive – cathexes.

An immediate corollary of this hypothesis is that the degree of primitiveness of the instinctual cathexes is closely related to the fusional processes, in the sense that it is inversely proportional to the degree of instinctualization of the libidinal cathexes. The more primitive the aggressive cathexes, the less these are fused with the libidinal ones. On the clinical level, we do indeed find that, the earlier the conflicts, the more these conflicts are characterized by destructive drive cathexes. Again, if we bear in mind that the primary aim of libido is to serve the economic and functional needs prevailing inside the self in early infancy, the hypothesis enables us to understand how, if these needs have not been appropriately met, the primitive urge of the self for its own survival will tend to remain as the dominant force, adversely affecting structural development, the formation of the sense of identity, the formation of the object separate from the self, and hence the development of the relation to the object. In adult pathology we can thus ultimately observe clinically how the whole of sexual activity – even if successful in some respects and apparently genital – may be placed in the service of the self's incessant and peremptory urge to survive, rather than in the service of the development of the object relation.

A useful distinction can be made in connection with this type of pathology in which the needs of the self are imposed on the entire mental structure (borderline cases, narcissistic patients, and per-versions). This is a distinction between the *instinctuality of the self* and *instinctual activity of the infantile ego*. The instinctuality of the self, as we have seen, characterizes the new omnipotence of the individual infan-tile self, and is directed outwards, at first indiscriminately, a–direction-ally or, as we might say, omni-directionally, for protection of the inside of the self, whose cohesion is maintained by the libidinal cathexes. The *instinctual activity of the infantile ego*, on the other hand, is turned towards an object in the outside world and tends to evolve in terms of process by fusion with libidinal cathexes and by complicated vicissitudes, which are gradually and increasingly aligned with the reality principle. The *instinctuality of the self* is omnipotent, dispenses with the dimension of time and therefore does not allow changes of kind, is ignorant of the requirements of the environment, and is concerned only with the security and maintenance of the internal space of the self. The *instincual activity of the infantile ego* is functionally posterior and tends gradually to admit experiences which lead to changes and hence to the sense of time

114

and of the real; it also seeks gradually to integrate the needs of the internal space of the self with the demands of external space-time. In all this, the instinctual activity of the ego necessarily encounters a type of drive anxiety, to be distinguished from a much more powerful and ego-paralysing type, 'loss-of-self' anxiety.

This distinction between instinctuality of the self and instinctual activity of the ego, each with its own type of anxiety, corresponds to some very interesting clinical aspects which, however, I cannot go into here as they would take us too far away from the subject of this paper. There are, however, two reasons, both relevant to my subject, for making this distinction. One is that it allows me to make some pertinent comments on the beginnings of the instincts, which bear on questions which have not yet been answered or on which opinions differ. It can then be stated that: (a) instinctuality seems to arise only at a certain point and not at the outset of early mental development; (b) it arises in the space of the individual self and makes an essential contribution to circumscribing this internal space and distinguishing it from an external space; and (c) it arises before there is any possibility of using it for a purpose and for an object.

The second reason is that this distinction may have something to do with a problem that has not by any means yet been solved – namely, the problem of how to define the self in relation to the mental structure and how to describe the relations between the two. We shall return to this problem shortly. First, we must go back briefly to the space of the individual self and its mental significance.

Anxiety, space and time in the individual self

The transition from the space of things to the space of the individual self constitutes an initial actual change in mental development after birth. The change is first experienced as a catastrophic loss of the total self, which is then transformed into a mutilating loss of the total self, with the survival of a circumscribed, evacuated, and impotent self, which subsequently recovers omnipotence, albeit with an instinctual character; this means that what appears as an initial change is actually the result of a tumultuous series of successive changes in the spatial experience, of such a kind as to introduce an initial element of process into that experience, and with it the dimension of time.

However, together with the dimension of time, the initial element of process introduces anxiety, and with it mental suffering, which perhaps peaks at the very moment of its onset. For anxiety appears as catastrophic, in the face of the experience of loss of the total self,

115

thereafter becoming loss-of-self anxiety in the self which has survived. In this way anxiety too enters upon a spatio-temporal evolutionary process. The loss-of-self anxiety is intended to protect the individual self from the first unrepeatable experience. It is obvious how it differs from catastrophic anxiety. The latter arises as a simultaneous effect and intrinsic part of a current catastrophic experience in the timeless space of the total self. Loss-of-self anxiety, on the other hand, is actively organized, on the model of the anxiety primarily experienced, in the temporalized space of the individual self. It is not part of any current experience, but presupposes an actual experience, with the *memory* of which it is connected, with the precise aim of preventing it from becoming current again.

All this involves an initial *use* of time which, however, it is important to note, is very far from the consciousness of time and the use made of it.

Now loss-of-self anxiety, which is at its peak at the beginning, tends to decrease in intensity as the individual self is gradually consolidated in its own space. The arising of the instincts and the consequent new omnipotence contribute decisively to this gradual consolidation. In particular, they contribute to a gradual consolidation of the boundaries of the self, which is accompanied by a growing sense of the delimited spatiality of the self. I do not here mean a spatial sense of the subject's own body, which comes about later, but the gradual formation of a *first mental image of the self*. This image seems to correspond to that of a closed form, a circumscribed space, which is originally two-dimensional. Later, when there is an ego, the child will be capable of making marks on a piece of paper; what he will spontaneously draw as soon as he emerges from the dysmetria of scribbling will be a roundish image, a circumscribed space. I have no doubt that this first creative expression has deep roots – namely, that this graphic image corresponds to the first mental image of the self. It is a concrete image, which derives from psychophysical experiences the child has had and suffered, and in this sense it can be best defined as a first mental representation of the bodily self [see Chapter 12].

A description of the functional activity of the instinctual self and the evolutionary processes which have onset within it would constitute material for more than one further paper. I have barely touched upon it, apart from earlier references, in the paragraph on primary mental activity. What I now wish to stress is that the individual self is a fundamental stage in the evolutionary process and that during the course of its own evolution it is possible in normal circumstances to discern the beginnings of the instinctual activity of the ego. This activity is accompanied from the beginning by a new form of anxiety, one that is therefore evolutionary in nature, which is well known to every analyst, for which I propose to reserve the term 'instinctual anxiety' or, more correctly, 'drive anxiety'. It arises as early as the relation of the self-ego (that is, an ego that is as yet barely distinguishable as such) with an external object distinct and separate from the self, concomitantly with the development of primitive oral drives (that is, ones which are barely fused with libidinal energy) directed towards the object, and with oral mechanisms – principally introjections (projections). In this first drive phase, which a patient may repeat in analysis, the infantile ego, so to speak, alternately enters and withdraws from the sensory-psychic area, which serves the needs of the self. When 'outside', the child is confronting instinctual experiences, and when 'inside', he is withdrawing from them. In this way he can magically obliterate the external instinctual stimuli when these become too painful [see Chapter 8].

Dependence on the external object exposes the child to loss of the omnipotence of the self. At this point it is the object that acquires the most threatening omnipotence. Withdrawal into the sensory-psychic mental area makes it possible to restore the omnipotence of the self and the sense of existing, thus enabling the child to expose himself again to the drive experience. On the other hand, dependence on the object exposes the child to the fear that the object might not be sufficiently stable, that it might be lost so that at that point the self, stripped of its omnipotence, might no longer be able to survive. In other words, the drive anxiety is only gradually distinguished from loss-of-self anxiety and confronted as such. For this to be possible, the loss-of-self anxiety must be sufficiently reduced to allow drive-anxiety to occur [see Chapter 8].

These brief notes may suffice to show how the initial drive activity of the ego – a structure that has barely formed at this point – is severely interfered with by conservative needs and by loss-of-self anxiety. It is my impression in this connection that the clinical significance of loss-of-self anxiety has not yet been adequately appreciated. I believe that it manifests itself pathologically in ways that are tremendously harmful to the mental structure and are extremely redoubtable in our therapeutic work: from subservience of the entire mental structure to the needs of the self on the one hand, to suicide on the other, and from the negative therapeutic reaction to the 'tunnels' of mental pain. The more fragile and necessitous the individual self, the stronger is the loss-of-self anxiety and the more peremptory, despotic, and indiscriminate the use made by the self of its own instinctual omnipotence in regard to the mental structure.

As we can see, my distinction between the instinctuality of the self and the drive activity of the ego has its clinical justification, and it thereby now disquietingly confronts us with the problem of definition of the self *vis-à-vis* the mental structure and of the relations between the two.

The difficulty in dealing with this problem is reflected in the variety of views to be found in the views of other writers. Hartmann treats it as a general concept, whereas Jacobson distinguishes the self from the images of the self. On the other hand, Winnicott writes of the formation of the self and of a distinction between ego and the self, clearly distinguishing the bodily from the mental. But in Kohut we note a contradiction in so far as the self appears to be regarded as a structure of the mind but at times not an agency of the mind.

In another context [Chapter 1] I spoke of a sensory-psychic area of the mind which had not previously been described. I believe that it serves in normal circumstances as a linking area with the functioning of the individual infantile self. Without that area there would be no thought, fantasy, identifications, identity, or creativity – all things that would not be possible without a self.

The hypothesis I should like to put forward is that the entire mental structure should be considered as a differentiated structure of the individual self.

8

Notes on the mind–body question

Read at a meeting of the Centro Psicoanalitico di Bologna in 1980, this paper was published in the *Rivista di Psicoanalisi* (January 1981) XXVII and post-humously under the title 'Notes on the body-mind question' in the International Journal of Psycho-Analysis (1987) 68.

What I am about to say might seem somewhat personal in nature. This is due to the fact that it is nearly impossible, in such a limited amount of space, to explore the entire range of an issue which is so vast and at the same time so consistently at the centre of psychoanalytical research. I will of necessity synthesize the body of the subject into its key structural points, keeping quotations to the indispensable minimum. Clearly, my long psychoanalytical experience will have a determining influence on the formulation of this synthesis, as will my personal position with regard to the question at hand. But in the process I shall attempt to make obvious what is strictly my own contribution. It is my intention, therefore, to describe, as based on current psychoanalytical knowledge, the initial phases of the mind's development and different-iation from the body, starting from intrauterine life.

Psychoanalysis considers mental activity to be the most highly differentiated function of the body, so differentiated, in fact, as to require the development of research methods specific to the study of its phenomena in and of themselves, as independent of their underlying biological predispositions. None the less, for psychoanalysis the body and mind form a functional 'continuum', the main element of which is a process of differentiation going from body to mind, but through which psychoanalysis, going by way of the mind, can ultimately arrive at the body. In Freud's words (1910b): 'Psycho-analysts never forget

119

that the mental is based on the organic, although their work can only carry them as far as this basis and not beyond it' (p. 217). This awareness permits psychoanalysis its own context for and perspective on those disciplines which deal with the workings of the body itself, as well as the possibility of gaining important information concerning the functional continuum. When in 1895 he abandoned 'The Project', Freud's pivotal insight comprised two essential aspects.

The first aspect was that the functional models he was attempting to describe in physiological terms could represent parallel models of mental functioning (which in this sense actually determine the physiological ones); and second, that in consequence it was an error to describe these models in bare physiological terms – rather, it was necessary to take a position which would permit their study in and of themselves in psychological terms. This was the only scientific psychology worth establishing; one that, as is evident here, could combine the idea of the mind as a highly differentiated function of the body and the concept of a complex and concomitant mind–body activity.

One general aspect of this 'continuum' which helps to give an idea of its complexity is that mental functioning, inasmuch as it is determined by bodily functioning, is influenced by it in differing ways and measures, and since mental functioning in turn influences the workings of the body, it can in some measure and manner determine them as well.

Before proceeding I would like to recall another aspect of the body–mind continuum: although it is true that the brain is contained in the skull, the same cannot be said of the mind. Like the nervous system, the mind is extant throughout the body. However, it would perhaps be more correct to say that in the organism understood as a functional continuum, certain functional models are present in parallel formations, both mental and physical.

What is most significant about this basic given, from which Freud himself started out, is that knowing the origin of a particular aspect of mental functioning allows us to observe and better understand the use which subsequently is made of it in the mind. For example: 'introjection' is known as the model of mental functioning parallel to the physical one of 'incorporation' (Glover 1939; Greenson 1954).

They are both basic models. But knowing the origin of 'introjection' permits the study of its mental significance and the normal or pathological variegations of its development which are totally independent of the corporeal model. It is important to keep in mind that even in normal development introjection 'differentiates itself' totally from incorporation. From this we can deduce that the basic model is parallel to, but differentiated from, the corporeal one, and therefore that mental functioning as distinguished from that of the body already exists

120

when a basic mental model is established parallel to the physical one. What we do not know, but hope eventually to find out from those disciplines which study corporeal functioning, is just how a physical functional model is converted into a parallel psychical one. The question is, in what way does physical functioning lead to the differentiated function of the mind?

What we do know at present, however, is that even in the individual growth process, the mind's development is a gradual accomplishment advancing from body to mind, a sort of emergence from the corporeal which coincides with the gradual mental acquisition of a sense of physical self. And since, as I have indicated, psychoanalytical research can only proceed in the inverse direction (from mind to body), the process of investigation has brought it ever closer to the early phases of individual development; that is, towards the initial stages of the mind's differentiation from bodily functions.

Long before it has the capacity to assimilate phenomena from external reality, the individual mind is able to follow in what I would call a 'focalizing' manner, the body's own functioning. Much remains to be learned about this primitive mental awareness, and I will return to this point before long. But still more has yet to be discovered about a form of learning which is present even earlier: that of foetal life. Meticulous scientific observation of foetal behaviour in the womb indicates a heretofore unsuspected level of motor and sensorial activity early on (from the end of the third month), as well as a familiarity with the space in which the foetus actively moves (Janniruberto 1980). The foetal organism appears, in fact, to be active and auto-promotional, even if its available space is extremely limited and protected as compared to the post-natal situation. Moreover, at the opportune moment the foetus seems actively to promote the process of his or her own birth, a process which otherwise (if the foetus is dead, for example) does not take place spontaneously.

How much of this learning is of a purely physiological nature is a controversial question. It seems reasonable to me to observe that the first parallel models of mental learning in this intra-uterine period are founded on models of physiological awareness, and that the birth process and the immediately post-natal situation promote active mental functioning based on these first parallel learning models.

This being the case, the beginning of the mind's process of differentiation from the body could be found at some point in intra-uterine growth. Apropos of this, it would appear that the establishment of a parallel model is impossible before that of the 'memory' of a physiological model. The memory, in fact, could play a crucial role in the passage from physiological to mental functioning, and in terms of development, it could indicate the presumable moment of intra-uterine life when this passage can begin.

In any case, there is no longer any doubt that mental activity is present and operational in the newborn, even if specific manifestations of it are difficult to demonstrate before the end of the second month *ex utero*. In recent decades psychoanalytical investigation has shed much light on the first weeks of post-natal life. The broad divarication that exists between organic functioning and mental functioning, at birth, is of primary importance. If a newborn child is physically an individual, it is because he is a self-defined organism, separate from his mother's body and distinct from other individuals. Mentally, however, he is none of this.

To be more precise, mental functioning is present at birth as differentiated, yet its development and refinement are activated, at the same rate as other bodily functions, by successive adjustments (necessitated by the birth process itself) to the internal physiological functions as well as to the surrounding physical environment. However, while the organism at birth can count on a certain degree of acquired physiological learning, and therefore supply, within certain limits, ready physiological responses adapted to the altered requirements of body functioning and environment, it cannot at the same time count on a comparable level of mental learning about its own physiological functions. In the light of this, it would appear that the parallel models of these functions tend to remain unchanged with respect to the upheaval which birth imposes on the priorly established (intra-uterine) organization.

But in reality, this is not how things stand. It is more likely that the divergence at birth exists mainly between the level of physiological learning in itself and the degree of mental learning about physiological functioning. One reason for this is that during growth, physiological learning necessarily precedes mental learning, which, as I will explore in greater depth presently, consists mainly in learning about physiological functioning. For as long as the foetal condition exists, this sequence can be considered the original expression of the mind–body functional 'continuum', and consequently it becomes admissible to deduce that such a sequence may give rise to basic mental learning prior to birth.

Earlier, in fact, I described the intra-uterine situation as spatially limited and protected in comparison to the post-natal situation, and referred to certain observations which would lead us to believe that the foetus has some sort of knowledge of the space in which he actively moves. One might say that the delimitations, the confines which the foetus learns physiologically, are also his own self-limits. If I were not hesitant unduly and prematurely to emphasize the mental, I might say that from its very origins the bodily self extends to a circumscribed space whose limits are also those of the self. Rather, I would like to demonstrate that certain behaviour patterns of the foetus can be understood as the expression of its physiological learning, the spatial limitations of which, lacking as they are in mental self-awareness, can only be those of the surrounding amniotic sac, consolidated by the uterine wall. If, in time, these models of physiological functioning make way, with the establishment of memory and of its mediation, for parallel functional models, it follows that these models constitute the primary basis for mental learning about physiological functions as contained within definite limits. We can consider this to be the fundamental body of knowledge existing at birth. Certainly we are, at this point, far from the possibility of even an initial mental self-image, intended as having an internal space enclosed within its own borders, which separate it from a limitless external space; but the mental use of memory which characterizes the mind's learning from the very beginning acquires new dimensions with the birth process.

Because of this process, which, following current psychoanalytical thought, we can take as a decisive turning point in individual development – the 'striking caesura', as Freud (1926) defined it – of crucial significance for the future, a series of sudden and important changes become visibly apparent in the organism's physiological functioning and in the surrounding environment, but of which no trace is evident mentally. Among the externally visible ones are crying, taking nourishment, breathing, and excretion.

Internally, secretion, the circulatory system, and the digestive process are activated. Peripherally, boundaries which previously limited the body's activity are lost, air takes the place of amniotic fluid, and the environment presents itself as diversified, inconstant, unfamiliar, and undefined. As far as mental functioning at birth is concerned, all of this certainly cannot be appropriated mentally as rapidly as it occurs physically. Besides the fact that mental learning is preceded by physiological learning (which in the intra-uterine situation is much more advanced), we must take into account that the establishment of mental learning models parallel to those of physiological functioning requires the mediation of memory. Thanks to the consistency and protective structure of the intra-uterine environment, and the physical delimitation of the foetus's physiological functions there, the development of a functional continuum is greatly facilitated. Moreover, in this environment the newly aroused mental function is in no way subjected to pressures from the outside.

What I wish to make clear is that the sharp contrast between a greater capacity to function physiologically and a lesser possibility to function mentally, which becomes acutely evident at birth, simply corresponds to the state of the functional continuum before birth. At this point the mind has absolutely no power to influence, much less determine, physiological functioning (to which, on the contrary, it is completely subject). This situation, of no extraordinary consequence during intra-uterine life, suddenly becomes of the utmost importance, and induces us to reflect upon the role of mental functions in the general functional economy of the organism. In the meantime, we can assert that birth promotes a strong incrementation of the differentiation process for mental functioning, of necessity accompanied by intensified mental learning about physiological functioning. This means that although, with birth, important changes take place in mental functioning as well, the subjugation of mind to body which characterized the pre-natal state will continue until such a time as the child's new initiative can give visible results; that is, not before the end of the second month of post-natal life.

Experience has demonstrated that, in the study of the human mind, it is more difficult to individuate and scrutinize what is normal, and therefore less obvious, than to study the evidence of psychopathology and move from this towards the norm [see Chapter 1]. When I wrote these words, I was referring not only to psychopathological aspects of adult life from which elements of mental functioning normal for the early days of life can be drawn, but also to a very early psychophysical syndrome not well-known as such: infantile rumination or 'merecysm' (Gaddini and Gaddini 1959) which comes to the fore no earlier than the end of the second month of life, and which permits us to understand the silent, intense activity that the infantile mind normally carries out in the first eight weeks after birth.

The syndrome shows that by the beginning of the third month, mental learning about physiological functions has already reached the stage not only of being able actively and autonomously to reproduce in the organism the functional model of taking nourishment (the nutritional act), but also of being able to alter it in such a way (so-called 'rumination') as effectively to control a serious pathological response (repeated vomiting caused by sudden and premature weaning) which otherwise could cause death. Once we understand its origins, we can see that the merecysm syndrome, long considered constitutional, an expression of mental retardation, or even as a 'phylogenetic regression' (!) (Gaddini and Gaddini 1959) is correctly described by paediatricians as a pathological syndrome, even if primarily a defensive psychophysical one in the service of survival. Mental retardation is thus the effect, not the cause of rumination.

The study of merecysm as a defence confirms Greenacre's (1958b) observation that 'the development of defensive measures in the human organism seems to proceed ontogenetically from early direct or reflex physical reactions which operate against the environment, to the complex structure of psychophysical responses'. But the infantile psychophysical syndrome of merecysm allows us to make some further considerations on this subject.

Earlier I mentioned the necessity of reflecting on the role of mental functioning in the general functional economy of the organism. Even from the little I have said till now, I think one can recognize that after birth, the physiological functions, forced as they are to modify their former functional models and exposed to an environment which no longer acts as the stable and precise boundary of their operation, are extremely vulnerable. For the newborn, in fact, the post-natal environment should virtually be able to substitute for these confines. Nothing could be so 'conducive' (in Winnicott's sense, though the original concept is Greenacre's) as the intra-uterine situation, since, defining as it contains, it allows as a basic given a maximum possibility of functioning. This is the origin of the newborn's primary 'need' for a boundary environment, a definition of itself in which to function simply and spontaneously. The absence of this free and secure functionality is at the base of the newborn's other primary 'need', which Winnicott called 'holding' (1961). The incapacity to maintain a seated position and to hold one's head erect, in the first months of life, is a concrete (physiological) expression of this.

The infantile organism, in any case, has only its own physiological learning to count on, plus the newly established and developing mental capacity to learn about it. For the infantile mind, all that the organism comes into contact with, and this is usually by touch, represents not the environment but the boundary of himself. Primitive perception in its biological model is physically imitative, and consists in modifying the body according to the stimulus. Consequently, what is perceived is the modification of his own body, and this is also what is learned physiologically. The mental model of primitive perception parallel to this biological one ('imitate in order to perceive') is 'imitate in order to become' [see Chapter 1] and is used by the infantile organism to become what he lacks. By this I mean that for an extended period of time, until the child is able to distinguish an 'object', distinct and separate from himself, to entrust himself to the outside world, the infantile mind is alert to providing for the 'needs' of the organism (and by 'need' I mean, here, the mental experience of something which has been physically lost). The infantile merecyst 'imitates', in this primitive sense, the lost experience of being nourished, 'nourishing himself' in order to reproduce the physical experience of achieving fullness.

In this case the psychophysical syndrome 'focalizes' like a magnifying glass the corporeal experience that at some point came to an end, but which has been preserved in memory. The clinical, pathological situation derives from the necessity to reactivate this memory, not only in the mind, but also in bodily functions. One might advance the hypothesis that merecysm, the necessity to reactivate, by way of the mind, the memory of corporeal functioning arises as an emergency situation, after which the circuits of physiological memory, severely altered in their habitual functioning by the pernicious direct response of repeated vomiting, are no longer able to re-establish, biologically, normal corporeal functioning.

All of this might induce us to describe the process of mental learning about the physiological as the mental learning of a primary reality, which is one's own body with its functions and physiological behaviour. This kind of description seems inadvisable to me, as it can all too easily draw us into the error of thinking of the mind solely as subject and the body as object only. From an ontogenetic point of view, it would perhaps be more correct to say that the body and mind are the organism, whose physiological learning process, at a certain point, because of the differentiation of the mental function, becomes aware of itself and so is gradually able to organize into a mental 'self', and to create a mental image of the corporal self.

I have often referred to the role of principal importance played by the memory in this process. Perhaps this is an appropriate moment to consider that physiological learning, as such, cannot come into existence apart from a memory of bodily functioning, which however has no need to acquire a mental quality in order to be active on its own. This is to say that through the memory of physical functioning it is possible to organize models of bodily functions, as well as their evolutions, including other behavioural patterns, always remaining within the biological circuit. In its initial phase mental learning draws from this pre-existent and continuing physiological memory, but in its own way, according to the principle of functional differentiation, and therefore should be described in these terms.

At the same time as a given physiological function is learned by the mind, it acquires signficance in a mental sense as well. Its mental quality consists in thus having a sense that physiologically it does not have: one that, bearing no relation to the objective reality of this function, can only be magical in nature. At this phase of functional differentiation, the learning process cannot be lived in the mind except in magical terms. As a result, for the primitive mind, the particular physiological

126

process we described is not learned but is actually produced by itself. In merecysm, as we have seen, the primitive mental function is in effect able to reproduce bodily – but with mental characteristics – the mentally appropriated physiological function. Under normal circumstances there is no need to go so far. If the lack (or absence or loss) is not so great as to determine direct bodily responses, or in any case before this can occur, the mnemonic mental reactivation of a phenomenon is sufficient attestation to its 'reality'.

The mind's memory is not continuous and unceasing, as is the physiological memory, and as a rule has no need of the reflex biological circuits which put memory at the service of the body. Mental learning in this phase is characterized by 'focality'; limited, that is, to a particular biological function, sometimes even to a detail. What is learned, and therefore what remains in memory, is necessarily but a fragment with respect to the unceasing flow of corporeal functioning; a fragment which is also a synthesis complete within itself, and which has, in this way, acquired its own mental significance in addition to that of being a magical product of the mind. It is an experience of the self which becomes, in the mind, self-created.

This is more easily comprehensible if we take into account firstly that the mind's memory is focal because mental learning is primarily focal, and second that the rhythmic, repetitious character of physiological functioning in relation to the environment, and the learning thereof, make an essential contribution to this focality. The physiological memory continually registers these rhythmically repeated functions. Mental learning, however, has to do with specific characteristics of functioning, including its repetitive quality, without actually engaging in repetition itself. This is also true for the mental memory. Since the learned function becomes the mind's 'creation', each repetition augments and reinforces, in the mind, its own magical creative omnipotence. Because of this, the primitive mind is unable to distinguish the actual repetition of an experience from its mental reactivation by memory. To the primitive mind, reactivating an experience deposited in the memory signifies its actual 'recreation' by the mind's own magical omnipotence.

The focalized learning of each function in relationship to the environment becomes, in this way, the creation of an experience of the self. For this reason, whether real or reactivated in the memory, each repetition contributes to the self's creative process, which is of essential importance in this first post-natal phase of mental development. Winnicott (1951) was the first to delineate this self-creative process in the early stages of life, and to show the importance that this 'illusion' has in the primary mental formation of the self when the child, who is

127

not yet mentally an individual, depends totally and absolutely upon the nurturing environment. Winnicott (1965) also demonstrated how much the environment (that is, the mother), in caring for her child, participates in safeguarding and nourishing his 'illusion', and how very psychopathogenic the neglect of this basic task on the part of the environment can be for the infantile mind.

The first mental formation of the self, then, should be considered the basic structure of the mind's differentiated development. Its formative process is characterized by the aggregation of fragmentary sensorial (that is, tactile, olfactory, and other) experiences of the self's functioning in relation to the environment. At this stage perception follows the aforementioned model of primitive imitation ('imitate in order to become') which can be translated as the simple, direct inclusion of its relationship with the environment in the experience of the self. Being primarily focalized, these experiences are fragmentary. They are not random but refer to particular repetitive functions that have acquired a definitive mental significance. Their repetition, like their mnemonic reactivation, is experienced magically as the possibility to recreate, each time, the experience of self. Winnicott (1974) properly referred to this initial phase of the mind's development as that of 'non-integration'.

'Non-integration' should not be confused with 'disintegration', a regressive phenomenon which presupposes a formerly existing state of integration, which would have been a more advanced stage. The use of the term 'assimilation' seems more appropriate to me for this phase, in order to indicate a functional phenomenon in the relationship with the environment, which, contrary to that of integration, does not imply any recognition of objective reality. In this sense even the objective reality of one's own body and its functioning, as we have observed, is ignored at the outset. The primitive mind tends to make concretely its own (to 'assimilate' into the self) what otherwise would be recognizable objectively. This phenomenon, in turn, should not be confused with 'denial', a mental defence mechanism which, however precocious it might be (certainly more so than that of repression), implies an active defence against the previously achieved objective recognition of a particular reality, and as such against a more advanced stage of mental development than exists in the primitive mind.

These distinctions are of no less importance technically than clinically. In its progress 'toward the corporeal', psychoanalytical investigation was able to individuate disintegration and denial far earlier than it could recognize non-integration or extension-assimilation. Similarly, research on the origins of object relationship much preceded current knowledge of the more remote terrains of relationship with the environment as a function of the self, or of the mental formation of the

128

self. Time was needed to reach even the first formulations of the concept of self in terms of a structural theory of psychoanalysis (Hartmann 1950), and more time had to elapse between Jacobson's (1964) study in the same vein and our current knowledge of the self's formation in the immediately post-natal period, which we owe above all to Winnicott's research. Bion (1961) also made an original and unexpected contribution through the psychoanalytical study of groups.

I have attempted to demonstrate how the stage of non-integration is brought into being gradually from the moment of birth to the point where it can actually be considered a stage: that of the first functional organization of the mind. The organism's extreme vulnerability during this period of time, its total and absolute dependence upon the environment, and the overwhelming prevalence of corporeal functions within the organism, encounter a magical and omnipotent mental function that seems practically oblivious to the necessity of objectively recognizing reality (as the mind is as yet incapable of such a recognition) and by means of which the mind is understood to 'create' a basic mental organization, magically auto-sufficient and validated by the prevalence of bodily functioning.

Even though part of this body is, in reality, a part of the mother's body, for the mental function's rapport with the environment it forms part of the experience of self. In fact, from the moment that, during birth, the amniotic membrane's stable, constant limitation (as reinforced by the uterine wall) breaks down, what becomes constant is the lack of a stable and sure delimitation comparable to what has been lost. This 'being without' is one of the strongest stimulants to primitive mental functioning, which tends magically to re-build and then reactivate, repetitively, the experience of having a definite limit to the self. The tactile sensations that a baby has while being nourished at the breast (especially in the oral and perioral zones and in the hands, which are ready to grasp the breast and anything within reach of the palms, such as garments near the breast) become in this way some of the first fragmentary (focalized) experiences stored away by the primitive mind.

Much later, in the autonomous invention of a transitional object (from about the seventh to the twelfth month) the mind reactivates and actualizes these original experiences in which some specific tactile detail is focalized with extraordinary precision and great specificity. Thus it has been possible to demonstrate that, when the transitional object is made of cloth, the choice of fabric corresponds so precisely to tactile sensations experienced by the infant at the breast or during early care that one can firmly establish whether the child was born in a cold season (when the garments associated with early care were of linen, silk, nylon, and so on) (R. Gaddini 1974). It is noteworthy that the

129

moment in which the infantile mind 'invents' a transitional object is the same one in which it is faced with the first serious, definitive loss after birth, that of physical contact with the maternal body as part of and frontier-line of the self. The similarities to birth as the physiological detachment from the maternal body are obvious. In any case it is extremely significant that at this point of mental development, the transitional object – new and transitory border and part of the self – is not a part of his own or his mother's body, indistinguishable from his own, but an inanimate object whose tactile properties re-evoke the first experience of having boundaries after the loss of the pre-natal boundaries.

The stage of non-integration has its beginnings in the first tactile experiences; it organizes itself little by little in the manner observed here, and tends progressively towards a degree of organization which is sufficient to allow the mental self, at a certain point, the experience of definitive detachment from the maternal body environment. Some degree of remittance of the role of corporeal functioning is implicit if the mental function is to be allowed objectively to recognize its body for the first time. This step, in a process which in mental terms closely repeats that of birth, is perhaps the most arduous and fatal in the entire process of differentiation of the individual mind. The first objective recognition of one's own separateness, in fact, upsets the magical, omnipotent, and primitive system of functioning, and produces its successive downfall. So detachment is equivalent to the permanent loss of the omnipotent self, and to admit one's effective separateness is equivalent to recognizing the extreme fragility and vulnerability of a self which appears mutilated in comparison to the magical self. As Bion has said, it is the 'catastrophe' (1961).

I will not, on this occasion, enter into the various qualities of all that can arise (in terms of psychopathology) during successive mental developments, according to just how this point has been reached. I think it more pertinent to the mind–body question not to lose track of what is verifiably psychopathological in this first period of development, which cannot but be expressed through the body. It has been quite some time since psychoanalysis established that for at least the first year of life (and perhaps it would be better to say the first eighteen months) mental disturbance is translated into bodily schemes or images which are really psychophysical; but it has not yet given sufficient attention, in my opinion, to the fact that there are so-called psychosomatic illnesses in this period which are, one might say, scheduled or dated. This means that they never intervene before a certain length of time has transpired after birth. I believe it is preferable to keep the term 'psychophysical syndrome' for this sort of 'illness'. Earlier, I paused to examine the syndrome of merecysm, pointing out, among other things, the fact that it never takes place before the age of eight weeks. To my knowledge, there is no psychophysical syndrome that occurs earlier than this. Even if it cannot be considered common (since it has to do with a whole series of particular events, among which is the imposition of detachment too suddenly and too early with respect to the mind's level of differentiation), this syndrome indicates that the principal suffering in this period is connected to the premature interruption of the experience of feeding.

I should add that any experience which is too precocious with regard to the natural course of the maturational process is potentially traumatic. I think we can also say that, in general, psychophysical syndromes of the first eighteen months (and perhaps even afterwards, until further development is under way), refer to a mental pathology having to do with detachment and separation. In consequence, these are made manifest in certain precise moments of primary development in which that problem presses urgently to the fore, and they express – in a sort of concrete language, pre-verbal and pre-symbolic (namely, by means of an altered bodily function) – a defensive mental content, specific to the moment of mental development in which the problem emerges.

One syndrome which is not manifested before the sixth month of life (and, exceptionally, a bit earlier) is atopical dermatitis. At this time – (when, if the relationship with the environment is sufficient, from the seventh month onward one can achieve the invention of a transitional object) – it is possible that even while detachment and separation are in progress one can express the difficulty or impossibility of proceeding further along the line of development, in somatically pathological terms. If this happens, in the following months there will be no trace of a transitional object, and the manifest pathology will have to do with the skin. Taking into account my earlier observations regarding the importance of the first tactile experiences at birth and their mental reactivation during the invention of the transitional object, one can understand how the transitional object becomes an evolutionary mental elaboration of the definitive loss of physical contact, while the appearance of dermatitis demonstrates that the confines of one's own skin (that of the separated self) are unable to hold and protect what it contains (as a matter of fact, the physical care required for dermatitis assures continuous contact) (R. Gaddini 1978).

In one of her last analytical sessions, a patient who a couple of years earlier in the course of treatment (at the age of *c.* 37 years) had experienced total relief from the dermatitis which had covered her neck, trunk, and upper limbs uninterruptedly from the time she was 6 months of age (and for which she had been hospitalized during the most severe episodes of eruption), brought forth two memories which had surfaced in her mind for the first time at termination. One memory concerned a sensation which before analysis had been accompanied by a feeling of great terror: it was the physical sensation that she could suddenly, actually, go to pieces. The other memory had to do with a 'strange' dream she had had at 18 years of age, at the time of her mother's death, and which had deeply affected the patient.

> *In the dream, she was a planet in dark, limitless space. At a certain distance, she saw another planet which was retreating rapidly. She followed it with her eyes, terrified by the knowledge that, when it had disappeared, she would shatter into smithereens and be scattered through space.*

The dream showed that mother's death had reactivated, in the patient's mind, the way in which she had lived the first detachment from her mother at the time of the onset of dermatitis. Her remembered feeling of 'going to pieces' went back to the then pathological relationship with her mother, and revealed that, until analysis, the patient had never been able to admit that she might overcome the risk of that detachment. Her ever-present dermatitis, always in need of care, gave concrete testimony to this. The patient's ability to share, at the end of analysis, the two memories which had always been omitted, showed that there was no longer any reason to harbour those fears. The former reserve, bound by omission, could now be broken. Now her skin would 'hold', and detachment from the analyst could be accomplished without danger.

The important psychophysical syndrome successive to atopical dermatitis would manifest itself no earlier than the end of the first year (more often in the first months of the second year), and would be that of bronchial asthma. The space available to me here does not permit me to explore this syndrome in depth, but merely to indicate it as one of the 'scheduled' syndromes and to note the fundamental diversity of its clinical formation, to which, I believe, two new aspects of detachment and separation make significant contributions: the initial phases of learning to walk, which contribute above all to the newly pressing emergence of the problem of detachment, and the simultaneous primary mastering of language, which contributes directly to the defensive organization of this psychophysical syndrome. Suffice it to say of this last that the functional link of speaking and breathing is, in my opinion, used by the infantile mind to reactivate – but usually in an altered way (in the body's concrete language) – one of the first functional links of which the mind has experience, which is that of suckling and swallowing at the breast while continuing to breathe. A bit later, in fact, but within that same second year of life, where the asthmatic syndrome has not taken hold, the syndrome of stuttering can occur.

In the serious stuttering condition of a 28-year-old patient for whom the concomitant exercise of the functions of speaking and breathing was extremely distressful, the complication of a significant tic (that of sucking his own tongue) thus continually recalled the original difficulty of breathing while suckling, through the impairment of simultaneous breathing and speaking. This patient, devoid of any sexual experience, was a foot and shoe fetishist who, before going to sleep in the evening, was in the habit of savouring the odour of his own feet.

The infantile syndrome of stuttering can, as is well known, spontaneously disappear at a certain point, never to reappear, meaning that the maturational problem which it expressed has in some way been mastered by the mind. In other cases the syndrome can continue uninterruptedly throughout life. But it can also happen that, having disappeared spontaneously after its first insurgence, it reappears in the fifth year of life or soon after. If this occurs, it usually stays for good. In the case of the above-mentioned patient, this is what transpired.

Finally, a disturbance in the other component of detachment and separation's urgent task at the beginning of the second year of life, starting to walk, can itself find concrete expression in a more or less prolonged delay in initiating de-ambulation. The child's first steps, besides confirming detachment and separation in a concrete way, constitute the autonomous self's first confrontation with unlimited external space. In a case of serious agoraphobia, I was able to establish that its successive organization was rooted in the infantile mental pathology relative to this first encounter with external space.

What I would especially like to emphasize here, however, is that at the beginning of the second year of life, breathing, speaking, and walking abide in a complex and reciprocal mental interrelationship which expresses its pathological aspects in apparently different psychophysical syndromes, whose significance harkens back to the reactivation of more primitive experiences: breathing while suckling at the breast, primary detachment and consequent separation, and the encounter with 'limitless' external space.

A striking example of how breathing, speaking, and walking can be exchanged for one another, confirming in this way their reciprocity and mental 'sense', became apparent to me through a case in supervision. At the start of analysis, the patient stuttered badly. Within a brief period of time, he entered a psychotic delusional delirium during which the symptom of stuttering disappeared. When, some months later, he emerged from the delirium (as treatment progressed), the

133

stuttering did not reappear, but the patient entered a state of deep self-loss anxiety which soon limited his ability to move. In his own words: 'A terrifying situation . . . I'm afraid. I feel phobic about walking. This must be what has become of the symptom of stuttering.' The patient went so far as to discontinue his analytical sessions temporarily because of his absolute incapacity to walk (move autonomously through space). Besides this physical limitation, self-loss anxiety was expressed in a concrete way by a feeling of 'coming forth from the eyes, really coming out of my eyes, seeing my body outside myself', or 'I feel bodiless'.

Maternal psychopathology is the prevailing factor in these infantile psychophysical syndromes, but within the maternal aetiology there are naturally situations on which objective factors exert a determining influence, such as a maternal illness which forces separation from, or worse, the permanent loss of, the mother. Another apparently objective situation not infrequently observed is the initiation of a new pregnancy while the child is in his first year of life, still less propitious if within the first six or seven months. The most auspicious situation, naturally, is that in which the mother, having brought the crucial experience of her detachment to its evolution and elaboration at the proper time, may allow the child to detach himself in turn and to proceed along the path of his autonomous development with her alongside. The invention of a transitional object and/or the intervention of transitional phenomena can be considered as steps of progress along this path, but not as a guarantee that those steps which should follow will necessarily do so.

It would be interesting to know the relationship of different infantile psychophysical syndromes within the same individual. I recall one patient who had been asthmatic since his second year of life, and for this reason was kept constantly at home and almost always in bed by his mother, until the age of 5, when his brother was born. This patient had also been affected, for as long as he could remember, by spastic colitis and atopical dermatitis.

What we consider to be the very first expressions of psychopathology come to the fore with the problem of detachment, of which they signal the principal stages. Detachment requires the infantile mind to pass from one functional stage to another, specifically from non-integration to effective autonomy. This repeats in a magnified way the passage from foetal functioning to post-natal functioning. In physiological terms, it is unthinkable that a newborn child could return to functioning as a foetus, but psychoanalytical literature provides no dearth of reported dreams from which we can divine that the theme of returning to the womb is part and parcel of the primitive mentality. It

134

is of particular importance to note that the inevitable experience of the 'catastrophe' can induce the autonomous self, in its fragile, impoverished state, to restore and strengthen the magical functions of assimilation and extension which characterize non-integration, and that these mechanisms, at that point no longer merely existing but actively organized as a defence, can spread to the relationship with the entire external world, remaining permanently as a basic function of the individual throughout adult life.

It is not my intention to refer, in this way, to a fact well-known to all psychoanalysts, that each organized stage of mental development, even if overcome by successive stages of development, never ceases to function in part (within average limits which can be considered to be the norm) but to the fact, replete with consequence, that an entire stage of mental functioning, the first stage in post-natal development, instead of becoming extinct, is restored and actively promoted as a defence, with the self's prime, categorical intention thus to ensure its own survival in the face of threatened annihilation. It is important to note that, when it succeeds, this is the first mental defence that is not expressed through the body. In a magical, omnipotent way, it functions in spite of the whole development of object relationship.

As a matter of fact, this organization can maintain its basic mode of functioning, even when all in the surrounding environment has changed from what was the original infantile situation. Above all, it retains the specific characteristics of its notion of space: a space occupied by fragmentary experiences of the self in relationship to the environment, where each part can seem the whole and the whole a part, where the self is fused with the environment and the environment is a facet of the self. Functioning as assimilation-extension continually pushes (objectively speaking) the limits of self beyond the self, which means that the limits of space are continually changing, undefined, lacking a definite form. The objective need of the other – whoever this might be – in this way remains constant and inalienable as the original need; but since the other is of value only as the functional limit of self and never as an objectively recognized 'other than the self', not even the need is ever recognized as such (in analysis this can be extremely frustrating for the analyst).

In this formless space, all is of the moment and everything is perpetual. Any change in functioning is unthinkable. And since this defensive organization has been placed in the service of survival by the self, it functions above all for the purpose of blocking recognition that detachment has occurred and that the separated self is inconsistent with it. (In this way, change, even in adult life, can continue to signify

135

possible catastrophe.) As a result the integrational processes are impeded and a sense of the dimension of time remains absent.

Primitive imitation is the psychic mechanism which originally forms the basis of assimilation-extension. This mechanism allows one to 'be' what otherwise should be recognized as 'other than the self' (as object) and therefore is destined for a particular kind of development and refinement when it clashes with the reality demands imposed by growth. As a matter of fact, without the identification process, which in itself requires recognition of an object separate from the self, imitation comes to replace the object. In intellectual development, imitation favours rapid learning 'by contact', the sort of learning which just as rapidly is lost, or which otherwise accumulates like fat for the obese, unintegrable. Sometimes these people are aware that they 'seem to be' what in reality they cannot be. They claim to feel as if they are always 'acting' and do not know 'who they are'. In truth, their continual need of the presence of the other in order to have a sense of themselves forces them to exist in terms of the other's form and space, so losing any real sense of self. Before substituting for identification, however, imitation takes the place of introjection, another mechanism which begins to function only when an object can be recognized as external and separated from the self. In analysis we need to keep in mind that the organization of non-integration as a defence cannot make way for the ability to introject, and so to internalize in a structuring way.

Clinical manifestations of this basic disturbance, which can be found in adolescents as well as in adults, are either of a prevalently psycho-physical or of a primarily mental order. In the first group, such manifestations can range from compulsive eating, which obeys the impulse to reproduce continually and concretely, the experience of feeding as a safeguard against the ever-impending catastrophe of detachment, to the alternation of eating and regurgitation, sustained by the fear that alimentation can be transformed into the dreaded 'incorporation'; or further, to mental anorexia, where eating becomes *ipso facto* incorporation and therefore always and in any case the forerunner of a new experience of the catastrophe. As we are able to observe, for the concrete (pre-symbolic) language of the body, incor-poration takes the place of the mental function of introjection.

I have previously [Chapter 1] indicated the fundamental importance of the mind's double use of oral functioning: a sensorial use, for such needs of the self as are connected mostly with sensory aspects of the mental experience of feeding, and which in truth are as yet little known to psychoanalysts (it is this magical, omnipotent use I have been speaking of till now; that is to say until we reached the experience of imposed detachment from the breast); and an object-dependent use, well-known to all since Freud outlined oral organization and after successive research illuminated the dynamics of the oral aspect of rapport with the object. Ignorance of this dual use of orality, corresponding to two distinct levels of functioning, leads to an error which is common even today: the interpretation of psychophysical syndromes of a sensorial nature in terms of object relationship, psychophysical syndromes like the ones just described which can influence bodyweight in sometimes dramatic ways, from irreversible obesity to emaciation, and which constitute extreme defences against the recognition of an object and the outside world (in defence of a detached self judged incapable of survival).

Decidedly more insidious and more difficult to recognize in analysis is an incapacity to introject unsignalled by accompanying somatic manifestations of a pathological nature. What is so insidious about this defence is that the transference is deep and silent, causing no apparent conflict of any kind. The analyst is placed in the role of the nourishing breast (not an object!) at the limit and border of the non–integrated self; that is, in the service of the massive, magical, and omnipotent defence mechanism organized by the self to ensure its perpetual survival. In place of the unachievable introjection, an intense imitative activity is developed which sustains the activity of assimilation-extension and transforms the analytic setting into a functional area for the self's magical omnipotence.

These silent operations are translated into manifestations which can mislead the analyst, involving him in quite pleasing and gratifying ways with the nourishing role which has been assigned to him, ways that can range anywhere from rapid imitative learning and the assumption, on the part of the analysand, of diverse aspects of the analyst's manner and behaviour (his way of expressing himself, speech inflections, at times even his way of dressing and other unthinkable details) to sometimes surprising intellectual development (but split, and so unrelated to the structuring and integrative processes). The seductive compliance of this kind of patient has a force comparable only to the seductive qualities of small children. What must not escape us is that these 'imitation introjections' raise a tremendous barrier to effective internalization within the analytical process.

A more advanced defence along the lines of acting-in, usually a very serious one, is the erotic transference. I mention it here only to emphasize its quality of closely imitating a real objectual rapport. It consists in actively producing conscious erotic fantasies regarding the analyst, as distinct, in fantasy, from himself, and 'verified' by physical sensations through which the sensorial experience of assimilation becomes sensual (erotic), and, for consciousness, sexual. Particularly striking in the erotic transference is the quality of active initiative present in fantasies of rapport and behaviour towards the analyst, a kind of activity which does not correspond to anything in real life, and which in fact is based on magic and omnipotence.

Better to comprehend this sort of 'activity', we should consider how it relates to anxiety. The most adequate term for the form of anxiety which follows the fearful experience of the catastrophe is, I believe, 'self-loss anxiety'. This arises when the self has separated, not before, and is consequent, not concomitant, to the 'catastrophic' experience. In this sense it is perhaps the most primitive weapon of defence, originally meant to prevent a repetition of the terrifying event; but the accompanying degree of anguish is such as to promote the organization of more efficient defence mechanisms whose chief purpose is to reduce and ward off self-loss anxiety, and which in any case are in constant reference to it. The more threatening and dramatic the experience of detachment has been, the more serious and difficult to contain mentally is the anxiety over possible loss of the self. Organizing a stable psycho-physical defence can be the only way of reducing the intensity of mental suffering. This is what we observed in the case of the patient with atopical dermatitis, but self-loss anxiety had continued to dominate the patient's mental functioning.

In the light of these observations, we can say that the psychophysical syndrome is closer to self-loss anxiety and in certain cases to the recognition of an object, than is non-integration when organized as a mental defence. The latter, in fact, leaves no room at all for recognition of an object, and as for self-loss anxiety, under this regime it can become so drastically reduced as to defy detection. In the long run, however, the mental cost of such instant efficiency is very high. Between these two basic aspects of psychopathology, non-integration's magical and omnipotent defence will reveal itself the more vulnerable for mental stability in the encounters with reality which growth imposes. Apropos of this we must keep in mind that this magical omnipotence is no longer the spontaneous function proper to the phase of non-integration, but active reproduction of that functional model for present-day defensive needs. What I mean is that the 'activity' of such an organization is under the vanguard of omnipotent and magical defence, and serves this end exclusively.

One reason for the greater vulnerability of this 'activity' in the defence lies in the fact that, while acting in the hope of avoiding every experience of self-loss anxiety, one is all the more apt to encounter directly the experience of detachment. Just when the defence is at its most 'successful', it is involved in the 'active' production of the specific

138

situation it was created to avoid (namely, confrontation with detachment). In this way, objective reality is turned upside-down. Instead of submitting to detachment, the mind thus becomes its omnipotent craftsman. It is an operation which magically empties detachment of its 'catastrophic' content in order to dominate it mentally. An example of this, one of which every analyst will have some experience, is that of the patient who somehow manages to miss the session which immediately precedes or follows a holiday break (and sometimes the simple, recurring weekend). Here we can see that acting out is a functional model which goes back to that of activity as a defence against objective recognition.

This example refers to a mere detail, but even a detail can give some idea of how alien defensively motivated activity is to any objective recognition whatsoever (a recognition which would put one in contact with detachment in a direct and concrete way, without the preliminary alarm, painful but useful, of self-loss anxiety), and, for this reason, how very pernicious it is. In fact, its working is so immediate and automatic, and so totally prescinds reality, that it can be fatal to the entire organism. If reality were to force habitual defensive activity to become insufficient – and so impotent for defence – by virtue of reality situations triggered by detachment, loss, or change; and the self were in this way to find itself directly exposed to what mentally (if unaided by objectivity) seems the definitive catastrophe, the real risk would become an extremely serious one. In fact, at that point, the functional model of defence activity could reach its paradoxical extreme, producing the catastrophe in a peremptory and omnipotent way (suicide, in reality terms) while magically intending to survive (that is, to avoid succumbing). The acute onset of psychosis can be in obedience to the same model.

I said earlier that, generally speaking, self-loss anxiety is useful. Now I would like to emphasize that it should be considered a normal phenomenon which intervenes at a certain point in development (as soon as a separated self exists) and which is accompanied, on the one hand, by an initial objective recognition of the self as within its own limits, defining internal space as separate from the external one, and on the other hand by the sense that this delimitation is the result of the mutilating loss caused by the catastrophe. The loss is that of the magical, omnipotent self and is often represented as the 'voiding' of the self, as in the above-described psychotic patient's feeling of 'coming forth from his eyes' or of being 'bodiless'. Another patient represented herself in a dream, with intense anguish, as emerging from the bath-tub (the maternal container or vessel caved in and flattened out).

Self-loss anxiety is connected with survival, a need which appears for the first time at separation. Anxiety, then, allows the first glimmer of recognition for a self which has survived the catastrophe, but which is emptied of its omnipotence, and is thus needy, defenceless, and exposed, with its very survival at risk. Most importantly, anxiety exists in ratio to the relative fragility and inconsistency of the self's newly acquired sense of boundaries and to the fear of being unable to hold together its remaining fragments and to prevent their dispersal in limitless external space.

There remains one more significant factor regarding self-loss anxiety to which we should give our attention: the fact that, with its insurgence, the mental processes are introduced to the dimension of time. Apart from the fact that, for the first time since birth, one can begin to consider an individual in mind as well as in body, something fundamentally different now intervenes in memory's functioning. As distinct, that is, from the mind's use of memory in the phase of non-integration, self-loss anxiety continually augments the memory of the catastrophe as a past event which must remain in the past, a 'before' which must never become 'now', but which rather must institute a 'past'. What I mean is that for the first time the memory becomes 'temporalized'. However, if detachment has been traumatic, this tem-poralizing function of self-loss anxiety may not take effect. In this case the memory maintains its actualizing activity, so that it always seems the catastrophic experience may happen 'now'. The pathological result is the continual expectation of the catastrophe. This, in my opinion, explains Winnicott's conclusion that 'there are moments when a patient needs to be told that the breakdown, the fear of which is destroying his life, has already occurred' (1974).

Whereas self-loss anxiety is at a bearable level and does not give way to pathological forms of defence, it represents a potent stimulus for the formulation of those positive defences which promote the self's organ-ization within its own borders. An essential task, to this end, will be a gradual coming to know one's body in objective terms. This gradual 'discovery' and recognition of one's own body is expressed in the graphic images which the child, step by step, renders himself capable of creating. Beyond the scribbling stage, the first image that the child spontaneously makes and draws is a roundish one, which I consider to be the first representation of the separated mental self (a space circum-scribed by a limit which separates it from external space). One cannot help but notice how altogether similar this form is to the one described above apropos of foetal functioning. The fundamental difference is that, while then the borderline united the child to the maternal body rather than separating it, now the frontier separates the individual from an external space in which the mother has an appropriate place.

As is well known, within that roundish image the child will eventually draw first the mouth and then the eyes. Usually he proceeds to indicate the limbs with essential lines sprouting directly from the head. Little by little, the rest will be indicated and perfected. What I mean to make clear is that the learning process is no longer focalized but is an objective recognition. At the outset I suggested that 'the mind's development is a gradual process going from body to mind, a sort of emersion from the body which coincides with the gradual mental acquisition of the bodily self'. Now we can add that this gradual mental acquisition of the body would not be possible, were it not preceded by the elaborate and strenuous process of emergence from a non-objective body, which is the functional unit of the child with his mother.

9

Early defensive fantasies and the psychoanalytical process

This paper was given to the 4th Conference of the European Federation of Psychoanalysis in Rome, March 1981. It was published in the *Rivista di Psicoanalisi*, 28 January 1981, under the title of 'Fantasie difensive precoci e processo psicoanalitico', and in the *International Journal of Psycho-Analysis* (1982) 63: 379–86.

Fantasy in its origin seems to be associated with an image, and above all with a visual image, and many fantasies can be found in dreams. Freud (1923) realized that visual thought precedes verbal thought in mental development, and the former is closer to 'things'. It seems to me that still nearer to 'things' we can find primitive mental experiences of the body which are made up of particular sensations connected to a specific function (originally that of feeding). Where necessary, these experiences are physically expressed, actively and specifically promoting that particular function which produced those sensations which the mind has already experienced. Since this necessity is generally linked to environmental failures, psychophysical response seems to imply a protective defence which aims to protect and preserve survival. Generally, enacting a particular bodily function also modifies it, according to the mental significance of the need. This closed circuit of body–mind–body most probably precedes the emergence of fantasy associated with the image. Thus, while the fact of an image being present was a guarantee of the reality of what was presented (Freud 1925), this guarantee seems itself to be furnished in the mind by the concreteness of the body. It seems to me certain that fantasy expressed through an image represents a more advanced stage than fantasy expressed by means of the body. I believe that when, at a certain stage, the presentation of an image interrupts the body–mind circuit, there is an essential change. In the first place, the image is much more economical for the mind than the enactment of a particular function of the body. In the second place, the image remains in the mind, where it can encounter dynamic vicissitudes of every kind, independently of bodily functioning, while that which is expressed through the body seems to remain enclosed within the body–mind–body circuit, and to be excluded from further mental work. Visual fantasy is capable of developing its organization, as can be seen in dreams. During analytical treatment one can assist in a gradual structuring of fantasies and dreams. By contrast, visual thought may regress due to serious psychopathology. At its earliest levels of organization, visual fantasy is obviously much nearer to 'things' than at more advanced levels.

When we deal with these earliest levels, we may mistake for image what is really enclosed within the mind–body circuit. For instance, it seems to me that we cannot be absolutely sure that what we have always described as 'hallucinatory image' is really that. It is clearly a very precocious fantasy, and therefore very near to 'things'. Moreover, we assume a fantasy exists from certain observable physical behaviour, which is enacted by the primitive mind as a defence against unfulfilled desires. These are exactly the characteristics of the body–mind–body circuit. It is possible instead that later on, when a child no longer needs to resort to the immediate psychophysical response of sucking and is capable, within certain limits, of delaying gratification, there is an effective hallucinatory image which comforts him during the delay. What, however, I want to emphasize is that the development of fantasy seems to begin with fantasies expressed by means of bodily functioning, what I would call 'fantasies in the body'.

Fantasies which intervene after these ones seem to be the earliest mental representations of the body self, and therefore they should be described separately as 'fantasies *on* the body'. Further on I will give some instances of them. As we will see, they are already linked to an elementary image of the body – usually a roundish shape – and precede the formation process of the sense of identity (Greenacre 1958a), and of what is known as the body image.

The occurrence of the 'fantasies in the body' accounts for the fact that mental pathology ordinarily becomes apparent in psychophysical syndromes (a term introduced by Greenacre 1958a); namely, within the body–mind–body circuit. What appears to be somatic pathology is a defensive fantasy represented in specific bodily functioning, with a corresponding change of functioning in accordance with its psychic significance. It is interesting to note, in this connection, that some psychophysical syndromes of early infancy intervene only at a certain period of time after birth. I am alluding here to those syndromes that I described in the course of the discussion of the body–mind question [Chapter 8].

I should stress here that in the first mental experiences of the body what matters seems to be not the organs themselves but the mental sense of their functioning. Further, we must take into consideration that psychophysical syndromes during the first eighteen months generally relate to a pathology of detachment and separateness. Consequently they manifest themselves at particular moments of early development, and express themselves in the altered bodily functioning in a mentally defensive content, which occurs at a specific time in development when this pressing problem emerges. In the work quoted above I have tried to describe the origin of the constituent elements of these precocious fantasies as they may be found in the analytic treatment of adult patients. In the present paper I have chosen, rather, to consider the way in which these fantasies operate in the psychoanalytic process, and the technical and theoretical problems which may arise.

A primitive fantasy expressed in the body can hardly be further elaborated in the course of development. The fantasy appears as if it were split. In reality it is the result of a gap in the process of integration, not of a splitting mechanism. In the psychoanalytic process, this difference may reveal itself as basic. From a maturational point of view, as Winnicott (1974) has indicated, the difference is between non-integration and disintegration. The latter presupposes the existence of a certain degree of integration, and is therefore a phenomenon which has regressed from a more advanced state. In infancy, the production of the somatic symptom comes from quite the opposite direction from the process of integration (R. Gaddini 1974).

In other words, the psychophysical syndrome is typically fragmentary and representative of a mental functioning which precedes the integrative process. At this level, splitting makes no sense. The defence, in this case, consists of opposing the integrative processes *in statu nascendi*, which takes place through the reactivation of the fragmentary functioning, which was lost through the integration. In the psychoanalytic process, we should therefore expect the following: (a) that the effects of one defence would be different from the other; and (b) that the reconstruction of the integration which was broken and damaged by the split – that is, the re-integration of the split parts – would be a process different from that occurring for the first time, from a non-integrated functioning to integration which would involve the integration of parts which were never previously integrated. Nevertheless, we may easily make the mistake of assuming something to be the result of splitting, even though it could not be because it had never been integrated.

In my view the role of anxiety may be of some help in distinguishing betwen the two conditions. Fundamentally, I am inclined to believe that the more unbearable the recognition of one's own separateness, the more overwhelming the integrative processes are. When separation has been traumatic and separateness, therefore, unbearable, the integrative processes greatly increase the anxiety of self-loss. On the other hand, when the quality of the separation has not been traumatic, and the separateness has been bearable, the integrative processes may take place more naturally and self-anxiety may undergo a progressive and definite reduction [see Chapter 8].

The role of splitting belongs particularly to the first type of case where the integrative processes promote unbearable anxiety of self-loss and the attempt is made to reduce such anxiety by means of disintegration, that is, through re-establishing the lost fragmentary functioning. This is the reason why, in the analytic process, the re-integration of that which is split provokes anxiety, the same anxiety which originally produced the split, and now makes re-integration difficult. In order to allow re-integration to take place, the analytical restoration of the infantile organization of the self has to reach the point of bringing the self to face this anxiety, which was originally unbearable. However, what really matters is that the damage produced to integrative processes by the split increases, instead of reducing, the pathological precariousness of separateness and, consequently, helps maintain the severity of the self-loss anxiety.

Perhaps non-integration (Winnicott 1974) can be defined as the first functional organization of the self, a fragmentary one, with which the infantile self finds itself at the moment of separation. The serious result of this unavoidable experience is that the separated self loses the protected situation of being held and must consequently maintain its own cohesion by itself in an external space which at first seems empty and limitless, and which will soon become monstrous and threatening. Patients often experience the anxiety of the loss of self in the form of a fear of physically going to pieces and getting lost in space. Fragments of the non-integrated self are related, most probably, to the experiences of bodily functioning by the primitive mind. Such experiences are necessarily fragmentary and selective, inasmuch as they refer to specific functions and to certain sensations; however, as I have said, the selection is based on the significance which subsequently established functions acquire in the mind. The body–mind–body circuit characterizes this primitive organization.

Integrative processes, the natural evolution of non-integration, established themselves in this fragmentary organization from separation onwards, but their initial development is made more or less difficult by

145

the way in which separation has been experienced, and by the consequent seriousness of the anxiety of loss of the self. In the pathology of separation this anxiety may reach unbearable limits, and integrative processes may then become threatening forerunners of a new and conclusive catastrophe. After a pathological separation, any thrust towards a change is experienced as a threat to survival. Due to the lack of other means of defence, the psychophysical syndrome is the only self-protective device which the fragmentary self is capable of producing.

This defence is elementary (although elementary does not mean simple) and it shows in a physical manifestation – in a specific pathological bodily functioning – a specific psychic disturbance, accompanied by pain. Since the cause of both the disturbance and the pain is in the environment, one might think that an appropriate intervention which modifies the environment should make the psychophysical syndrome disappear. In fact, this can occur when the cause can be understood and an adequate intervention takes place. For instance, it has been demonstrated that if a ruminating baby is given into the exclusive care of a nurse who is capable of looking after him as the mother would have done if she had been able to, rumination may rapidly disappear (Gaddini and Gaddini 1959). Analogously – except where the syndrome does produce irreversible functional alterations in the body – one can see that a psychophysical syndrome aroused in early infancy, which lasts for the rest of the person's life, can sometimes disappear during analysis, not so much because of our interpretations, but because the analytical process was able to re-establish a mother–infant situation which allowed certain natural processes and experiences to take place for the first time. The impression that one has is that the psychophysical syndrome disappears simply because it is no longer necessary. One could say not only that its disappearance is not accompanied by anxiety of loss of the self but that it is actually a product of the reduction of such anxiety.

Unlike what occurs in the case of splitting, where reinstating integration requires a re-experiencing of that painful anxiety of self-loss which at the time had made the split necessary, in the case of the psychophysical syndrome the therapeutic process seems to proceed in the direction of a favourable start and development of the integration processes up to the point where the self is able to emerge from the dead-end of non-integration. Usually it is a long process, in which obstacles are encountered which seem, and sometimes are, insurmountable. The dead-end consists of the fact that the pathological anxiety of self-loss is constantly fed from two opposite directions. On the one hand it is fed by the precariousness of the non-integration state itself (the terrifying fantasy of going to pieces and being annihilated in space). In infancy, in conditions which are not pathological, anxiety most probably contributes to the beginning of the integration processes, and these contribute to its progressive reduction. On the other hand, the pathological anxiety of the loss of the self is also fed by the tendency towards integration, which implies the fearful recognition of a permanent separation. Integration, in pathological conditions, thus appears as a fatal step beyond return, which is the move from survival, however precarious, to final catastrophe.

It may be useful therefore to distinguish these two contrasting and coexistent aspects of pathological anxiety of loss of the self; namely, anxiety of non-integration and anxiety of integration. Obviously, it is the latter which represents the true pathological aspect; it is stronger than anxiety of non-integration, it prevents the natural developmental process and contributes in an essential way to maintaining the non-integrative state as an extreme defence.

What follows concerns a female patient who is 43 years old, and married without children. Analysis had been going on for about two years when the patient decided to leave for London for ten days, as a reaction to the separation caused by the Christmas holidays. I shall report some of the things that she said during the first session after her return.

Now I'm okay, but when I was in London I didn't feel very well, and if I could have, I would have returned on foot instead of waiting those ten days. I was surrounded by very affectionate people, but I had to pretend that I was all right. I even had to take a tranquillizer three times a day. I only went out twice, once to buy my return ticket. What I felt was my usual sensation of being broken up, of not being unified, not having a centre, going to pieces, and so therefore I couldn't go anywhere, and was not able to reciprocate affection, so I wasn't interested in anything at all. Now, since arriving at your house I have felt as if I were a whole again. There, I was constantly afraid of not returning, and therefore I couldn't even think about the time or about the days which separated me from my return. I had the strongest fears which I wasn't able to control. I was afraid of a strike, a war . . . I often felt as though I were outside the situation, outside myself. . . . A horrible thought occurred to me, I thought that in order to die one must first reunify oneself. If I thought about killing myself, that would mean that I had been able to gather myself together. You certainly can't die disintegrated, can you? You must be a unity to die. [She cries.] But why did you let me leave like that? Without skin? I was also a bit upset with you. In England, at the worst moment, I thought about painting, in order to feel better, and

147

in fact I succeeded in painting three little pictures; and when I looked at them I felt a lot better. It was as if I could see myself, as if I could see that I existed. I recognized myself more than if I was looking at myself in the mirror.

As can be appreciated, in the suffering of non-integration there is no place for conflict. The reason for this is that, for the fragmentary self, no object can exist as an object. It cannot give way to wishes and drives but instead it must only obey necessity and need. The object becomes the limit and definition of the fragmentary self, the skin which confines, defines, and shapes it. This is the essential importance of contact. The roots of this importance are remote, and go back to pre-natal life, when the foetus was surrounded by a precise and stable boundary, the amniotic sac, which is fortified by the womb. That protective boundary allowed the foetal organism to develop and function freely. The loss of this boundary at birth presumably contributes to the primary need of physical contact that the neonate shows, and to the storing of tactile sensations in the primitive mind.

This is certainly one of the most precocious among the mental experiences of bodily functioning. Tactile sensations create the sense of the limit of the self, and therefore contribute in an essential manner to the formation of the sense of self. But unlike the continuous and constant boundary of pre-natal life, the post-natal environment is discontinuous and inconstant. The original tactile experiences are therefore fragmentary. What, in adequate conditions, gradually transforms the discontinuity of the boundary into a greater and more consistent continuity is the repeated and dependable rhythm of the tactile experiences at the breast, together with the quality of the associated maternal care. If these factors of continuity are lacking, the boundary of the self will remain precarious and insufficient after the separation, and the need for contact will become permanent. Consequently, mental activity will have, above all, to organize protective defence of the self, in order to ensure its survival. It is in this sense, I believe, that the need to make permanent the fragmentary state of non-integration should be understood, as well as the need to make, by means of contact, a magical and repetitive experience out of the integration which is not possible.

The protective defence fantasy on which the experience of contact is based is that of being able to create, each time, the original lost situation when there was no need to differentiate the other from the self, and the experience of the boundary of the self was, in the fantasy, produced by the self. As I have already written [see Chapter 8], the objective need of the other, whoever this is, therefore remains constant and unavoidable; but since the other's worth is to be a functional limit of the self, and the 'other as distinct from the self' is not objectively recognized, the need, too, is not recognized as such.

In analysis, this may be particularly frustrating for the analyst.

It seems to me that the basic fantasy of the repetitive experience of contact belongs to what I have already described as fantasies in the body, and that these should be included within the body–mind–body circuit fantasies. Rather than translating itself into images it translates itself into physical behaviour, in an effort to reproduce magically the lost bodily sensations of self-containment. This is perhaps in line with two phenomena that Marty and De M'Uzan (1963) have rightly isolated in psychosomatic patients and which they have descriptively defined as an absence or scarcity of fantasy activity, and as 'pensée opératoire'. The fantasy of perennial survival – that is to say, the lack of the dimension of time – and a particular actuality of space are an intrinsic part of non-integration. I cannot enter here into these important aspects of non-integration but will limit myself to describing briefly certain fantasies which pertain to them and which are of interest in the psychoanalytical process.

The drive for survival originates in the infantile self as a natural result of separation. To survive separation and to organize oneself for an autonomous life are part of the developmental tendency. Under pathological conditions, however, the drive to survive can become, as we have seen before, the principal goal of mental activity, damaging the integrative processes which could have reached an organization sufficient to cope with the process of growth and with an effective autonomous life. Thus, whereas the psychoanalytic process is disposed to favour the natural tendency to develop, which entails the passage from the need to survive to the desire to live, the pathological non-integration opposes the force of need, which does not give way to any desire, least of all that of living which appears as an extreme danger. 'It is horrible even to think about', said a 41-year-old patient who, after seven years of analysis, was with great difficulty arriving at the crucial passage. 'It is horrible that at the time when one is born one realizes, for this precise reason, that one must die.' This patient had never married nor had any children, but she had had two abortions, one at the time of an earlier psychotherapy and one a short time after the beginning of the actual analysis. This time, however, she had been able to perceive the repetition of her acting out, and to understand her profound tendency to abort the internal growth process of the self.

When she had spoken the words I have just quoted it was easy for me to make her notice that, in her description, the whole of life was lacking, the life which lies precisely between being born and dying. This omission, so to speak, was due to the fact that she was not really speaking as she thought, about physical birth and real death, but about the recognition of the boundary of the separate self (psychological birth), and the breakdown of her fantasy of eternal survival (final catastrophe).

Faced with the same problem, another patient *dreamed of having a doll in her hands whose head she had to change* [the patient had a workshop for restoring antique dolls]. *However, this doll's head was a real child's head, and the new head had to be like this. 'How is that possible?' the patient wondered in the dream. At the moment when the head was removed the doll-child would die for ever.* This very beautiful and intelligent patient was sterile (the lifeless body of the child-doll). Only after a long analysis, at the age of 42, did she become pregnant for the first time, and had a baby.

As may have already been noticed, the patient to whom I first referred associated not her individual life but suicide to the integrated unity of the self. In reality, when, in the analytic process, one feels that a developmental change in the state of non-integration is imminent, there is a danger that the extreme defence of suicide may be acted out, especially in patients who have already attempted suicide before the analysis began. I would say that this type of suicide has a lot to do with the body–mind–body circuit, a circuit in which the essential function of the mind generally seems to be to protect the life of the organism. In a paradoxical way, the suicide is the extreme form of withdrawing from the catastrophe. On the other hand, to survive suicide may, at times, be an essential turning point in the development of the psycho-analytic process.

So far, I have had frequently to refer to the idea of space. It seems to shape itself gradually in the mind, from the time the first fragmentary mental experiences of the body occur. It is generally with separation that the idea of an internal space circumscribed by a boundary shapes itself, together with the idea of an unlimited external space beyond the boundary in which a part of the self which has detached itself from the self (breast) is located. The intermediate space described by Winnicott (1952) is located between the self and the breast. We have already seen how much the early pathology has to do implicitly with the idea of space and how much it can upset the formative process of the idea of space. We have also seen how this formative process is linked with the first mental experiences of bodily functioning which are fragmentary and selective, and how the development of fantasy, primarily in the

150

service of defence, proceeds from the body experiences. I have already described the fantasies in the body which, lacking images, may be revealed through a functioning of the body activated by the mind, and altered to a greater or lesser extent according to its psychic meaning. The idea of space can be inferred in an indirect way in these rudimentary fantasies, or proto-fantasies.

Before concluding this paper I would like to emphasize that the gradual process of fantasy development seems to be essentially linked to the idea of space in the developmental process. The earliest image of the self is linked to this idea, that image which in dream fantasies and in the child's very first graphic expressions is represented by round forms which do not usually refer to objects, but to the detached and separated self. These ones are the earliest 'fantasies on the body'. which should be distinguished from the preceding 'fantasies *in* the body' (see above). I would like to cite an example.

A patient *dreamed of being 'something like a round shape, about the same size as an omelette or a cake, that floated in the sea'. This sea was not very big, since he could see his mother standing upright, on firm ground, motionless in front of the round image that was himself.* The strangeness of the dream, according to the patient, was that he *was* that round thing in the water as well as the person who was watching the scene with increasing anxiety. *In fact the round image in the water 'was reducing itself by crumbling away as if it were consuming itself'. The patient looked on in terror, as he became smaller and smaller. His hope was that his mother would do something to save him before he was completely annihilated. However, his mother remained motionless, looking at the round form which would soon disappear.* Before this happened, the patient woke up in great anxiety. In the session he commented on what he described as 'a space of water': 'Certainly it was not a sea, but it appeared to the "me" that was immersed in it as greater than a sea, an ocean.'

It is not surprising that the dreams in which the first mental image of the body self appears are usually accompanied by anxiety of self-loss. These dreams usually occur at a very advanced stage in the analysis, when, during the psychoanalytic process, the danger of having to recognize one's own separate individuality, and having to abandon non-integration as a defence, is very near. However, dreams of this kind also intervene in certain life situations which approximate to the original anxiety of self-loss. In this connection I should like to describe the use that a patient made of a dream of this type, because even though she had the dream many years before the beginning of her analysis it played a significant role in the psychoanalytic process.

This was a 30-year-old female patient who, from the age of 6 months, was affected by atopical dermatitis which spread over her

151

neck, chest, and arms. She had been hospitalized several times because of it, in its more severe phases. Obviously this was not the reason why she had started psychoanalysis. For this patient dermatitis had become so complete a part of herself that she was unable to think of her existence without it. For the rest, her life as well as her internal organization were so seriously unsettled that she had been considered by a psychiatrist as having a split personality. However, psychotic episodes had never played a part in her life, whereas her dermatitis had become so acute at times that she required hospitalization.

In analysis, this patient's capacity for internal work was extraordinary. When the analysis was reaching its termination, after a little more than nine years, one of her achievements was that the dermatitis had completely disappeared. This apparently silent and unnoticed disappearance came about only gradually, but then decisively and rather rapidly in the second half of the seventh year of analysis. While this was happening, she never talked about it and only once spontaneously remarked that her skin was 'much better than usual'.

In a session during the last week of analysis, the patient talked about her dermatitis again, declaring that it had actually disappeared a couple of years ago. She made me observe that she was wearing a woollen sweater next to her skin, which would have been quite inconceivable earlier in her life. After a short silence she said,

> There is something that I've never told you, only because it never came into my mind. Before analysis I often had a terrifying idea which made me suffer a lot. This idea was that I could literally go to pieces at any given moment. It was a horrible physical sensation.

After a pause, she continued,

> There is another thing I never told you, which only comes to mind now, after so many years. It's a strange and fearful dream which I had after my mother's death [this happened when the patient was 18]. *In the dream I was a kind of planet in dark and infinite space. In the distance I saw another planet, which was moving rapidly away. I was extremely frightened. I knew, in the dream, that when the planet had disappeared I would be completely shattered and I would be lost in that dark space.* I woke up in great anxiety. This dream deeply impressed me, and often came back to my mind during the months that followed my mother's death.

During these same months her dermatitis had become very acute, and she had had to be hospitalized.

The dream was therefore the representation of the infantile experience of separation which determined the first appearance of dermatitis as a protective defence of the self. This representation was obviously brought on by the actual death of the mother. It became clear to me that, in that session, the patient was discovering the connections which linked together some fundamental experiences of her self which had not been integrated previously. Her efforts also implied a synthetic retrospective view of the entire analytic process. Only now was the patient able to bring together within herself the original infantile experience – that is, the necessity of maintaining the non-integration and the dermatitis: on the one hand, the dermatitis expressed the anguished defence fantasy expressed in the dream and afterwards in the terrifying idea of going to pieces, and, on the other hand, the necessity of assuring the survival of the self by means of continuous cutaneous contact, which compensated for her own fragmentary boundary. The omission throughout the entire analysis of these two very pertinent memories corresponded to the vital need she felt to use the analyst as the limit and boundary of the self. Finally, the fact that she had now reported these memories demonstrated that she no longer had to feel her everlasting fears. In this sense, the disappearance of dermatitis had been the first signal of a dramatic reduction in the anxiety of loss of the self. But, with great caution, she had kept these memories within herself for two more years, in order to consolidate her newly acquired gains. Now she could allow her reserves to be set free. Now she knew that she could count on her own skin for her limits and her boundary, and that her separation from the analyst could take place, without the fear of not surviving. Now at last the patient was convinced that she could start living.

10

Acting out in the psychoanalytic session

The emphasis which is laid here upon the importance of the earliest experiences does not imply any underestimation of the influence of later ones.

(Freud 1919)

Given at the 32nd Congress of the International Psychoanalytical Association in Helsinki, July 1981, the paper appeared in the *Revista de Psicoanalisi* (Association Psicoanalitica de Argentina) (1981) XXXVIII 6, under the title 'El acting out en la session psicoanalitica'. It was published in the *International Journal of Psycho-Analysis* (1982) 63: 57.

Whereas acting out in the session may be a clarifying indicator of the way things are in the psychoanalytic process, the study of acting out in the session in terms of the psychoanalytic process can be very helpful in clarifying problems regarding early development of the mind. In fact, acting out is part and parcel of early development and, along with other early functioning models, is in turn integrated into more evolved models, towards an adult model of action. However the adult model is to be understood, I think we can agree that the action implies a satisfactory development of reality testing, identification, and object relationship, with all that this implies, and that in infantile acting out none of these objectives has yet been reached. Thus, there is no such thing as adult acting out, but there are adults who use acting out. For this reason, in the psychoanalytic process we can find ourselves having to distinguish acting out used as a defence, which goes against the process, to the extent of nullifying or breaking it, from acting out in terms of the process, reproducing original infantile acting out, whose model defensive acting out has maintained and stabilized, but for aims which are different and in fact opposite to the original ones.

In terms of early development, acting out takes place before action, before activity, and before thought, so that, paraphrasing Freud's quotation from Goethe, 'Im Angang war die Tat', 'In the beginning was the Deed' (Freud 1913), we could say, 'In the beginning was the Acting out'. Acting out tends to remove from oneself, and thus remove from the mind, whatever cannot be contained and worked through inside oneself. In early development and in the psychoanalytic process this may work as an effective regulator of the tensions that go together with integrating processes, and may therefore contribute to the organization of a separate self with its own inner space. When acting out is working as a defence against development (and against the psychoanalytic process) the opposite is true. Acting out then tends to eliminate and not regulate tensions; it tends to maintain a state of 'non-integration' (Winnicott 1974), thus counteracting the process of integration; it tends to prevent objective recognition of oneself and separation; it tends to counteract the recognition and organization of an inner space; it tends to counteract recognition of one's own autonomy and one's real dependence. Acting out leaves out reality; it is magic and omnipotent.

Taken as a kind of functioning, acting out could be defined as the representative of an early mental organization, which tends above all to keep itself unchanged. Needs are intended for this purpose, therefore they come first and are peremptory, with no consideration for reality. Acting out is mostly used in the service of needs, and much less in the service of wishes.

This mental organization is originally part of primary development. It organizes itself during the beginning months of life, and precedes structural functioning. It is the fragmented and non-integrated mental organization which exists at the crucial time of the experience of separation. This experience has less to do with the moment mother stops breast-feeding the baby, and much more with the overwhelming time when the child has to realize its being separate, and with the capacity to deal with this change. This experience, which seems to repeat in early development the caesura of birth (Freud 1926), marks in fact the first change, which is surely the greatest and most terrifying of all successive changes; furthermore, it marks the beginning of mental processes which are fundamental for further growth. It really behaves as a 'mental caesura' in the early development of mind.

I have dealt with these early fundamental processes in the preceding essays [see Chapters 1 and 8]. I have then stressed the need to be alert to the presence of fears of integration as much as fears of disintegration. I have also drawn attention [especially in Chapter 7] to the importance of distinguishing between anxiety affecting the self and ego anxiety. Such considerations are of relevance to our understanding of acting out.

A pathological organization of the self actually gives rise to pathological effects in the structure *in fieri*. The ego, whose function would be to structure and develop autonomous trends, and to develop object relationship, may be coerced to the extent of putting them in the service – prevalent or exclusive – of the needs of the self. Superego may become a fierce watch-dog, which allows only the satisfaction of the self's needs, and forbids the ego to experience any wish towards an object. Instinctuality itself may be compelled to serve the self's needs. Acting out, stabilized as a defence, is used to put the entire executive apparatus, consciousness included, in the service of the magic and omnipotent autarchy of the self, instead of serving autonomy.

Naturally, the self which rules omnipotently over the developing structure is really a self struggling against having to recognize its own fragility, its own state of need, its own integration anxiety, and the anxiety of going to pieces and disappearing into space (non-integration anxiety). The latter, however, is a sort of lesser evil, which may be counteracted by magic omnipotence much more successfully than integration anxiety. The need to reinforce the dangerously precarious boundary of the self continuously seeks satisfaction through attempts at kinds of contacts which may easily be exchanged for a relationship to an object, but in which the object does not really exist as such but simply as the limit and boundary of the self.

The continuous acting out in the session of a patient, A, was that of extraordinary mobility on the couch, with frequent changes of position and a continual tendency to uncover her body, both by pulling her dress or skirt well above her knees and moving her uncovered legs in various directions and by making her breasts as evident as possible. In marked contrast with this apparent obvious erotization of the analytical session, there was no evidence of an erotic transference. On the contrary, the patient seemed to impose a condition of anonymity on me. I was not allowed to be someone. Clearly the pseudo-sexual acting out in the session had an equivalent in the external pseudo-sexual acting out, in which the patient was continuously involved, and constituted a massive defence against the relationship. Uncovering her body was equivalent to expanding it and stretching it out until she felt its boundaries, the safe limit of herself. The continuous changes of position on the couch and the movements of her limbs had the same meaning, and obeyed the same necessity. In consequence, I was not allowed to exist as a separate object, but only to serve this need.

This patient had taught me that her sexual acting out was a sort of imitative sexuality, through which she intended to appear to other people and to herself as an adult woman, but which in fact she used to fight against and prevent an object relationship; a sexuality which was set in motion by need and not by desire, even though in her conscious mind need might seem to be desire. In a characteristic way this patient liked physical contact and not penetration in a sexual relationship. Through the physical sensations of her sexual acting out this patient realized the unconscious fantasy of a nutritional contact and containment of the self, and thus produced magically in her body a feeling of selfness that her mind did not possess, and which it did not intend to possess. What this patient could not in fact bear was the objective recognition of her own separation and autonomy. In the same way, she was not able to recognize the existence of an external object which was distinct and separate from herself. What could have been an object became one with herself in her sexual acting out, the boundaries of herself, which contained her.

Parallel to her sexual acting out this patient went in for an eating acting out. She ate not in order to feed herself but to fill herself. She did not know what appetite meant, nor satiety either. Through her compulsive eating she created a feeling of self-fullness in her body, which was intended as a substitute for, but it also maintained, the mental sense of an empty and inconsistent self. For this reason, an incapacity for introjection and for a structuring internalization corresponded to the compulsive eating and excessive body weight. All this was represented in the psychoanalytic session, which the patient tended to experience as a physical contact, which enabled her to feel contained and filled.

In sharp contrast to acting out which aims to nullify the psychoanalytic process, there is, as I said before, acting out in terms of the process. This kind of acting out is generally more subdued, less evident than the first. The problem is that psychoanalytic work can arouse in the ego, enslaved by the need of the self, a great fear of being attacked from inside the structure. Participation in psychoanalytic work can only take place in secret, in a sort of clandestinity. If the psychoanalyst is not alert enough to realize this, he may have the impression that nothing is happening. But the patient has no intention of doing anything to correct this impression. More than that, what is meant to appear is just that nothing is happening. The messages which the patient's ego sends resemble those which the shipwrecked person throws into the sea closed in a bottle. Besides not being evidently addressed to the analyst, they are usually disguised and made cryptic like the latent contents of dreams. They are coded messages for whoever can decipher them. Acting out can be used in a case like this, like a container which doesn't give rise to suspicion, thanks to which the secret message can find its way to the outer world, evading censorship.

The degree of empathy that such a situation requires from the psychoanalyst is out of the ordinary. Continuously subjected to frustration, the psychoanalyst may in fact collude with the defences organized around the self, and think that nothing is happening and nothing relevant can happen. If instead he is able to notice through indirect signs (in dreams, behaviour, associations) that a certain amount of work is unconsciously being carried out, he may feel pleased and may want to tell his patient the good news. To his surprise, he will see the patient withdraw into silence, and if he persists, he will find himself attacked by the patient in a sardonic and depreciative way. Actually, it is as if he said, 'Well, what do you understand? You think you understand things that don't exist, that you make up in your imagination. Do you think you are very clever?', and so on. Obviously the worst thing the psychoanalyst can do at that moment is to feel resentful, and to want to show the patient he is right. In other cases, in which the patient's ego suddenly sees its own clandestine work made public, a negative therapeutic reaction may be set in motion, through which the ego tends to show its powerful inner enemies that what has emerged is not true, that nothing has happened, which is clear from the fact that not only is the patient feeling bad but he is getting worse. This is what possibly happens, I think, when we hear that a negative therapeutic reaction followed an interpretation by the psychoanalyst, which emphasized some kind of progress. Paradoxically, the more correct the interpretation the more negative the patient's reaction will be, the reason being that the interpretation reveals just what was not meant to be known inside. Paraphrasing Glover (1955), this could be described as the anti-therapeutic effect of exact interpretation.

What is required of the psychoanalyst is not an easy task, but it is essentially important. He must make himself available and reliable for that unconscious part of the patient that is working. He must help it not to come out into the open but, on the contrary, to protect its clandestineness. He must learn to discover and to decipher the oncoming messages, without making them public. He must accept a kind of communication which is, and must remain, a one-way communication. In other words, he must accept a clandestine therapeutic alliance. The only return communication, no less cautious and silent, which is worthwhile, is that his clandestine ally comes to trust him, to make up his mind that there is somebody out there who is able to understand him and protect him, someone he can count on, when, properly grown up and strengthened, he can come out of his clandestineness less terrified. The psychoanalyst will have to know how to wait for this to happen.

The following example is about a case in supervision, a young woman patient, B, married, but whose marriage had not been consummated. This patient, during the first phase of analysis, was visibly terrified. For over a year she could not lie down on the couch. Nevertheless, from the beginning, the analyst had had the impression of a desperate request for help, which went beyond what the patient expressed. After some months when it seemed to the psychoanalyst that the patient was looking forward to the sessions, and that the attachment with the analysis was strong enough, the patient began to be late, even half an hour late, and sometimes to miss the session completely. It took some time to understand that this acting out of the patient was officially intended to reduce the time of the session, and occasionally to cut it out completely, in obedience to the inner necessity of minimizing the attachment to the analysis, and to show that psychoanalysis was not important to her at all. In this way the patient managed to protect and maintain her attachment to the analysis without arousing inner suspicion. Naturally, it would have been very easy to make the mistake of interpreting the acting out as a defence against the analysis, but the problem is that it would have been a much more harmful mistake to reveal the latent purpose of the acting out with an interpretation.

Sometimes in the psychoanalytic process there is a crucial phase, in which the patient gradually becomes aware that the psychoanalyst is different (separate) from himself, and that consequently he is different (separate) from the psychoanalyst. To describe what can happen in this phase would require another paper. It is enough here to keep in mind that, for the first time in this phase of the process a collapse of omnipotence may be experienced, and the anxiety of loss of the self can emerge. There are patients who, approaching this phase, take the inner decision to stop the treatment. For example, one patient, C, dreamed at this point that she was talking to me on the telephone when the door-bell rang. 'Excuse me a moment', she said, 'I am going to open it and I will be right back.' Having opened the door she found that her husband was there (the patient had seemed to be convinced that she had to separate from him). So, she came back to the telephone and said, 'I'm sorry, I must leave you; my husband has arrived, and I must be with him.' The analysis had to be interrupted some months later.

Of course the inner decision may be acted out in the psychoanalytic session. Another young woman, D, married, but unable to have sexual intercourse with her husband from the very moment of the wedding (before, when they were engaged, they had occasionally had intercourse) appeared to be a wilful, assured, and active woman. Really, this was in large part due to her use of omnipotence and acting out. She had sucked her thumb until shortly before getting engaged. However, her husband had noticed that she still did it at night, in her sleep. In the fourth year of analysis, coming close to what I have called the crucial phase, this patient asked me one day to change the time of a session. I said that, unfortunately, this wasn't possible for me. She accepted, but was clearly displeased. Ten days or so later, she repeated a similar request, but to have the session on a different day. When I told her that I was sorry but I couldn't, the patient reacted violently, accusing me of not considering her external activities at all, and announced her decision to stop the analysis, and having said this she got up and went out without saying goodbye. A few days later she rang me up. She was in a very good mood and very nice. She said she regretted what had happened and asked me to excuse her. She thought however that for now it might be better to stop the analysis. After the summer we would see. Of course, I heard nothing more from her.

When the analysis is not stopped, and the psychoanalytic process enters the crucial phase, one of the important phenomena is the changed perception the patient has of the analyst and of him/herself. Before reaching this point, one patient, E (a supervised case), went through almost a year of acting out directed against the analysis, to the extent of arousing serious doubts about her possibility of continuing. At last the problem was discussed in a session. In the following session the patient came back to the problem, saying that in the previous session she had felt that the psychoanalyst had changed, was different from the way she knew him, and that he had been keeping her at a distance, and she had felt hostility towards him, so that she felt they had been set against each other. The next session she brought a dream.

> *She was entering a room where there was a sort of reception, and she saw, among other friends, an important person she had met some years before and whom she had once taken on a whole day's sightseeing tour of her city, which he didn't know very well. She went up to him gladly to greet him, but he, unexpectedly for her, was cold and detached, and accused her of not being seen or heard of for almost a year.*

The patient vaguely realized that the dream must have had something to do with the previous session, but she embarked on a series of associations regarding the outer world. At one point, she suddenly stopped speaking and stayed in silence, motionless, for a couple of minutes. Then she lifted her hand and she stroked herself gently on the neck, toward the nape. At that point she came to, and started speaking

160

again. The psychoanalyst did not so much notice this gesture as the sudden silence.

But in the following session the patient, with a self-awareness she had never shown before, spoke about some decisions she had taken, which would bring to an end certain situations which had lasted about a year, among which was one of breaking off a relationship she had established and experienced in that period with a man, with whom she had no real relationship except a sexual one, and about whom she had hardly ever spoken in analysis. Then she went back to the previous session, because she had to let him know, she said, about something very strange that had happened to her in the session. What she said was that, when she had suddenly stopped talking and kept still, it had been because she had suddenly had the clear feeling that the psychoanalyst was moving his hand towards her and was about to touch her. Everything had seemed so real and she had been so sure about it, that she had stayed still, waiting for this contact. When, after some minutes, she realized that what she was expecting hadn't happened, she had automatically moved her hand towards her neck, where she had expected to be touched.

The patient had reached the threshold, so to speak, of the crucial phase about a year before, but only now she realized, inside herself, that all the acting out of that period in the outer world had served the purpose of saving her from the crucial problems of her inner world. The dream showed that the patient was now able to let go of those defences and come back to herself, and to face the painful problem of separation, which she experienced as diversity, change. It was no surprise that in the session, speaking about her dream, the patient felt overcome with anxiety of loss of self, and that the impulse to re-establish in the session a unifying contact with the psychoanalyst had the power of a hallucination. But the patient had nevertheless had objectively to recognize a separation, which left the psychoanalyst next to her, but outside her, and left her contained within the real confines of her own skin.

The appearance of silence is, however, one of the constant phenomena of this phase of the psychoanalytic process. What usually happens is that patients who for years haven't had the slightest difficulty in speaking in the session, start to feel that difficulty, which is usually connected with increasing tension. Under these initial silences is the sense of being separate and the anxiety of loss of the self, and there is also the sense that the use of words as a unifying link – the acting out of language – no longer produces its usual magic effects. Now words can have their meaning, which may reveal what the patient never

161

intended to recognize. The patient's, E's, sudden silence, and the substitution of language with hallucinated fantasy had something to do with these painful feelings.

With two different patients, at a distance of some years between them, it happened that, at an advanced stage of analysis, the patient one day suddenly refused the couch and went to sit in an armchair opposite me. For one of them, F, this happened during the session, while the patient was silent for some minutes. These long pauses or silences had started happening recently, and had been accompanied by disturbing tension. The patient suddenly got up from the couch and went to sit in the chair.

The other patient, G, instead came into the analytical room one day, went as usual to the couch, but instead of lying down stopped a moment to look at it, then turned round and went to sit in the armchair. This patient too, previously very talkative, had recently started to be silent in the session. But, unlike patient F, patient G, some sessions before her acting out had said something about silence, which had struck me, and which now came back to my mind. In that session the patient had been silent for some minutes, when, suddenly, and with unusual irritation, she said: 'Perhaps my being silent is a reaction to your not speaking'. I told her I realized how painful silence was for her, and I added that, whatever the reason for her silence, the fact that she had broken it counted perhaps more than if I had broken it. 'For you' – said the patient after a while – 'silence is different, it can never be total, as it is for me.' I asked her what she meant.

When I am silent, and you don't speak either, you can still see me. So, silence for you is never total. But I can't see you, and if, when I don't speak, you don't speak either, everything disappears and silence becomes overwhelming. It's horrible. I feel as if I am disappearing into it.

What she was describing was anxiety of loss of the self. Since her silences continued to occur, she was finally compelled to act. Acting out was therefore consciously intended to prevent this unbearable experience from happening again. Now that she could look at me, she would no longer be dissolved in total silence. It was important, I think, that she had been able to express her feeling in words. The same kind of anxiety, but to a greater extent, was underneath the acting out of patient F, but she had no words to describe it. Though this anxiety had given rise in both patients to the same kind of acting out in the session, basic mental organization was in fact very different in each of them.

In both these patients, however, acting out in the session constituted a change of the setting, and could therefore formally appear to be directed against the psychoanalytic process. Really, it was in both cases a kind of acting out which was meant to allow them to continue the analytic work. Patient G stayed in the armchair for about ten more sessions, until one day she came to the session and, without a word, spontaneously went to lie down on the couch. Patient F, on the other hand, never went back to the couch. Anxiety of loss of the self gradually increased, and the patient's mental pain became a stable phenomenon for a long time, apparently paralysing any inner work. In fact, in spite of appearances, and of what she herself tended to show, I came to realize that the clandestine work which I have described above was going on. The narcissistic structure of this patient was clearly represented by her in a dream some years later, when she was getting close to finding a way out.

In the dream,

> she was with another young woman at the foot of a round hill. This woman was showing her a little house on top of the hill. She explained to her that that was her house, and boasted about its advantages. 'Up there' – she said, among other things – 'I am saved from any disturbance. Nobody could ever reach me.' A little incredulous, the patient asked her for an explanation. 'It looks to me' – she said – 'as if anybody can climb the hill and get to your house.' 'No they can't, it's impossible,' answered the other triumphantly. 'Look down there' – she said, pointing at the bottom of the hill – 'from the bottom to almost half way up the hill it is covered with shit, which goes all round the hill, so that nobody can manage to reach me.' The patient was puzzled for a moment. 'Well' – she said then – 'all in all it may be easier, and perhaps even better, to talk to someone.'

As one can see, this patient's childish sexuality, which she placed in her dream at the bottom of the hill, where the hill was in relation with the surrounding world, had not been able to serve the purpose of relationship, but had instead been serving a self which, in a magic and omnipotent way, had itself to be one and the same with an enormous self-sufficient breast (the round hill). In this way her instinctuality (her ego) had lost its original trend towards object relationship, and found itself obeying the opposite aim, which was to be a barrier to the outer world, and protect the timeless survival of the self. Only now something was emerging in this patient, apart from the self's imperative needs; namely, an autonomous wish towards an object.

11

The pre-symbolic activity of the infant mind

This paper was presented to a seminar on 'The Psychological Development of the Infant Mind, Present Orientations and Perspectives' at the Goethe Institute, Rome, in 1984, under the title 'L'attività presimbolica della mente infantile'. Unpublished.

My subject will not be symbols but what precedes them in the infant mind and somehow paves the way for the capacity to symbolize. The actual utilization of this capacity will be the task of the ego. Here, however, I shall be concerned with an earlier form of mental activity, which, although more elementary, is anything but simple, and I shall refer to it by the term 'basic mental organization' (BMO).

This paper necessarily appears theoretical, but it is fundamentally clinical – that is to say, the concepts here put forward are based on clinical experience and aspire to clinical verification of their soundness.

By 'basic mental organization' I mean the primitive mind as gradually organized in the period extending from the biological process of birth up to, and including, the mental process of separation, a process which has been called 'psychological birth'. For this reason, the BMO can also be defined as the mental organization which the individual has at his disposal at the moment of his psychological birth. I have discussed the formation of the BMO in detail in *Notes on the Mind–body Question*. In a subsequent paper, 'Il Sè in psicoanalisi' (The self in psychoanalysis), I used this term 'officially', having already used it informally for some time, first to avoid the confusion that still surrounds the term 'self' in the psychoanalytic literature, and second because it seems to me to cover more correctly the phenomena, which are as elementary as they are complex, involved in the earliest organization of the mind – although I have no doubt that the main purpose of the formation of the

BMO is the achievement of an initial mental image of the bodily self. When this occurs, it may thus be said that the body as a whole has acquired a mental 'sense' which normally constitutes the first sense of self to be achieved.

However, before discussing the mental sense, I should like to add that the first definition and description of what I now believe can be called the BMO was that of the 'sensory-psychic area' of the mind [see Chapter 1], the first fruit of research which had already been under way for many years. I have deliberately used the term 'organization' rather than 'structure', because it is a characteristic of the processes which give rise to the BMO that they are so elementary that they do not require any already formed structure and do not initially give rise to any structure, in the sense given to the term by Freud. The BMO may be said to be a form of mental organization which precedes the structural organization of the mind described by Freud (1923); it is therefore primitive and elementary, but capable of a specific form of functioning of its own, with which it is important to be acquainted (*Il Sè in Psicoanalisi* [The self in psychoanalysis] E. Gaddini 1984a: 562).

However, the need to use this term became manifest only after the description of the processes which extend to the point of constitution of a separate self had been completed. What then happens is that the disruption involved in the process of separation ultimately leads to a situation that tends powerfully to activate mental functioning and is in all respects comparable with the initial activation of the mind in the immediate post-natal situation, after the process of birth has disrupted the pre-natal phase. The physical change in the environmental situation – the principal activating factor of mental functioning at this time – is now paralleled by the no less dramatic and clear-cut change in experience of the environment: the sensation of a separate self that is fragile and whose boundary is uncertain, having just survived the catastrophe of detachment – which has substantially modified the accustomed form of psychical functioning – and that of a dark and limitless external space in which it is possible to be obliterated for ever. To the physical change in the organism and the environment, which initiates mental functioning at birth, there now corresponds a psychical change in the self and in the environment capable of activating a mental organization which has meanwhile come into being. The activating force which in fact connects the two situations is probably the survival urge. It is, I believe, legitimate to say that, in the human individual, the onset of mental activity is necessitated by the urge to survive, and that it is therefore necessary at the beginning to the survival of the organism after birth and to that of the newly formed self at psychological birth.

What is particularly striking in the separation process is how far what the organism experienced only in terms of physiological disruptions in the process of birth now comes to be assumed into the mind and thereby to acquire mental sense. Again, the early months of the neonatal period may be said to bear the same relation to the process of separation as the period of intra-uterine life to the process of birth. The problem of memory plainly arises.

It seems to me that two hypotheses can be made in this connection. The first can be based on the law discovered by Freud (1895) that the earliest models of mental functioning parallel the models of physiological functioning. On the basis of this hypothesis, the initial activity of the mind could be taken as necessarily having the object of modelling the bodily experiences of the first months of life on the physiological prototypes of intra-uterine life, and the experiences of the separation process on the physiological prototypes of the process of birth. The second hypothesis more properly concerns memory. There are very early psychophysical syndromes, the study of which has shown that the mental function of memory is operational from the moment of birth. Whereas this has been fairly definitely established, we are much less sure about the moment at which mental functioning actually begins. If memory, and hence mental activity, began not at the moment when the neonate sees the light but as a result of the powerful sensory stimuli of the process of birth, it would then be possible, when particular reactivating experiences occur, to recognize the reactivation through the memory of similar sensory experiences. I shall not espouse either of these hypotheses because, as things are at present, both can be accepted or rejected. However, if one or other of these hypotheses proved to be true, this could not alter the description so far given of the BMO in any way.

It is not surprising that the main aim of the BMO is to serve the needs of the self and to defend these needs at all costs against any event, thing, or situation that appears to threaten them. Nor is it surprising that the BMO is primarily conservative, tending to oppose any change that is not initiated and organized by itself, to serve its own functional ends. However, what is perhaps unexpected is the exiguous and elementary nature of the functional modalities available to the BMO at the outset, compared with the scale of the tasks it is called upon to perform.

These modalities are conditioned by the way the BMO was formed. So far as we know, the BMO is the result of the mental learning of the body – that is, of the sensory experiences relating to specific bodily functions. From this point of view, it corresponds to what I originally called the 'sensory area' of the mind [see Chapter 1]. Sensory activity – and here I refer to sensations – dispenses with perceptions, makes use

166

of sensations and thus implies imitative functioning [see Chapter 1]. The predominant sensation of imitative functioning is that of contact, because of the importance at the beginning of life of physical contact for the sense of self and for the subject's own existence. All the sense organs may be said to function originally as contact organs. Sight and hearing in particular function as contact organs in the physical situation of distance. Whereas visual or auditory perception draws attention to distance, visual or auditory sensation magically abolishes distance, transforming it into contact.

This use of sight and hearing as continuous contact organs, in ways still discernible to a greater or lesser extent in adult life, can definitely be observed in analysis. Every psychoanalyst will have experienced the situation where the sound of his voice is much more significant to the analysand than the words he utters and their meaning. One female patient even told me that she had a few times attained orgasm while I was speaking. Every analyst will also have observed how patients sometimes suddenly notice details or objects in the consulting room which have in fact always been there in front of them. In such cases, we usually say that a person looks but does not see. This may be a correct description of the phenomenon, but does not explain it. It must be borne in mind that this 'not seeing' means using sight not to perceive but to make contact, and that this operation of contact obliterates the existence of the real object in so far as it makes it possible to 'become' the object. As we shall soon see when we come to discuss the mental sense of the 'fragment', every detail of the consulting room stands in this type of mental activity for the analyst, and the analyst is present in every detail of the consulting room. The visual 'dis-appearance' of the detail is 'identical' to the disappearance of the actual person of the analyst, with whom the patient is thus only performing a contact operation and not having an object relation.

A young female patient who was a successful interior decorator one day came into the consulting room and suddenly stopped in front of a bas-relief of Gradiva that stood beside the door of the room. She said with a kind of worried surprise: 'Good gracious, so you also have this bas-relief?' I pointed out that it had always been there, even if she had never seen it. Somewhat dismayed, she lay down on the couch and told me that in the last few days she had thought of getting herself two bas-reliefs of Gradiva (with which she claimed to be familiar inde-pendently, without knowing anything about Jensen or Freud's study [1906], and putting them in the entrance hall of a house she was decorating, one on the right-hand wall and the other opposite, on the left-hand wall, so that one figure would appear to be entering the house and the other to be leaving it.

I had occasion to distinguish elsewhere [see Chapter 8] between physiological learning, which is bound up with physiological memory, and mental learning, which is associated with mental memory, and I gave a detailed description of the functioning of mental memory, showing its intimate connection with the mental sense of bodily functioning and how this accounts for the fragmentary nature of primitive mental learning.

However, it would be wrong to construe these fragments literally as incomplete parts of the subject's self. The mental sense of each fragment – that is, of the sensory experiences relating to a specific functioning of the body – concerns simply the self. The idea of 'a part of self' does not yet exist in the formative phase of the BMO. The mental presentation during this phase of a particular sensory experience merely bears witness to the presence – the existence – of self. It may be added that this existence of self, for the infant mind, is magically produced by itself. Every time such an experience presents itself – for example, the rhythmically repeated sensory experience of feeding – the mental sense of self created by itself is re-presented. If the experience in its absence is magically reactivated in fantasy, this does not alter its mental sense during this phase. In other words, the experience activated in fantasy is not distinguishable from the real experience.

The fragment that stands for the self – and hence the self experienced in each fragment – is a basic functional model which can later also be found in adult life in dreams and fantasies and which has been described in bodily terms as the use of a part for the whole, or by the improper term of 'identification' with a part of self. The same functional model is in my view to be found in certain group situations, and in particular in what Bion described as a group 'in itself'. Each of the members of the group is a fragment that stands for the whole, and the whole is in each of the members. Since Bion's creative development began with the group and eventually led him to the individual, he came to speak in theoretical terms of an 'internal group' existing in each individual. Winnicott (1958), on the other hand, as the title of his extraordinary book tells us, travelled 'through paediatrics to psychoanalysis' (of children and adults) and was the first to introduce the concept of 'non-integration' and to identify it as a stage in the infantile development of the mind. I shall retain this term here, although I consider that non-integration is a magical integration, which precedes the prolonged and laborious process of integration, for which, however, it paves the way with its own model. In non-integration, the multiple is not distinguishable from the single; later, the multiple will tend to be integrated into the single.

168

At the moment when the BMO begins to function, its fragmentary nature is, of course, not integrated. However, something fundamental has happened amid the disruptions of the process of separation which has decisively altered the sense of the multiple as one and hence of the fragment as self. Precisely by way of this magical integration, the mental sense of the experience of separation cannot but be first and foremost that of a total obliteration of self. It is only the experience of the self which survives, which presents itself to the mind with an extremely painful sense of a mutilation, of the loss of a 'part of itself' and at the same time the loss of the magical omnipotence whereby the self continuously created itself. Now the fragments are the pieces of self which have survived the catastrophe, immersed in a dark and infinite space, in which they can be absorbed and scattered for ever. There now appears the dominant urge to hold the residual fragments of self together, to maintain and protect the state of survival: an urge which will condition the entire initial activity of the BMO.

During the phase of which we are now speaking, what is perhaps the most immediate defence, because it relates to the catastrophic experience, the sense of mutilation and the collapse of magical omnipotence, is the appearance of the *loss-of-self anxiety*. This is distinguished from the catastrophe. The commonly heard term 'catastrophic anxiety' is confusing. It is not the anxiety that is catastrophic; the anxiety is a defence against the catastrophe. I believe that the foundation of a temporal dimension of the mind is laid by this anxiety, which can be regarded as the most primitive anxiety and the matrix of the subsequent forms of anxiety. A different use of memory comes into play for the first time. Whereas hitherto memory has served only to make present the sense of self – in other words, re-creation in the memory of an experience has served for magical re-creation of the sense of self, and hence to fuel a sense of self which has always remained current and timeless [see Chapter 8] – memory cannot now perform this function because this would be tantamount to making the catastrophe present again. For the first time, therefore, memory must serve for the preservation of something outside, in a space different from that of the current experience. This is perhaps the first form of a recollection – namely, of something that memory must preserve and no longer make present.

Loss-of-self anxiety initially serves to prevent this making-present. It is for this reason very important, not least because it greatly affects the manner in which integration takes place. It quickly becomes differentiated into two aspects, which condition the processes of integration with two opposing tendencies: on the one hand, the tendency to maintain the fragmentary, unintegrated organization, and, on the other, the thrust towards integration, which, however, would change something in the unintegrated organization. In pathological conditions, the thrust towards integration may be so severely impeded as to be practically obliterated. This happens when any change in the fragmentary organization is apprehended as the harbinger of a new and final catastrophe. In individual analyses of adults, this may result in the complete stalling of the analytical process, a process whose trend is, of course, in the direction of integration. This differentiated form of loss-of-self anxiety tends to prevent and impede the integrative processes, and I have called it 'integration anxiety'. On the other hand, the state of non-integration is, as I have mentioned, weak and fragile, and the risk of failing to hold together the fragments of the self may become very serious in pathological conditions. I have given the name 'non-integration anxiety' to this differentiated form of loss-of-self anxiety which tends to preserve the fragmentary state and to prevent the fragments from bursting asunder and becoming scattered for ever in the darkness of infinite space. This is where mental processes not yet containable in the mind can readily become somaticized.

There are adult patients who tell in very obvious terms of their anxiety about falling to pieces, losing themselves in space, being unable to keep themselves together. Non-integration anxiety is at the root of various psychophysical syndromes of infancy, especially those concerning the skin, which is experienced as the precarious boundary of the self. However, the separate self seems to coexist much more readily with non-integration anxiety than with integration anxiety. This is understandable considering that the former tends to preserve the status quo while the latter aims to prevent changes connected with the evolutionary process. Clinically, as in infancy, integration anxiety is the more pernicious of the two, because it opposes growth, and the analytical process in therapy, and for this reason fuels the catastrophic expectation. It is perhaps this anxiety that underlies the much feared negative therapeutic reaction (Limentani 1981).

Again, non-integration anxiety has as its direct aim the survival of the self, but it fuels the danger of fragmentation, of falling to pieces, of coming unstuck, of not keeping oneself together.

This oscillation between integration and non-integration, or rather between integration anxiety and non-integration anxiety, is truly dramatic in some patients in analysis, to such an extent as dangerously to restrict the therapeutic possibilities and, I would say, the mental processes as well. The technical problem is how to remain at an appropriate distance to satisfy these people's need to make contact without thereby arousing in them a threatening prospect of integration, which may disrupt the patient's precarious sense of self, and which he therefore rejects. The paradox in which the patient is caught up is along the lines of 'I cannot be with you and I cannot be without you'. The therapeutic problem is therefore precisely this calibrated distance which must allow the patient gradually to reduce the non-integration anxiety and, as a result, the integration anxiety. There is, however, no doubt that integration anxiety is the last kind which can be reduced: a pre-condition for its reduction is that a security organization in the self, an organization of the boundary, shall have been sufficiently well constituted; the analyst must be able to constitute this boundary, a task in which the mother has failed, and thereby make subsequent steps possible, which can take place at this point.

Before the experiences of separation disrupt the mind's equilibrium, the baby's mental sense of feeding is of a nutritive contact with himself produced by himself. In other words, the mouth replaces the function maintained stably by the umbilicus with the cord, even if the stability is now afforded by other factors, such as the rhythm and reliability of the environment. My point is that the mouth has no instinctual significance during this phase. There is therefore no 'incorporation', no 'intro-jection' or 'projection', no 'cross-identification' and no 'projective identification'. These concepts refer to phenomena which are yet to come. What is relevant now is that when, with separation, feeding in reality comes to be distinguished from contact, the BMO will not accept and acknowledge the change; it will resolutely retain the mental sense of contact as actual feeding by the self, and will actively continue to seek the lost physical contact in order magically to renew the mental sense. This failure to distinguish between contact and feeding has an unexpected consequence: when physical contact is objectively difficult or impossible to achieve, feeding is used as contact, just as sexual relations can be used as contact or as food. This may well account for the well-known fact that, where we have a baby who is an overweight little 'guzzler', there is often also an over-solicitous environment (mother) with, however, little capacity for contact. But there are other aspects to this need for contact, which we shall have to discuss.

I would say that need is a – indeed, perhaps, the – fundamental element which constitutes the starting point for primitive mental activity, and about which that activity is organized. The transition from the physiological to the mental implies the sudden lack of something of specific importance, which did not exist as such until it fell within the general automatic mechanism of physiological functioning. It is as if the transition to the mental, at least in the human species, at this point entails the sense of 'having to provide from one's own resources'. It is indeed the case that a kind of total and necessarily magical autonomy reigns in the primitive mind of the individual, in stark contrast to the actual complete dependence on the environment during this period. Need is the requirement to supply something which, because it is lacking, takes on an immediate importance such that it could be defined as a matter of life and death. This accounts for the mental force of need, which, unlike wishes – which will emerge in the future in the ego – usually presents itself as imperious, peremptory, and above all not amenable to any discussion. In the psychophysical economy of the infant organism, finding and implementing ways of supplying the needs which emerge during the separation process constitutes the essential task of the functioning of the BMO.

Indeed, to some extent, before the separation the relationship with the environment in effect acts as a substitute for pre-natal physiological functioning. The difference is that the infant mind feels that it can magically satisfy the needs of the self – what Winnicott called 'illusion'. With the separation, this kind of omnipotent autonomy – let us call it autarky – is objectively shaken. Subjectively, however, this gives rise to a powerful mental effort to organize, to try to reinforce and maintain the subject's own autarky and to 'prevent' the repetition of a catastrophe, and with it a final annihilation of the self.

The first need is to keep the fragments of the self together. There is now after all the sense of the dark void without any conceivable limit, within which a part of the self has become lost, and there is also a sense of a limit of the self, which was supposed to keep the fragments together but did not succeed in preventing the loss sustained. The limit, or boundary, could open or break again, allowing the self literally to fall to pieces in that black, limitless void. If a 4- to 6-months-old baby contracts dermatitis, it is because he has mentally apprehended the skin, from experiences of physical contact, as the limit of himself, and he is therefore expressing the primitive fantasy of the break-up of the self in that part of the body. I have discussed elsewhere [see Chapter 9] these fantasies 'in the body', which precede the appearance of the visual image in the mind. The point I wish to emphasize here is that the date of the dermatitis, in the pathological situation it expresses, may also be indicative of the degree of pathology. As I stated in the above paper, the psychophysical syndromes of early infancy are dated because they correspond to primitive mental precipitates of bodily experiences during the development of the BMO. This functional mind–body model will later be found in the development of the ego, in the mental precipitates described by Freud. Where dermatitis occurs, its onset is usually not before the age of 5 or 6 months. If it appears at 4 months, this in my view suggests that the mind has been compelled to organize the expressive-defensive syndrome precociously. I consider this to be a more severe sign, because it indicates that the separation process took

172

place early – a very important factor among those likely to make this process traumatic.

This is bound up with the date of commencement of an organized mental activity. Of course, what I have said about the dermatitis, which could not occur unless a mental organization sufficient to constitute the defensive psychophysical syndrome existed at that point, also applies to the BMO. The BMO normally begins to function at the end of the process of separation – that is, from the sixth month on. However, if the mental disruptions of separation are set in train precociously by a detachment situation, the infant mind will have to confront them while still in a state of relative immaturity, with traumatic effects on the subsequent development of the individual. So far as we know at present, the earliest age at which the mind can organize a psychophysical syndrome is eight weeks. Before that point, the response is an uncontrolled, self-destructive organic pathology.

The beginnings of organized mental activity thus arise from the survival of a sudden catastrophe, the danger that this catastrophe might recur and finally obliterate the self, and the subject's urge to save himself and maintain his survival. Operationally, this activity is therefore characterized by fantasies associated with the mental sense of bodily experiences (fantasies *in* the body) and defence of a precautionary nature. We should not be misled by the word 'precautionary'. This has nothing to do with a capacity to foresee, which will only develop later, in the ego, but concerns an expectation of something terrible, something which, moreover, has already happened. Any rudiments of temporality we might wish to trace back to this point would concern rather an initial distinction between present and past. The disruption of separation has for the first time brought about a change. The current situation is not that which prevailed formerly. However, I wonder whether this description might apply to the situation as it appears, and not as it is. If what is past could actually become past, the dreadful expectation of its recurrence would not need to occupy the present, thus preventing it from becoming present. The fact is that the possibility of a present and a past does not yet exist. All that exists are bodily experiences whose mental sense is always current, even if they may be present or absent. Memory serves not to 'recall' but to make present what is absent. Nor is the mind yet able to distinguish the presence of an experience by actual repetition from its presence by re-activation in fantasy, through memory. In both cases there will be 'true' presences produced by the subject himself. The problem of the catastrophe is that it has been undergone and was not produced by the subject himself. Like every other mental sense, the catastrophe is a true and current fact, but its absence or presence is not the result of the omnipotence of the self. This is the reason for the terrifying character of this inconceivable expectation. It implies the certainty of the recurrence of the catastrophe and the impossibility of knowing the moment when it will recur. The subject survives, with the certainty that he will not manage to survive.

We are bound to see in this the prototype of what will appear later in life as a serious depression, capable of inducing suicide. It is an obligatory point of growth in early infancy, and the various ways in which a baby can succeed or fail in emerging from this first blind alley in his life will determine his subsequent fate. The environment is of paramount importance at this point. If the illusion — namely, magical omnipotence — has been duly fuelled, the baby may now be able to encounter hope. The capacities to hope, trust, and believe probably belong at birth to the potentials inherent in incipient mental function; as potentials, these capacities are deemed to be possibilities. My point is that the mental quality of these potentialities means that their development is not then automatic but is only modulated by the relationship with the environment. There are in fact babies in whom hope cannot arise at this crucial moment because of the vicissitudes of the relationship with the environment. This means that even when they find themselves undestroyed physically in reality, they will continue to see themselves in a state of bare survival, and will then seek to organize their minds in terms of the primary aim of maintaining their survival and causing it to persist as long as possible. As adults, these subjects generally have no possibility of living lives of their own, except in appearance. They succeed in acquiring a sense of self only if they manage to maintain contact with someone. This in no way contributes to fuelling an autonomous sense of self; on the contrary, it prevents such a sense from arising. The dominant unconscious idea is still, as then, that in a situation of detachment the ultimate catastrophe always looms with the same ineluctability. Any situation, thing, or person which might somehow modify this sole and terrible certainty is therefore immediately rejected as a serious danger.

One of the situations construed as highly dangerous is that of somehow being defined. Any definition of oneself is equivalent to the situation of detachment. It is therefore necessary for the subject to keep his own identity vague at all times, or to express an apparent identity, obtained by imitation in contact. The subject can, for example, belong to a group, in which the same opinions are shared by all: this allows him to have a kind of identity with the other members of the group and towards the world outside the group.

A love relationship can, of course, be no more than a semblance. In reality it is a 'contact relationship' (I call it so knowing that the two words are contradictory, but it seems to me that the phrase nicely expresses the contradictory coexistence of the manifest and the latent reality). This pseudo-relationship is normally one of mutual contact – that is to say, the choice of partner is never a matter of chance. This corresponds to the fact that the possibility of being abandoned cannot be risked, as it would be catastrophic. With this fear, others never venture into a relationship at all unless it be contingent and brief. The fear that the relationship (always conceived as contact) might be transformed into separation may become so intense that any relationship must be avoided at all costs. This is also relevant to syndromes like anorexia, in which being prepared to eat would mean accepting the possibility of existing independently. The other side of the coin is the continuous urge towards physical contact, which may be manifested either in sexual acting out, serving the unconscious purpose of a feeding physical contact of the self, or, where this is lacking, in the compulsive eating of bulimia, which is also a form of acting out, in which, as mentioned above, feeding of oneself stands for feeding by contact.

All these are only a few of the many possible manifestations of the need to keep any definition of oneself vague, in order to protect the separate self from a final catastrophe. It seems to me quite wrong to call these manifestations 'defences'. The term 'protective manoeuvres' (Tustin 1981) is in my view more correct. They in fact have a provisional, contingent character – one of changeability equivalent to the plasticity of the self (and not to its capacity to change, which cannot exist). What is perhaps the most extraordinary event that normally takes place in the self surviving after the separation – the mutilated self, stripped of its magical self-creative omnipotence – is the emergence of the instinctual drives. It is indeed at this point that the instinctual drives, which are certainly present at birth but in non-functioning form, emerge – that is to say, begin to function. Before this, there is no need for the drives, but the instincts must be ready to emerge if they are unfortunately compelled to do so – for instance, if the separation is unduly early. What I mean is that the emergence of the instincts in the self usually follows the separation, as one of its effects. If detachment and separation occur too early (the norm is around 6 months), the emergence of the instincts will also be early, and the earlier they emerge, the more pathogenic the consequences for subsequent development are likely to be.

The function of the emergence of the instincts seems to be primarily that of providing the self, impoverished and mutilated as it is by the separation, with a reinforced sense of itself, which is accompanied by a

175

kind of new magical omnipotence connected with the functional presence of the drives.

As to pathology, the problem of the earliest months of life, in the phase of fusion, is precisely the amount of libido the mother has been capable of promoting in the mental organization of the baby, and whether the baby, once detached, will therefore have sufficient libido at his disposal to keep himself together. That is one thing. Another is that the aggressive cathexes are omni-directional and thus not directed against an object. They are against everything and nothing: against the outside, against the space outside. Sometimes the analyst in the analytical situation is not attacked as an object but as the outside world, and he must then be capable of understanding that he is not an object, because otherwise he might believe himself to be in dynamic object situations, which, however, do not yet exist.

The activity of the BMO seems to be directed principally towards preserving and consolidating the self that has survived the disrupting drama of separation, and towards autonomously achieving a sufficient degree of stability. On the other hand, external reality becomes more pressing as the perceptual capacities gradually develop, and with them the first introjections. Fragments of reality are then introjected, and this gives rise to the process of integration between imitations and introjections – that is to say, to the first dawning of the ego.

------------------------------ 12 ------------------------------

The mask and the circle

Presented at a scientific meeting of the Centro Psicoanalitico di Bologna in September 1985 and published in the *Rivista di Psicoanalisi* (1986) XXII, 2, under the title 'La maschera e il cerchio'.

Consciousness and the mental continuum

On the basis of the knowledge of the dream-work we have acquired from *The Interpretation of Dreams* (Freud 1900) and later publications, I may begin by recalling that with respect to consciousness the manifest dream is the mask of the latent dream. The importance of this fact transcends the specificity of the dream-work and applies to everything we usually understand by consciousness, as opposed to everything that is not.

The dream is after all a particular state, in which this distinction appears obvious. However, the limits of the consciousness to which we customarily refer are not easy to define. What we experience as the state of consciousness appears to be capable of changing into different states, the most conspicuous of which is the state of dream consciousness, which we contrast with what we call the waking state. There may be other states in the non-REM phases of sleep. Others have at any rate been described. Beyond their distinguishing diversity – now precise and decisive, now blurred and barely perceptible – which is suggestive of a discontinuity in the psychical world, the possibility of moving from one state to another is indicative of a continuity in the mental sphere comparable to that of the physical world, in which there occur states that appear to be extremely different from one another, giving rise to an obvious discontinuity due solely to the fact that the phenomena of transition from one state to the other are not easily recognizable (the law of continuity).

177

The body–mind continuum

The present state of our knowledge admits of little doubt that the mental sphere can be conceived as a continuum. However, a difficulty of present-day research is that it is sometimes required to define where and how the mental continuum ceases to be such – in the sense that it borders, or even encroaches, on the biological – and where, conversely, what appears as biological in fact belongs to the mental sphere. I believe that in this connection we must distinguish, not the mind from the body – as philosophy, religion, and psychology on the one hand and medicine on the other did before the advent of psychoanalysis – but instead a *body–mind continuum* from a *mind–body continuum*, and a virtual area in which these two continua somehow overlap.

Plainly, in order to exist and function, the body does not have an absolute need for mental activity, while the latter is conceivable only in so far as a bodily organism exists and functions. But this does not imply that the body is separate from the mind; on the contrary, it means that a *body–mind continuum* exists, and this accounts for some of the great interest currently shown by psychoanalytic research in the forms and stages in which mental activity commences in the organism, and also for the still persisting error of considering mental activity in biological terms – an error to which the psychoanalysts themselves, especially in the United States, have in part contributed, and which has led many outside psychoanalysts to believe that psychoanalytic investigation is based on biological foundations. Only a few years ago, Freud was still described by an American author as the 'biologist of the mind' (Sulloway 1979). In the present state of our knowledge, it seems very likely that the body–mind continuum already begins to form during foetal life.

The mind–body continuum

Unlike the *body–mind continuum*, the *mind–body continuum* is the expression of a mental continuum that includes the body in the mind. In the mental continuum, the body exists only in so far as the mind exists and functions. Even when the mind is dissociated from the body, as occurs in certain forms of somatic pathology, it must be remembered that the dissociation is a mental operation and that the dissociated body is the body as understood mentally – that is, the body of the 'mind–body continuum'.

It follows, therefore, that psychoanalysis is not 'biological' but that it is extremely interested in the mental sense of the biological. When we say that the first sense of self is bodily, we mean that this is the *mental sense* of the bodily self. If this is clear, it also becomes clear that present-day psychoanalytic research on primitive mental activity and on the early organization of the mind does indeed touch upon phenomena at the confines of the biological, but with the sole aim of ascertaining how far the mental continuum extends, or rather, where and how in the area of overlap a biological phenomenon or process acquires a mental quality.

Primitive mental phenomena

It is legitimate to assert in this connection that mental phenomena recognizable as such exist from birth on. This means that the mental sphere is ready to function immediately upon full-term birth, because the body–mind continuum has previously formed. Psychoanalytic research on the area of overlap can therefore be approached from either the mind–body side or the body–mind side. An example of the former type of research is that which Frances Tustin (1984) has undertaken for many years in London with autistic children, and in particular her recent studies of autistic tactile *forms*, whereas the current research of Mario Bertolini (1984) in Italy, which compares the tactile sensory activity of premature babies with the equivalent pre-natal activity as revealed by ultrasound recordings, adopts the body–mind approach.

However, the characteristic feature of primitive mental phenomena is that they are rooted in the mental sense which certain bodily experiences acquire through the sensations arising from these experiences. In other words, it is the sensations which are translated into mental 'sense', or rather allow certain experiences to acquire a mental sense. In this way, from birth on, the mental sphere gradually and fragmentarily acquires the 'sense' of the body, which has nothing to do with the objective reality of the body but is very much bound up with the gradual organization of a first 'sense of self', which is necessarily bodily and necessarily fragmentary [see Chapter 8].

The circle

The first 'mental learning' thus consists in this primitive acquisition of a sense of self. I have described this process in detail elsewhere, showing among other things that it is closely connected with the primitive 'mental memory', which differs from the 'biological' memory. It is only at a certain point, after a 'basic mental organization' [see Chapter

11] can be said to have been formed (that is, after the sixth month), that the sense of self is reflected in the mind in a visual image, which may therefore be regarded as the first representation of the bodily self as an image, a first *form* of self. This form is round, and will be expressed graphically by a child as a circle (Gaddini 1959), as soon as the scribbling phase is over. The child will trace this circular image quite spontaneously, and it will also be the first image that the child is able to express graphically. This calls for some comments.

When a child draws a circular shape on a piece of paper for the first time, he *does not know* consciously what he is actually doing. But after he has drawn it, this form is perceived, exists in consciousness, and from then on becomes recognizable. As a result, the child will hence-forth be able to draw the same form whenever he wishes. In other words, consciousness will be able to make use of it. In descriptive terms, we may say that the child has achieved the capacity to draw a circular form and to recognize it as such. However, as we have learnt from Freud, a description, for all that it may be correct, is not the same as an explanation. We now know that this capacity is the end result of a long and complicated set of mental processes, no trace of which is to be found in the child's consciousness. What he *publicly makes known* of himself is what has entered into his consciousness in his internal administration – that is, *what he has made known* to himself. Note that this is not the representation of the bodily self through *the mental image* but only the *graphic representation* of that image. It is worth dwelling for a moment on the point that this graphic representation is only seem-ingly a simple or innate form and considering the meaning it comes to assume in consciousness.

The first point to be made is that this first graphic image is, by virtue of its very spontaneity, a child's earliest creative expression, and may therefore be regarded as the actual origin of creative expression in consciousness (but not of creativity, which has much more remote origins, in the early months of life). It is interesting to note, too, that this particular graphically represented *form* does not differ from the mental image of the bodily self which precedes it except by the concealment of the concrete sense that this image had in the mind. Now that it is deposited graphically in the external world, it is in effect detached from its mental sense. Creative expression thus begins with an abstract image (but one which is autobiographical, although this aspect is concealed).

To appreciate the true significance of this fact, it should be borne in mind that the child usually draws this image at the end of the second year of life, when the sense of self has become consciousness in the developing ego. However, this has not been reflected in *consciousness of self* in the image of the circle. Clearly, compared with the primitive image of the bodily self, which was an operation of the basic mental organization, the circle is an operation of the developing ego; it is a symbol, the first graphic symbol 'invented' by the child.

Digression on the symbol

Evidently, if it is to be possible for symbolic activity to begin, the mind must be capable of being no longer occupied exclusively with the body. This confirms a discovery of Winnicott's (1951b) – which is an integral part of the discovery of the transitional object – that is not taken sufficiently into account when the origin of the symbol is discussed. The transitional object already has this fundamental characteristic of not being part of the bodily self, as well as that of being found/invented by the child before the ego begins to structure itself, when the basic mental organization is still operative. What is lacking at this point, but commences with the transitional object, is the extraordinary economic capacity which the symbol created by the ego possesses (the transitional object is the first effective reducer of loss–of–self anxiety), and a clear recognition of the external world, in which to place and use the symbols created. Subsequently, the important fact is that the symbols can be produced in the ego and then learnt and used for reality purposes.

I do not know whether from the psychological viewpoint the circle can be regarded solely, or at all, as a geometrical figure. As stated, it is first and foremost a symbol, and in particular the symbol of a mental image, whereby an initial form was given in the basic mental organization to the bodily self, experienced through sensations. In the consciousness of the ego, however, it may well be that the first graphic symbol created by the child of the man may have subsequently given rise in the man into which the child grew to the development of other graphic symbols, abstract like the first symbol, and to the mathematical and geometrical elaboration of space and time. My point is that, once symbolic activity has begun, it may evolve scientifically, and this scientific evolution may apparently diverge from, but also coexist with, that of artistic creativity. The profound tendency towards reconstitution of the lost fusion may also lead to mystical idealization, the symbol of the circle then giving rise to magic and religious circle symbolism.

Be that as it may, what is important from the time of graphic representation of the circle, is the work the developing ego continues to do on the body, with quite different possibilities from those of the past. The new instruments of the ego are the perceptions, instead of the sensations. They enable the child to perceive the form of his own body in space, starting with the head and face. The child then begins to represent graphically what he perceives of himself. The circular image thus becomes the head, in which the mouth and eyes are represented. The child gradually comes to draw the familiar doll-like simplified human figure. And so on and so forth. Perceptions first of the mother's face and then of her person (separate from the person of the father) develop concomitantly.

This work of the ego removes the first mental image of the bodily self further and further from consciousness. The subsequent development of the ego and all the processes inherent in growth cause that image to recede to greater and greater depths and to become increasingly inaccessible. I would say that as a rule, for the consciousness of the ego, everything that has preceded it in the mind is considered to be a danger to its own structural functioning. There are, of course, valid reasons for this.

The ego between self and object

It is not a mere play on words to say that the natural task of the ego is primarily that of allowing the self to emerge out of itself – that is, to put the self in relation to the external world or, as we are accustomed to say, although anticipating matters somewhat, in relation to the object. The formation of the object is in fact a long process, which entirely occupies the second and third years of life. I believe that psychoanalysis has been wrong to date the Oedipus complex back to these years, in which I would speak only of the *primal-scene process* and the *triangular situation*. The importance of this phase will be clear from the above, because it is the phase in which the early development of the ego takes place, or, alternatively, is impeded to different extents, reduced, or arrested in positions intended no longer to put the self in relation to the object but – in the limit – to form a structure erected to defend a self damaged at the outset, to whose needs the ego thus ultimately finds itself predominantly subjugated. The survival of the self becomes the sole guarantee of survival of the ego.

Pathology of the structure and dream consciousness

This means that, in the period of its own development, the ego must also organize any pathology of its own, from the most common to the most severe. Later, one of the tasks of the dream consciousness will be to block access to consciousness of the most dangerous contents during sleep, either by disguising them so that they become incomprehensible or by interrupting them and generating anxiety. During the process of analysis, however, I would say that it may become one of the main functions of the dream consciousness to act as a bridge, allowing the most remote contents to draw gradually nearer to consciousness. There are thus cases in which the most dreaded primitive pathology of the self – the feared madness in the structure – may come to be represented in dreams. The same mental image of the bodily self, with its primitive pathology, may in this way be found in the dreams of adults, usually at very advanced states in their analyses.

The round image in dreams; primitive anxiety

The representations concerned are usually analogical (I am deliberately not calling them 'symbolic'), and therefore highly diversified, but they are all clearly round in form, and have in common the fact that the dreamer usually 'knows' in his dream consciousness, often with great anxiety, that this form is himself.

The anxiety aroused in these cases is particularly intense. The alarm to which it gives rise is understandable if its primitive quality is considered: these dreams very closely concern early loss-of-self anxiety, the most primitive anxiety there is and, I would say, the matrix of subsequent forms of anxiety. The anxiety is thus about 'falling to pieces' (that is, of being unable to keep together the fragments that make up the self) and about being lost for ever in a limitless space or sea, or about being annihilated by falling for ever. [Examples of dreams showing the presence of such fantasies can be found in Chapters 9 and 10.] This primogenial anxiety normally arises in the self immediately after the catastrophic experience of separation, and may therefore be regarded as the first elementary operation of the basic mental organization, intended to safeguard the survival of the separate self by a continuous but necessary painful vigil. Before the separation, the fragments of the developing self were held together by fusion with the mother-breast; after the separation and the catastrophic experience, keeping the residual fragments together becomes an immediate and imperative task of the separate self, on which its own survival depends. It is at this point, that of the separate self, that the basic mental organization commences.

In this terrible and fundamental way, an individual is psychologically born. Long before the complex structural organization of the ego, with its conscious, preconscious and unconscious aspects, becomes available and capable of mentally acquiring the dimension of time, the duration of life, and the reality of death, there exists from the beginning in the elementary mental organization of the infantile self the anxiety of loss-of-self, bound up with the mental sense of annihilation and survival.

Separation and vulnerability

It is readily understandable that, because it is so elementary, primitive mental functioning is particularly vulnerable, the more so the sooner after biological birth, and that it is also very vulnerable indeed during the process of separation – namely, at the time of psychological birth. A premature separation for this reason alone becomes traumatic, and the earlier the trauma, the more serious it is. However, a separation may be equally damaging if, although formally occurring at the appropriate time, it was never accepted by the mother, and hence by the child.

In fact, when infantile loss-of-self anxiety takes on a pathological quality, it becomes more or less seriously pathogenic for the entire subsequent process of development. The early development of the ego will thereby be damaged in various ways. Certain psychophysical syndromes, which may already arise in the first months of life as an expression of the pathological situation, may then persist throughout life in the form of somatic illness, limiting the domain of the ego. Any moves by the ego towards growth, and in particular the processes of integration, are impeded, curtailed, or completely prevented by the pathological loss-of-self anxiety, which causes any change in the already precarious situation to appear as a new and final catastrophe. In a word, the structural organization of the ego will find itself in the position of having to settle accounts more or less painfully with the previous basic mental organization, just as the latter had to settle accounts with the way things had gone before, from birth to the process of separation.

In general, psychopathology may therefore be said to originate in the basic mental organization and to organize and manifest itself in the structure of the ego. Exceptions are certain psychophysical syndromes, which may become organized and manifest themselves already in the basic mental organization, or even before. As for the ego, there is a difference between the time when the pathology is organized – generally, the second and third years of life, precisely the time that corresponds to the first structuring of the ego – and the time when it becomes manifest, which varies considerably, from infancy to adolescence and adulthood.

Another point must, however, be made. While the psychophysical syndromes may arise before mental activity is structured, mental illness in its most devastating aspects directly threatens the ego from the moment when the latter begins to become structured. Psychosis, whose origins pre-date the structuring of the ego, may become organized and may thus break out irrevocably as soon as the early basic mental organization is formed or even before.

The mask

It follows, in my view, that all the rest of the psychopathology we find structured in the ego, in all its forms, is the result of the ego's capacity to confront the threat that loomed at the beginning. The counterpart of loss-of-self anxiety in the ego is anxiety about its de-structuring, the fear of madness. Paradoxically, the pathology structured in the ego is intended to safeguard the ego's structure. In reality, however, the cost of this safeguarding is inversely proportional to the stability of the structure. During sleep, by way of the dream consciousness, the ego seems to allow itself to become psychotic, while its own structure remains unharmed. The nocturnal psychosis is in fact a temporary mask which serves to keep the true psychosis latent. It would not be too far from the truth to say that the whole of non-psychotic psychopathology in its many different forms and aspects is a mask for the psychosis latent in everyone. Unlike dreams, however, individual psychopathology is a permanent mask — the face that everyone possesses.

Changes in psychoanalytic patients up to the present day

Given at the 4th Symposium of the International Psychoanalytical Association, Taunton, April 1984, and published in *Changes in Analysts and their
Training*, Monograph No. 4, International Psychoanalytical Association,
under the title 'Whether and how our patients have changed up to the
present day'. It was published in the *Rivista di Psicoanalisi* (1984) XXX, 4,
under the title 'Se e come sono cambiati i nostri pazienti fino ai nostri giorni'.

Introduction: objectivity and objectification

If it is true, as we believe today, that the individual is not the automatic
result of his genetic constitution but is, rather, the result of his development – that is, of his interaction with the environment in which he is
born and grows up – then we must accept that individual psychopathology changes, as does the human individual, in accordance with
the socio-cultural environment in which it is formed (Rangell 1975).
In fact, the epidemiology of mental illness varies quantitatively and
qualitatively from one society to another and in one and the same
society in time, as that society gradually changes. However, the evaluation of these variations is very difficult, because it calls for an 'objective'
description of the mental disorders presented to us, such that they can
be catalogued and classified in a statistically usable form. In other
words, it is necessary to *invent* statistical diagnostics.

The most conspicuous recent example of such an approach is the
DSM-III of the American Psychiatric Association (1980). This necessarily entails serious distortion and coercion of a reality which is by its
nature subjective and therefore 'astatistical' to turn it into something
objective and amenable to statistics, while at the same time being, as
those responsible for DSM-III say, 'atheoretical'. What is important is

the description of a particular mental disorder as it manifests itself, and the assumption that it must manifest itself in this way in every individual. 'A common misconception' – as the authors correctly point out – 'is that a classification of mental disorders classifies individuals, when actually what are being classified are disorders that individuals have.' This means that the individual does not exist as such. He acquires significance only as the 'carrier' and not as the author of a given mental disorder. Consequently, 'for most of the DSM-III disorders . . . the etiology is unknown'.

All this is, of course, poles apart from psychoanalysis, according to which the study of individual psychopathology requires that the situation in which the phenomena are observed should essentially be the clinical situation – that is, one which is inherently 'experiential' and not 'experimental'. The experience in this situation is inevitably reciprocal and in no way comparable to what happens in a laboratory, where there is an observer on the one hand and phenomena to be observed on the other. Hence the data accruing from research on the human mind can never be defined as 'objective', and must for this reason be continuously and as far as possible 'objectified'. This necessitates prolonged training. The personal analysis of the future psychoanalyst and the years of supervision of his early clinical experience should lay the foundations for his achievement of an objectification capacity of his own. After training, however, years of clinical experience are required for this capacity, first of all, to reach a level of reliable sufficiency and, eventually, to develop further.

I should like to distinguish two stages in this necessary process of objectification which every psychoanalyst must undergo. The first is specifically limited to a given clinical situation – that is, to the objectification of subjective experience in a particular therapeutic relationship. The more the analyst succeeds here, the better he will be in a position to allow the patient gradually to objectify his own experience in the clinical situation. Hence this first stage is an essential component of the psychoanalytical process. The second stage is that of objectification at the level of research and scientific communication. Admittedly, therapy and research coincide in psychoanalysis, but it is equally true that, much more often than might be thought, research fails to be pursued and communicated. The transition from the first to the second stage plainly demands effort and dedication different from one's investment in the therapeutic experience. Therapeutic objectification is carried out together with the analysand, but scientific objectification is done by oneself; again, still on the emotional level, scientific communication involves self-exposure and self-definition *vis-à-vis* others. In intellectual terms, it involves complex operations, such as the establishment of possible connections between data gathered selectively from those objectified in different clinical situations, or the performance of logical operations leading to possible theoretical formulations which are based on previously objectified clinical data and preclude subjective involvement in the given clinical situation.

For all this, as the twentieth century approaches its end and psychoanalysis is about to complete its first century, psychoanalysts may legitimately wonder whether and how their patients have changed over the course of time. They do not, of course, put this question in a statistically objective form. In asking it, they know that they must take into account first of all the ways in which the psychoanalysts have changed *vis-à-vis* their patients. Second, they must remember that the psychoanalysts' patients, apart from every other aspect, are an absolute minority compared with the number of 'psychological' patients in a society, just as the psychoanalysts are an absolute minority compared with the psychotherapists of all kinds and origins who have emerged since the appearance of psychoanalysts. Third, they must consider that psychoanalysis has had a quite disproportionate impact on our culture compared with the number of psychoanalysts existing in it, and that if what is happening in that culture could be represented in a single individual, it would have to be recognized that this 'culture-individual' is imbued with a profound and irreducible ambivalence towards the psychoanalysts.[1]

Hence, before some of the 'potential' patients actually become patients of the psychoanalysts, it must be remembered that the relationship between them and the psychoanalysts is mediated by the culture of the society in which they live. I shall endeavour as far as possible to describe this mediated relationship as it appears to me, and show how it in some way operates to select the psychoanalysts' patients. I shall also examine some massive and apparently objective changes periodically encountered by the psychoanalysts due to extraordinary and long-lasting social upheavals, and shall try to show what part has actually been played by external events in these occasions.

Another point which will become obvious is the importance, in spite of all countervailing factors, of the gradual and more tacit evolution of patients with time, as the psychoanalysts' diagnostic capacity has improved and the field of their therapeutic intervention has gradually widened. A fact which is perhaps worrying, which must, however, be considered by psychoanalysts, is the clear trend displayed by individual psychopathology to become more severe over the course of time, up to the present day. This poses a serious problem for the immediate future. I shall consider this problem in my conclusion.

The culture mediating between psychoanalysts and patients

It is an established fact that there is an absolutely disproportionate discrepancy between the relatively small number of psychoanalysts in a society and the cultural impact of psychoanalysis on that society. I tend to see this discrepancy as a defensive manifestation of alert and alarm on the part of our culture when confronted with psychoanalysis. It resembles the behaviour of some patients at the beginning of their analysis. They tell everyone they are in analysis, talk about psycho-analysis everywhere, try to start discussions on psychoanalysis in society, defend it vigorously against any attacker, and so forth. The cultural impact of psychoanalysis becomes comprehensible when it is realized that a psychological dimension never existed in any society before psychoanalysis made its entry.

The debate is gradually becoming more serious and more cautious among intellectuals, who are, of course, the principal vehicle for cultural dissemination as well as, in a way, for the spreading of informa-tion at a profound level. After a moment's disorientation, the culture's defences are reorganized, new and appropriate weapons are forged to confront what appears to the unconscious consensus of the majority as an enemy not comparable with any other known enemy – one capable of laying bare and disarming the security defences deployed to guard the deep and dangerous places which had been intended to remain forever inaccessible and unknown. Yet the impact remains, bearing witness to society's need to stay constantly awake and alert. All the same, as a result of this impact, superficial psychoanalytical information is tending to spread widely. In this way, psychoanalysis seems to be conquering language, usage, and many of the outward aspects of life. People use psychoanalytical jargon in interpersonal relationships; they interpret one another's slips and behaviour on the spot, and so on. Behind all these manifestations lies a profound and generalized defence, whereby everyone magically becomes an analyst.

I have come to recognize this defence, when it occurs in the analytic situation, as one of the most insidious and formidable of all, and I have called it 'imitative transference'. According to the biologists, imitation is a mental operation which is exclusive to man. I have no difficulty in accepting the truth of this thesis. Imitation in animals is an instinctive behaviour and not a mental operation. However, the common error is to believe that a mental operation consists solely in copying what someone else does so as to achieve a certain object. In human beings, this is accomplished only if the imitation is complemented by the urge to internalize – that is, by introjection. It is this integration of imitation and introjection which leads to the most highly evolved capacity for

189

identification. Imitation is an elementary defence with the function of protecting the self. Introjection, on the other hand, implies the capacity to recognize the object as external, and oneself as separate from the object – hence the primitive dynamic of eating and being eaten, described in different ways by Bertram Lewin (1950) and Melanie Klein (1952). One introjects instead of incorporating, to make what is outside oneself become part of oneself. Hence introjection is also a magic and primitive defence, but its omnipotence is limited by the anxiety of losing the object for ever after incorporating it and of not being able to survive without the object (in my opinion, this is the first appearance of the sense of real dependency). Two types of omnipotence should therefore be distinguished: in the first, which is total, one flees from instinctual anxiety by magically becoming the object; in the second, which is instinctual and magically more limited, one is obliged to recognize the object and to encounter the anxiety of real dependency for one's own survival.

I consider that imitation plays an essential part in the relationship between psychoanalysis and the culture which surrounds it. The 'imitative transference', which I referred to above, calls for a minimum of specification for the same reason and because it has to do with patients and candidates. In analysis it is formidable because it is a potent and tacit defence. It is insidious because it presents itself with all the most convincing aspects of a desirable positive transference. For this reason it is all the more insidious in a training analysis. It may take a long time before the analyst realizes that the patient (or candidate) is constantly imitating him. He uses his words and turns of phrase, assumes his attitudes, and imitates his style of dress. The biggest difficulty arises because the patient imitates him particularly in his absence – that is, outside the consulting room. For example, he quite often meets people previously unknown to him who, after only a few minutes, tell him their life story and problems. The patient listens seriously and in silence, making the same 'ummmm' noises as his analyst, and if necessary intervenes in the same way as his analyst would have done. Sometimes the patient describes some of these episodes to the analyst, expecting to arouse his approval. In some cases the analyst comes to hear through other people that the patient (candidate) is behaving outside the analysis as if he were himself, using his own phrases and vocal inflexions. In this way, the analyst is tacitly and constantly relegated to becoming an instrument of the patient's (or candidate's) own needs and is annihilated as a separate object. As long as the patient (candidate) succeeds in his magic and omnipotent way in 'being' the analyst, he will not run the risk of encountering the problems which would arise if he were to recognize the analyst as separate and different from himself (introjection, conflict, anxiety, real dependency, and, above all, loss of magic omnipotence).

Conversely, until the analyst is able to realize that what appears to be transference is a massive defence preventing the transference, he will continue to feel himself the object of a constant, admiring attention, which will induce him to feel favourably disposed and approving towards the patient (candidate). Hence the counterpart of the patient's (candidate's) urge to gratify him and gain his approval will be the actual gratification of the analyst and his attitude of approval.

When we come to think of it, all this bears an extraordinary resemblance to what happens in the culture of a society when a group of analysts appears in it. Variations in the local characteristics of the culture and the time at which psychoanalysis appeared in the countries concerned do not alter the substance of the interactional phenomena which then commence. At the centre of these phenomena is the massive use of imitation, which allows anyone who uses it to 'become' an analyst. At this point everyone magically possesses psychoanalysis and is on equal terms with everyone else – in particular, with psychoanalysts, who are therefore not 'different'. Imitation is used particularly in intellectual defences, and just as a child at school who uses imitation instead of introjection can learn quickly (but without being able to retain what he learns for long) and go to the top of the class, the imitators of the psychoanalysts hold forth about psychoanalysis in newspapers, journals, and learned tomes; they organize conventions and national and international congresses – just as if they were born psychoanalysts.

Another characteristic of imitation is rapid 'contact' with others, in place of the impossible 'relationship'. I believe that imitation is the basis of the identity of the crowd, where the term 'identity' means 'identicality', 'everyone the same', 'all as one and one as all'. What are imitatively called congresses are more often crowds of intellectuals of every kind and degree and age, united by the magic use of the imitative defence. The name of Sigmund Freud resounds everywhere, as if each person were thoroughly acquainted with him. In reality, actual knowledge of Freud is the least important thing. But pronouncing his name magically gives value to oneself. In Italy, in the last few years, once the name of Freud was spoken, that of Lacan followed almost in the same breath – but the speaker's knowledge of Lacan was no less illusory than that of Freud. It is simply that by 'being' Lacan, one was allowed to say or write unintelligible things freely in the most obscure way possible. One of Lacan's ideas immediately became clear to all – his assertion (in the way it was understood) that anyone is free to decide to become an analyst. This is a legitimation of the imitative defence, by

191

which Lacan himself was eventually swamped, and against which he tried to react before he died by disavowing his followers and through them the entire cultural movement which had made use of him. In fact, naming Freud and *becoming* Lacan was the mirror image of what Lacan had done, calling himself the *école freudienne*.

A final characteristic of imitation is that it favours imposture. Phyllis Greenacre (1958a) has given us an excellent study of the personality of the impostor, who takes the possibilities of imitation to the utmost limit, having no capacity for identification and no sense of self. He therefore organizes imitative representations and lives the part concerned; to be true, however, these representations must appear so to the outside world. This compels the impostor to construct a whole series of imitative situations, each of which must support the others, until a kind of imitative coherence is created. Sooner or later, reality often exposes the imposture, and at this point, depending on the situation, the impostor may suffer legal sanctions. But more often he simply moves elsewhere and commences his obligatory imitative activities afresh. Hence, in order for an impostor to be unmasked as such, it is necessary for what he purports to be to exist authentically in external reality. However, it is precisely this which enables the impostor to act out in this way. He relies on his artefacts being taken for the genuine article for a shorter or longer period before his deception is exposed. The following account is a good example of this type of imposture.

During the 1960s in Italy, a young Jew managed to complete an entire training analysis and already had a number of patients in supervision before it was discovered that he was an impostor. His ability to gratify the analyst was out of the ordinary. His imitative transference had never been recognized – on the contrary he had become the training analyst's favourite candidate. The training analyst was old, also Jewish, and his family had Austrian origins. German was his second language. Among other things, the 'candidate' produced in his analysis memories or dreams in which vague and confused memories appeared – which made them all the more fascinating to the analyst – of a German concentration camp to which he said he had been taken. It was only after the end of the analysis that the analyst was forced by incontrovertible information *from the outside world* to realize that he had been the victim of an impostor.

The responses generated by psychoanalysis in culture are such that analogous manifestations in an individual would be considered pathological. The problem is that, as Freud clearly understood (1930), interpersonal relations in a society have progressed much less than the relationship which one may have with oneself or which may exist between two individuals. I believe that the foundations of interpersonal relations in society, which cannot yet be regarded as being concerned with objects, lie in the individual mental activity preceding the functioning of the ego, which we are now beginning to get to know. But these relations are a function of the ego. The mental activity which precedes it even if it is individual, is not sufficiently individualized.

This means that a mental activity which may be at the root of an individual's pathology may, when confused with the individual in the group, simply become the basis of his social functioning, and this may deprive the individual pathology of its sense. If thousands of people take part in a peace march, the crowd forms part of the individual just as the individual forms part of the crowd, and everyone with good reason feels 'normal'. Any pathology in each individual is temporarily outweighed by the strengthening of the basic mental activity which is imitative and united. On the other hand, when the individual confronts an environmental demand by himself – an examination or any other reality task – it is his individual (structural) pathology which is strengthened. Even in the common situation of a reality task which faces everyone, each person is alone in having to confront it.

This may account for the particular defence to which pathologically 'immature' persons resort in order to avoid the fact that the demands of the outside world give rise to anxiety. It is a defence which takes the apparent form of 'socialization', and is in reality an attempt at 'concealment in the social' of one's own individual pathology. Like all defences, it may be relatively effective or ineffective. It may fail as a result of events in external reality, on which such individuals depend in ways which closely resemble infantile dependency.

My point is, of course, that the relationship between the individual and the society in which he lives is largely determined by the individual's relationship with objective reality. The problem is to estimate to what extent an individual (today perhaps represented by a growing majority) is compelled to use social reality as a mother in the service of his own infantile needs, and to what extent, conversely, he is sufficiently structured to be able to sustain effective autonomy in acknowledgement of real dependency. The defences deployed in the former case often tend to organize an apparent autonomy, which could be defined as autarkic. Compared with autonomy, autarky is based on need, and on imitative, magic, and omnipotent functioning.

The advent of psychoanalysis in culture, precisely because its impact on that culture is like that of a stone falling into a pool, also gives rise to a change in the relations between the culture and the individuals participating in it. Psychoanalytical knowledge of the internal world reinforces anxiety about the dangers threatening from within in everyone outside the circle of the psychoanalysts. By joining in the cultural response to psychoanalysis described above, each person can relieve his own anxiety, ostensibly by valid operations of participation in external reality. Of course, this does not prevent other individuals (usually a minority) who are more autonomous and less afraid of themselves from engaging in the cultural debate in more conscious and realistic ways. This minority probably contributes in some way to weakening the defence of concealment in the social manifested by individual pathology, at least in some people who, having become more painfully aware of their pathology, dispense with cultural mediation and enter into a direct relationship with the analyst.

In other cases, this happens because the defence of self-concealment in the social, kept up for a time, eventually proves insufficient for reasons associated with the individual's pathology. Still others, before this can happen, act out the unconscious imitative fantasy and endeavour to become therapists, without expending anything of themselves. There are many inferior analysts who subject others to pseudo-analysis, not with therapeutic intent but with the common aim of making the other into a therapist. When they have reached the stage of acting out, the problem becomes that of perfecting it. In this way, the imitation of psychoanalytic training begins. And so on. Finally, there are those who embark on analysis with a 'real' psychoanalyst, having decided consciously that this is the 'serious' way to become a psychotherapist. These are in general pseudo-patients, and imitative transference is virtually the rule. The task for an analyst who does not wish to aid and abet a delinquent unconscious plan may be no less arduous than the similar task which may be encountered in a training analysis.

Psychoanalysts and their patients

It is my impression that the defences organized by the ego of each individual during growth to achieve as far as possible participation in the adult world, were upset for the first time during this century by the First World War. Psychoanalysts then observed a change in their patients for the first time (Eitingon 1922). It is clear that the individual structures most subject to risk must have been worst hit. However, I believe that psychoanalytic experience does not show that the structures least subject to risk are the majority. The pathology which emerged from the First World War was considered by psychoanalysts primarily as hysterical (conversion and anxiety hysteria) and phobic. The abundance of clinical material indeed favoured the trend for the psychoanalysts of the time to study the two neuroses, and also anxiety, and these studies led Freud (1926) to his second theory of anxiety. In reality, it seems to me that legitimate doubts are now arising about the diagnoses of the time, considering that the range of possible diagnoses was greatly limited by the contemporary state of psychoanalytic knowledge. For example, it was not then possible to distinguish a psychosomatic event from a conversion symptom. The apparently protean aspect of hysteria could have been largely due to pathological manifestations which would not at all suggest hysteria to us today. The shift of interest from neurosis to character had not yet taken place. Psychosis was in general not mentioned.

There were, of course, many changes in the twenty years between the two wars, from the surprising re-formulation of the theory of the instincts (Freud 1920) and the revolutionary structural theory (Freud 1923) to the recognition and study of the mechanisms of defence of the ego (A. Freud 1936), the transference and, more tacitly, the counter-transference, and in general the study of the theory of technique (Fenichel 1941), with particular emphasis being placed on interpretation. This is not to mention the compulsory institution of training along the lines of the Berlin Psychoanalytical Institute and the growth in the number of psychoanalysts and the geographical area of dissemination of psychoanalysis. I tend to attribute the shift of interest to the study of the so-called 'character disorders' (Reich 1933) more to the growth in clinical experience of the psychoanalysts than to a change in the patients. At the same time, there was renewed interest in narcissism (Freud 1914), and interest focused for the first time on psychogenic somatic disorders as distinct from conversion symptoms (Alexander 1939). 'Psychosomatics' extended the more limited concept of 'organ neurosis' to the study of the personality. Object theories arose and began to develop in Europe (Fairbairn, Melanie Klein) as did the psychoanalytic psychology of the ego in America (H. Hartmann and colleagues). Child psychoanalysis (Anna Freud 1929; Melanie Klein 1932) and psychoanalytic psychotherapy of the psychoses also arose. This twenty-year period ended with the death of Freud.

There now followed a second attack from the outside on the defences of the ego – namely, the Second World War – and once again the psychoanalysts observed a change in their patients at the end of the war. In my opinion, this finding was very similar in significance to the change observed at the end of the First World War. Even if the diagnostic and technical level of psychoanalysts was now much more advanced than it had been then, the change observed consisted principally in a quantitative increase in the syndrome in which they had been most interested at the beginning of the war – namely, the character neuroses. The diagnostic field was in any case much wider, covering not only character neuroses but also perversion (Gillespie 1952), narcissism, somatic disorders, and so on. Hysteria continued to impress, but the evolution of the concept, too, was indicative of a change in the psychoanalysts rather than in the patients. For example, an 'hysterical character' was now recognized (Siegman 1954), and at the same time the fact that hysterical symptoms could be found in other types of personality. The existence of 'oral regression' in hysteria was also recognized. The study of character neuroses was in fact arousing renewed interest in orality, but in a different way from the studies which followed the First World War (Glover 1925). Oral regression was now frequently observable in cases of character neuroses. Primitive orality was now described in dynamic terms by B. Lewin (1950) and by M. Klein and her school, and there was also interest in narcissism, perversion, and psychosis. Plainly, the pathology of persons with character neuroses, child analysis, and psychoanalytic psychotherapy of the psychoses were revealing to the psychoanalysts deeper and more remote levels of activity than those hitherto known. Again, the study of the counter-transference, greatly enriched by the institution of the supervision of candidates, contributed greatly from 1950 onwards (Heimann 1950) to the achievement of a more thorough understanding of the psychoanalytical relationship.

Special mention should be made of the fact that, also in the immediate post-war period, there was a new concept of the 'self' (Hartmann et al. 1947; Hartmann 1950), and this was to play an important part in the subsequent development of psychoanalysis. Hartmann's intention was to cleanse the ego (the principal subject of his study) of everything which did not fundamentally belong to it and which was constantly confusing its definition. As distinct from the ego, the 'self' is the result of the whole formed by the psychic structure and the body. Images of the self may arise in the ego, but the ego is not to be confused with the self.

During those post-war years, D.W. Winnicott (1958) carried out his own psychoanalytic research on children and adult patients, and gradually discovered and described a primitive and elementary mental activity preceding the functioning of the ego and the other psychic agencies. For this reason, he referred to this first expression of psychic life by the term 'self'. Hence it may be said that whereas Hartmann wanted to distinguish the ego from the self, Winnicott's aim was to describe a self and distinguish it from the ego. Hartmann was endeavouring in this way to perfect Freud's structural theory; Winnicott was conducting a systematic psychoanalytic enquiry into early infancy, which led to new discoveries being placed alongside those of Freud. Other authors (Greenacre 1958b; E. Gaddini 1969) were inde-

196

pendently proceeding in the same direction – the discovery and exploration of an as yet unstructured mental area.

This was in my opinion the most advanced psychoanalytic research in the twenty years from 1950 to 1970. What happened after the death of Freud was that research was conditioned by Freud's final formulation of psychoanalytic theory – the theory of the instincts (1920) on the one hand, and the structural theory (1923) on the other. This inherited dichotomy was paralleled by a dichotomy in research: on the one hand, the development of a psychoanalytic psychology of the ego, conceived and directed by H. Hartmann, and on the other the development of a theory of instinctual relations with the object, conceived and directed by M. Klein, which had its origins, provocatively as it seemed, in a total acceptance of the controversial death instinct. Hartmann's research was primarily theoretical and was dominated by the fundamental concern that Freud's theoretical formulations were not scientifically acceptable. Hartmann therefore considered that he must amend and perfect them, starting from a scientifically valid theoretical model, which was the biological model. It may be objected that Hartmann's attitude here was based on a mistaken methodological approach. No scientific discipline can theorize on the basis of a theoretical model which is alien to it, as is the model of another scientific discipline. If this were to happen, we should have to conclude that the former, for its part, is not a scientific discipline. But according to R. Schafer (1970), this is precisely what Hartmann thought.

Another objection that may be made to Hartmann is that he considered that theory should precede and inform clinical experience, and not the other way round as Freud thought. In other words, Hartmann did not consider that a scientific theory worthy of the name is built upon experiential data, and that in the study of the human mind, these data can only be gathered from the clinical situation. It is obvious that a theory constructed in this way will turn to clinical experience for preliminary understanding, but this also implies that it is confronted with clinical experience, which may confirm it or amend it.

A final possible objection to Hartmann is that he arbitrarily postulated the existence of an aggressive instinct, not confirmed by any scientific enquiry, with the sole intention of substituting a scientifically (biologically) acceptable concept for Freud's last formulations on the life and death instincts, which he found unacceptable, and that he equally arbitrarily decreed that the vicissitudes of the supposed aggressive instinct were entirely similar to those of the libido (A. Freud 1972; see also Chapter 2).

Unlike Hartmann, Melanie Klein did not start in her research from arbitrary postulates about aggression but simply adopted the contro-versial death instinct without any discussion. [A detailed discussion of these issues will be found in Chapter 2, 'Aggression and the pleasure principle', where the author argued that Melanie Klein and her followers have accumulated impressive clinical evidence on how aggression is at work at the beginning of life, adding that there is nothing in the large volume of work of these analysts to confirm or deny the Freudian conception of the death instinct.]

At any rate, apart from the problem of a theoretical formulation of aggression, which still remains open, it can be said that unlike H. Hartmann, M. Klein and her group always based their theory on clinical experience. If they never put the theoretical problem to them-selves as regards aggression, this is presumably because they considered the Freudian theoretical formulation of the death instinct to be valid. On the other hand, they constructed theories on the development of object relations which are important additions to the theoretical field of psychoanalysis. Since these theories are based on data from clinical experience, they can be modified only by subsequent clinical experi-ence – that is, by subsequent knowledge.

This is what is, in fact, in my opinion, happening. For example, the Kleinian psychoanalysts have placed the origin of the relation to the object at the moment of birth. The breast is immediately an object for the newborn, even if a 'part-object', and is therefore invested from the outset with instinctual charges and the associated conflicts. This pre-supposes an ego, albeit primitive.

A consequence of the dissemination of these Kleinian theories is that phenomena, which are in reality much more advanced (starting from 'projective identification') and call for the functioning of a psychic structure which is not yet in existence, are still described as being neonatal or very close to birth.

Now, however, we can take it for granted – following the research of Winnicott and other psychoanalysts – that the object and the relation to the object are formed gradually, in parallel with the infantile formation of the self, during a period which precedes the phenomena described by the Kleinian theories; and that the processes of that period, which are intrinsically elementary, do not yet call for a mental structure, and still less for an instinctual activity and conflictual experi-ences. Following a different route, and starting from primitive percep-tion, I demonstrated the mental priority of sensations (prior to structure) over perceptions (beginning of structure) and described the origin and pre-structural functioning of imitations (associated with sensations) as opposed to introjections (associated with perceptions); this led me to the same conclusions as Winnicott as to the absence of instinctuality and of any kind of conflictuality in these processes. Hence the argument that used to be opposed to the Kleinian theories – that there was in principle an objectless phase – was no less inexact than the Kleinian theory that the ego and the object are present at birth.

It should be remembered that post-Kleinian psychoanalytic research has been conducted by individual psychoanalysts, unaware of one another's work. In using the term 'post-Kleinian', I am referring not so much to the chronology of the research as to its intentions and results. In this sense, even the systematic research of M. Mahler and the less systematic but exceptionally acute and illuminating research of P. Greenacre, both in the United States, can be regarded as post-Hartmannian. What is chronologically post-Hartmannian in the United States (R. Schafer on the one hand, and H. Kohut and O. Kernberg on the other) appears to me to be not so much new research as the necessary but difficult attempt at liberation from the heavy shadow of H. Hartmann.

The characteristics which unite the new workers can be defined as follows: (a) their research is personal; (b) none of them has felt the need to surround himself with followers and to contend as a group with other psychoanalysts; (c) their research focuses on the very earliest days of life, when the mind–body problem is absolutely dominant and a psychic structure is not yet present.

In this sense, as it happens, the data afforded by the new psycho-analytic research completely bear out what Freud (1914) had supposed to be necessary: 'We are bound to suppose that a unity comparable to the ego cannot exist in the individual from the start, the ego has to be developed.' The new research concentrated on infantile psychosis and on borderline and narcissistic patients, who could often during the 1960s be regarded as suffering from serious character disorders, as cases of latent psychosis, or as psychotics.

This is how an eminent American scholar and research worker, P. Greenacre (1966), described on the basis of her own experience the difficult diagnostic problem which, as early as the beginning of the 1960s, faced an analyst who was confronting the new situations, which still escaped the attention of the conservative analyst:

> The group of patients on whom I shall concentrate, however, does not belong to the anxiety hysterias or other anxiety and phobic states or the compulsive neuroses, which form the bulk of the conservative analyst's practice. Probably some clinicians would call them psycho-pathic or at least impulse-ridden characters. But in general they are not conspicuously impulse-ridden except under the pressure of analysis, and even there it is mainly within the transference

relationship. Others would tend to put them in that general group of the 'borderline' cases. But this seems too often not to define where the borderline approximately lies, or what is partially divided from what by it. I have thought that some were character neuroses with special deformations of the ego development. But I have also thought that some might be cases of major hysteria, a group which we have thought of as hardly existing any longer. It is possible that this is a clinical group that does exist but has been excluded from our vision by reclassification and the difficulty of their treatment. . . . It might be thought that these patients were psychotic from the way in which emotions entirely incongruous to the setting in which they are expressed are allowed to color the total picture and to dominate the behaviour usually without any apparent even superficial insight into their inappropriateness. Certainly the psychotic patient distorts reality in the interest of his displaced emotional reactions. But if the distortion invades the sensitive transference relationship, it generally has colored and continues to color aspects of reality relationships elsewhere as well. In these patients, reality outside of the trans-ference relationship is hardly at all involved or impaired.

(1966: 149)

It was only after the social upheavals of the last years of the 1960s that analysts were forced to note, for the third time this century, that the patients had changed. Instead of character neuroses, the majority of patients in the 1970s were borderline cases and narcissistic personalities. On this occasion too, it is clear that what was considered to be a 'change' was primarily a quantitative phenomenon. There had been an absolute increase in the psychopathological forms which had already emerged in the previous decade, on such a scale that a number of psychoanalysts concentrated their attention, and in some cases their research, on them.

Conclusion: the problem

On the basis of our comments on the previous 'changes', the following initial conclusions should be drawn:

1 The patients are changing continuously, even – and particularly – if the psychoanalysts, who are themselves continuously changing, do not notice this as a general and 'objective' phenomenon.
2 When particular external events play havoc with the life and organ-ization of society over a period of years – as has happened no less than three times during this century – this seems to catalyse and

200

trigger in constitutionally weaker individuals the expression of a psychopathology which would under normal conditions of life have been better, if not entirely, contained and therefore less conspicuous.

3 The pathology which emerges as a consequence of exceptional external situations is never 'new' and unforeseeable; the syndromes concerned are normally ones which had increasingly become a focus of interest for psychoanalysts in the period leading up to these situations but which, as a result of the trigger events, become fully manifest and assume, as it were, epidemic proportions; hence this is what is new and unforeseeable compared with the normal situation.

4 It is therefore legitimate to say that exceptional external events have on each occasion compelled psychoanalysts to take stock of the changes in progress in individual psychopathology, thereby in effect providing objective confirmation of the results of their clinical experience.

It may be added that sufficient time has now elapsed to permit a retrospective view of the changes which have taken place in both patients and psychoanalysts. To sum up, it seems to me that, as regards the patients, there has been a progressive expansion of psychopathology, in the sense of the variety of forms which can be recognized and diagnosed, and a progressive deepening of this psychopathology, in that the aetiological and pathogenic factors which can be identifed have become increasingly remote and profound, and therefore capable of influencing the development of the whole personality. The psychoanalysts, for their part, have gradually refined their diagnostic and technical capacity and thereby widened the range of indications for therapeutic intervention. It is a fact that psychoanalysts today are as a matter of course treating patients who would for a long time have been considered inaccessible to psychoanalytical therapy.

It is at this point that the problem is posed. The problem is to discover the direction in which the forms of individual psychopathology are evolving. The conclusions that can be drawn from our review of the last few decades seem explicit enough. The prevailing forms show a trend towards increasing severity. The objective test represented not by the psychoanalysts but by exceptional external events has shown the prevailing forms to be, first, hysteria; second, character neuroses; and third, borderline forms and narcissistic personalities, succeeding each other at intervals of twenty or twenty-five years. If all this is true, as it seems, it is as though we were being swept along willy-nilly faster and faster towards the brink of a cataract.

What I am about to say is not the solution to the problem but what seems to me to be a plausible interpretation of these apparently objective data. It involves the sense of psychoanalysis and of the work of the psychoanalysts, and consequently the sense of the psychoanalysts' patients.

Another way of looking back over the past is from the point of view of psychoanalysis, which began by departing from psychosis and has now come very close to encountering psychosis again. I consider that this path has not been determined by the patients but that, on the contrary, the patients are determined by the path of psychoanalysis. This path is probably determined by the clinical situation – that is, by the work of psychoanalysts; and by the fact, which has always been known, that the therapeutic situation is also the only valid situation for research. Whether they like it or not, psychoanalysts are an army of research workers who for the first time in human history have been enquiring systematically for about a century into the pathology of mental functioning, and through it into natural mental functioning. During the course of this enquiry they have unwittingly described a journey, outlined by their gradual discoveries and experience along the way.

Human psychopathology was always a wasteland of knowledge before the psychoanalysts, following Freud, began to penetrate it. Among the many things that Freud taught the psychoanalysts is a sense of the scientific and gradual nature of research. There is no point in running on ahead. Those who have done so have got stuck on the way. The wasteland of knowledge has to be conquered inch by inch, in the realization that the journey could not be planned. The journey took its own gradual course; it proceeded automatically on the basis of the knowledge acquired up to that point, and has continued to direct itself up to the present day. I feel it is important to understand this journey now. It is now clear that madness loomed over the wasteland of knowledge, and that it was madness which had made it a wasteland. It should now be clear that psychoanalysis has proceeded towards an understanding of madness, which is dreaded by all. It is not our patients who are going towards madness but the psychoanalysts who, with their help and duly armed with experience, are getting closer and closer to that understanding which has been feared since time immemorial. The use we make of our patients has been made possible by the use they make of us, by the fact that no one else could help them in the way that we can, and by our own investment of ourselves in the long relationship that we maintain with them. We are together, our patients and ourselves, on the journey through the wasteland.

202

Note

1 Seven or eight years ago, a well-known Italian idealist philosopher, Ugo Spirito, wrote an article on psychoanalysis in which he emphasized that the unconscious was the greatest discovery of the century, which he credited to Sigmund Freud. However, he continued by saying that the unconscious was by definition unknowable, so that the psychoanalysts were scoundrels because they pretended to ignorant people that they knew the unconscious. His conclusion was that if he had been Minister of Education (as his mentor in fact had been during the Fascist era), he would have 'persecuted' the psychoanalysts.

Bibliography

Adler, A. (1908) 'Der Aggressionstrieb in Leben und in der Neuroses', *Fortschrift Medicine*, 26.

Alexander, F. (1939) 'Psychoanalytic study of a case of essential hypertension', *Psychosomatic Medicine*, 1: 139–52.

American Psychiatric Association (1980) *Diagnostic and Statistical Manual: DSM-III*, Washington, DC.

Bertolini, M. (1984) 'Fusione, separazione, funzione dei genitori', Atti del Congresso 'Il Trauma delle Nascita', Rome: IES Mercury.

Bick, E. (1968) 'The experience of the skin in early object relation', *International Journal of Psycho-Analysis*, 69: 484–6.

Bion, W.R. (1961) *Experiences in Groups*, London: Tavistock.

—— and Rickman, J. (1943) 'Intragroup tensions in therapy: their study as a task of the group', *Lancet*, 2, 27: 678.

Bradley, N. (1967) 'Primal scene in human evolution and its phantasy derivatives in art, psychology and philosophy', *Psychoanalytic Study of Society*, I, V: 34–79.

Britton, R. (1989) 'The missing link: parental sexuality', in R. Britton, M. Feldman, and E. O'Shaughnessy (J. Steiner, ed.) *The Oedipus Complex*, London: Karnac.

Deutsch, H. (1942) 'Some forms of emotional disturbance and their relationship to schizophrenia', *The Psychoanalytic Quarterly*, 11: 301–21.

Edelheit, H. (1974) 'Crucifixion fantasies and their relation to the primal scene', *International Journal of Psycho-Analysis*, 55: 193–9.

Eidelberg, L. (1948) *Studies on Psychoanalysis*, New York: International Universities Press.

Eitingon, M. (1922) 'Bericht über die Berliner Psychoanalytische Poliklinik', March 1920 to June 1922, *Internationale Zeitschrift für arztliche Psychoanalyse*, 8: 506.

Federn, P. (1952) *Ego Psychology and the Psychoses*, London: Imago, 1953.

204

Fenaroli, L. (1974) *Gli Alberi d'Italia*, Florence: Martello.

Fenichel, O. (1937) 'The scopophilic instinct and identification', *International Journal of Psycho-Analysis*, 18: 6–34.

—— (1941) 'Problems of psychoanalytic technique', *The Psychoanalytic Quarterly*, New York.

—— (1945) *The Psychoanalytic Theory of Neurosis*, New York: Norton.

Ferenczi, S. (1909) 'Introjection and transference', in *First Contributions*, London: Hogarth Press, 1952.

—— (1932a) 'The language of the unconscious', in *Final Contributions*, London: Hogarth Press, 1955.

—— (1932b) 'Suppression of the idea of the "grotesque"', in *Final Contributions*, London: Hogarth Press, 1955.

Freud, A. (1929) 'On the theory of analysis of children', *International Journal of Psycho-Analysis*, 10: 29–38.

—— (1936) *The Ego and the Mechanisms of Defence*, London: Hogarth Press.

—— (1972) 'Comments on aggression', *International Journal of Psycho-Analysis*, 53: 163–71.

Freud, S. (1894) 'The neuro-psychoses of defence', *Standard Edition of the Complete Psychological Works of Sigmund Freud* (1950–74), SE 3: 43–72, London: Hogarth Press.

—— (1895) 'Project for a scientific psychology', SE 1: 283–393.

—— (1900) *The Interpretation of Dreams*, SE 4–5.

—— (1905) *Three Essays on the Theory of Sexuality*, SE 7: 125–244.

—— (1906) 'Delusions and dreams in *Jensen's Gradiva*', SE 9: 7–97.

—— (1910a) 'The future prospects of psychoanalytic therapy', SE 11: 139–53.

—— (1910b) 'The psycho-analytic view of psycho-disturbances of vision', SE 11: 210–18.

—— (1911) 'Psychoanalytic notes on an autobiographical account of a case of paranoia', SE 12: 3–85.

—— (1912) 'Recommendations to physicians practising psychoanalysis', SE 12: 109–21.

—— (1913) *Totem and Taboo*, SE 13: 1–162.

—— (1914) 'On narcissism: an introduction', SE 14: 3–104.

—— (1915a) 'Instincts and their vicissitudes', SE 14: 109–40.

—— (1915b) 'The unconscious', SE 14: 166–216.

—— (1915–17a) 'Mourning and melancholia', SE 14: 237–59.

—— (1915–17b) *Introductory Lectures on Psycho-Analysis*, SE 16: 243–440.

—— (1916–17) 'The libido theory and narcissism', in *Introductory Lectures on Psycho-Analysis*, SE 16: 412–31.

—— (1917) 'A metapsychological supplement to the theory of dreams', SE 14: 219–37.

—— (1918) *From the History of an Infantile Neurosis*, SE 17: 3–103.

—— (1919) 'A child is being beaten: a contribution to the study of the origins of sexual perversions', SE 17: 175–204.

—— (1920) *Beyond the Pleasure Principle*, SE 18: 1–16.

—— (1923) *The Ego and the Id*, SE 19: 3–68.

—— (1924) 'The economic problem of masochism', SE 19: 157–72.

—— (1925) 'Negation', SE 19: 235–42.

—— (1926) *Inhibitions, Symptoms and Anxiety*, SE 20: 77–178.

—— (1930) *Civilization and its Discontents*, SE 21: 64–148.

—— (1937) 'Letter to Marie Bonaparte', 27 May 1937, Appendix A, letter no. 33, in E. Jones, *The Life and Work of Sigmund Freud*, vol. 3, New York: Basic Books, 1957.

Friend, M. R. (1976) 'The role of family life in child development', *International Journal of Psycho-Analysis*, 57: 373–81.

Gaddini, E. (1959) 'Imagine corporea primaria e periodo fallico: considerazioni sulla genesi dei simboli di forma rotonda', in M. L. Mascagni, R. De Benedetti Gaddini, and R. Cortina (eds), *Scritti* (1953–85).

—— (1969) 'On imitation', *International Journal of Psycho-Analysis*, 50: 475–84.

—— (1972a) 'Aggression and the pleasure principle: towards a psychoanalytic theory of aggression, *International Journal of Psycho-Analysis*, 53: 191–7.

—— (1972b) 'Oltre l'istinto di morte (Beyond the death instinct)', *Rivista di Psicoanalisi* XVIII: 179–88.

—— (1974) 'A discussion of Dr Edelheit's paper on crucifixion fantasies and their relation to the primal scene', *International Journal of Psycho-Analysis*, 55: 201–4.

—— (1975) 'Ricerca, controversie ed evoluzione della tecnica terapeutica in psicoanalisi (Therapeutic changes in psychoanalysis: research controversies and evolution), in G. Tedeschi (ed.) *La Psicoterapia Oggi*, Il Pensiero Scientifico, Rome, pp. 10–25.

—— (1981) 'Paths through the creativity of Bion' (in English and Italian), *Rivista di Psicoanalisi* XXVII, 3–4 Monograph issue in memory of W. E. Bion.

—— (1984a) *Il Sè in Psicoanalisi*, in Atti del Congresso, 'La nascita psicologica e le sue premesse neurobiologiche', Rome: IES Mercury, 1984.

—— (1984b) 'L'Ultimo Bion (Ultimate Bion)', in M. Mascagni, A. Gaddini, R. De Benedetti Gaddini (eds), *Scritti* by E. Gaddini 1989, pp. 663–9.

Gaddini De Benedetti, R. (1974) 'Early psychosomatic symptoms and the tendency towards integration', *Psychotherapy Psychosomatics*, 23: 26–34.

—— (1977) 'Psychodermatology in children', *Proceedings of the 4th Congress of the International College of Psychosomatic Medicine*, Myoto, pp. 197–8.

—— (1978) 'Transitional objects and the psychosomatic symptom', in

S. Grolnick and L. Barkin (eds), *Between Reality and Fantasy*, New York: Aronson, pp. 110–31.

—— and Gaddini, E. (1959) 'Rumination in infancy', in L. Jessner and E. Pavenstedt (eds), *Dynamic Psychopathology in Childhood*, New York: Grune & Stratton.

—— and Gaddini E. (1974) 'Transitional objects and the process of individuation: a study of three different social groups', *Journal of the American Academy of Child Psychology*, 9, 2.

Gillespie, W. (1952) 'Notes on the analysis of sexual perversions', *International Journal of Psycho-Analysis*, 33: 397–402.

Glover, E. (1925) 'Notes on oral character formation', *International Journal of Psycho-Analysis*, 6: 131–54.

—— (1939) *Psychoanalysis*, London: John Bale Medical Publications.

—— (1955) 'The therapeutic efficacy of inexact interpretation', in *Technique of Psychoanalysis*, London: Baillière, Tindall & Co., pp. 353–66.

Greenacre, P. (1958a) 'Early psychical determinants in the development of the sense of identity', *Journal of the American Psychoanalytic Association*, 6: 612–27.

—— (1958b) 'Toward an understanding of the physical nucleus of some defence reactions', *International Journal of Psycho-Analysis*, 39: 69–76.

—— (1958c) 'The imposter', *The Psychoanalytic Quarterly*, 27: 359–82.

—— (1966) 'Problems of acting out in the transference relationship', *Monographs of the Journal of the American Academy of Child Psychology*, 1: 144.

—— (1973) 'The primal scene and the sense of reality', *The Psychoanalytic Quarterly*, 42: 10–41.

Greenson, R. R. (1954) 'The struggle against identification', *Journal of the American Psychoanalytic Association*, 2: 200–17.

—— (1966) 'A transvestite boy and a hypothesis', *International Journal of Psycho-Analysis*, 47: 396–403.

Hartmann, H. (1950) 'Comments on the psychoanalytic theory of the ego', *Psychoanalytic Study of the Child*, 5: 74–96.

—— Kris, E. and Loewenstein, R. M. (1947) 'Comments on the formation of psychic structure', *Psychoanalytic Study of the Child*, 2: 11–59.

—— (1949) 'Notes on the theory of aggression', *Psychoanalytic Study of the Child*, 3–4: 29–37.

Heimann, P. (1950) 'On countertransference', *International Journal of Psycho-Analysis*, 31: 81.

—— (1955) 'A contribution to the re-evaluation of the Oedipus Complex: the early stages', in M. Klein, P. Heimann, R. Money Kyrle (eds), *New Directions in Psycho-Analysis*, London: Hogarth.

Jacobson, E. (1964) *The Self and the Object World*, London: Hogarth Press.

Janniruberto, A. (1980) 'Studi ecografici sulla vita prenatale', presented by A. Milani Comparetti at the Psychoanalytic Centre, Bologna, 9 May.

Jones, E. (1953) *The Life and Work of Sigmund Freud*, 3 vols, New York: Basic Books, and London: Hogarth Press.

Klein, M. (1932) *The Psychoanalysis of Children*, vol. 2, in *The Writings of Melanie Klein*, London: Hogarth Press, 1975; paperback, New York: Dell Publishing Co., 1977.

—— (1952) *Developments in Psycho-Analysis*, London: Hogarth Press.

—— (1957) *Envy and Gratitude and Other Works*, vol. 3: 25–42, London: Hogarth Press, 1975; paperback, New York: Dell Publishing Co., 1977, and London: Virago Press, 1988.

Lewin, B. (1950) *The Psychoanalysis of Elation*, New York: Norton.

Limentani, A. (1981) 'On some positive aspects of the Negative Therapeutic Reaction', *International Journal of Psycho-Analysis*, 62: 379–90.

Mahler, M. (1968) *On Human Symbiosis and the Vicissitudes of Individuation*, vol. I, *Infantile Psychosis*, New York: International Universities Press.

Mahler, M. S. and La Perriere, K. (1965) 'Mother–child interaction during separation–individuation', *The Psychoanalytic Quarterly*, 34: 483–98.

Marty, P. and De M'Uzan, M. (1963) 'La Pensée opératoire', *Revue Française de Psychoanalyse* (special issue), 27: 345–56.

Rangell, L. (1975) 'Psychoanalysis and the process of change: an essay on the past, present and future', *International Journal of Psycho-Analysis*, 56: 87–99.

Rapaport, D. (1951) *Organization and Pathology of Thought*, New York: Columbia University Press.

—— (1953) 'On the psychoanalytic theory of affects', *International Journal of Psycho-Analysis*, 34: 177–98.

Reich, W. (1933) *Charakter Analyse: Technik und Grundlagen für Studierende und Praktizirende Analytiker*, Vienna: Selbstverlag d'Vorf.

Richter, H.-E. (1976) 'The role of family life in child development', *International Journal of Psycho-Analysis*, 57: 385–97.

Ritvo, S. and Provence, S. (1953) 'Form perception and imitation in some autistic children: diagnostic findings and their contextual interpretation', *Psychoanalytic Study of the Child*, 8: 155–61.

Sachs, H. (1947) 'Observation of a training analyst', *The Psychoanalytic Quarterly*, 16: 157–68.

Sander, I. W. (1977) 'The regulation of exchange in infant–caregiver system and some aspects of the content-context relationship', in *Interaction, Conversation and the Development of Language*, New York: Wiley & Sons, 1977.

Schafer, R. (1970) 'An overview of Heinz Hartmann's contributions to psychoanalysis', *International Journal of Psycho-Analysis*, 51: 425–57.

Schilder, P. (1950) *The Image and Appearance of the Human Body*, New York: International Universities Press.

Siegman, A. (1954) 'Emotionality: a hysterical character defense', *The Psychoanalytic Quarterly*, 23: 339.

Spitz, R. (1955) 'The primal cavity: a contribution to the genesis of perception and its role for psychoanalytic theory', *Psychoanalytic Study of the Child*, 10: 215–40.

Stern, D. (1985) *The Interpersonal World of the Infant*, New York: Basic Books.

Stoller, R. J. (1966) 'The mother's contribution to infantile transvestic behaviour', *International Journal of Psycho-Analysis*, 47: 384–95.

Sulloway, F. J. (1979) *Freud: Biologist of the Mind*, New York: Basic Books.

Tustin, F. (1981) *Autistic States in Childhood*, London: Routledge & Kegan Paul.

—— (1984) 'Autistic shapes', *International Review of Psycho-Analysis*, 11, 3: 279–91.

Vaihinger, H. (1924) *The Philosophy of 'As If': A System of the Theoretical, Practical and Religious Fictions of Mankind*, trans. C. K. Ogden, London: Kegan Paul, Trench, Trubner & Co.

Weiss, E. (1960) *The Structure and Dynamics of the Human Mind*, New York and London: Grune & Stratton.

Winnicott, D. W. (1951a) 'Growth and development in immaturity', in *The Family and the Individual Development*, London: Tavistock, 1965.

—— (1951b) 'Transitional objects and transitional phenomena', in *Through Paediatrics to Psychoanalysis*, London: Hogarth Press, 1975, pp. 229–43.

—— (1952) 'Psychoses and child care', in *Through Paediatrics to Psychoanalysis*, London: Hogarth Press, 1975, pp. 219–29.

—— (1957) 'The child and the family', in *First Relationships*, London: Tavistock.

—— (1958) *Through Paediatrics to Psychoanalysis*, London: Tavistock Publications.

—— (1961) 'The theory of parent–infant relationship', in *The Maturational Process and the Facilitating Environment*, London: Hogarth Press, 1965.

—— (1964) 'A review of C. G. Jung: *Memories, Dreams, Reflections*', *International Journal of Psycho-Analysis*, 45: 450–4.

—— (1965) *The Maturational Processes and the Facilitating Environment*, London: Hogarth Press, 1965.

—— (1971) *Playing and Reality*, London: Hogarth Press.

—— (1974) 'Fear of breakdown', *International Review of Psycho-Analysis*, 1: 103–7.

Name index

Abraham, K. 49, 52, 53, 94
Adler, A. 107
Alexander, F. 92, 195
American Psychiatric Association 186–7

Berlin Psychoanalytical Institute 195
Bertolini, M. 179
Bick, E. 4, 103
Bion, W.R. 14, 17, 108, 129, 130, 168
Bonaparte, Marie 6, 43
Bradley, N. 68, 74
Britton, R. 8

De Benedetti, Renata, *see* Gaddini
De M'Uzan, M. 149
Deutsch, H. 19, 24

Edelheit, H. 68, 74
Eidelberg, L. 19
Eitingon, M. 194

Federn, P. 19, 21, 25
Fenichel, O. 1, 10, 22, 195
Ferenczi, S. 19, 23, 25, 27, 56
Freud, A. 6, 9, 25, 46–7, 93, 94, 195, 197
Freud, S. 9, 16, 54–60, 64, 94, 113, 155, 178, 180, 191; on aggression/aggressive energy, instinct viii, 6–7, 35, 40–1, 43, 47, 48, 58, 59–60, 65, 73; anxiety 195;

compensation mechanism 41, 73; death instinct 48, 49, 59, 60; dreams 15, 177; ego 56, 58, 60, 199; identification 18, 23; instincts 44, 49, 55, 58, 195, 197; interest 56, 58; interpersonal relations in society 192; and Jung 91–2; on libido/libidinal energy, cathexes 7, 41, 42, 44, 57, 65, 81; life instinct 49, 50; mental functions 52–3, 54; mind-body continuum 119–20; narcissism 24, 55, 57, 195; object/relationship 22, 24, 27; oral organization 137; pleasure/unpleasure 35, 36–7, 38, 39, 40–1; primal scene 68; scientific psychology 54, 60; signal anxiety 87; space 10; spatial fiction 106; structural theory 106, 165, 195, 196, 197; therapeutic technique 95, 96; therapy and research 51; 'things' 111; and time 107; and visual thought 142
Friend, M.R. 83

Gaddini De Benedetti, R. 2, 16, 28, 77, 124, 129, 131, 144, 146
Gaddini, E. vii–ix, 1–17, 28, 62–3, 68, 77, 124, 146, 196
Gillespie, W. 196
Glover, E. 91, 94, 99, 120, 158, 196
Goethe, F.W. von 155
Greenacre, P. ix, 6, 14, 16, 94, 125,

Subject index

acting out 154–63; as defence 13, 139, 154, 155, 156–7, 160; eating 157; as mental caesura 155; as process 154–5, 157–8; as regulation of tensions 13, 155; as process 154–5, 157–8; as regulation of tensions 13, 155; sexual 74, 81, 156–7, 175
action, protomodel of 37
adaptation 23
adolescence 78
affects, formation 38
aggression: arousal 7; death instinct as 7, 49; economic aspects 7, 50, 52; as instinct 7, 46, 47, 48, 50, 59, 60, 93, 99; and libido 6, 7; and narcissistic libido 44; as part of sexual instinct 47–8; repression of 73; as response 99; sublimation of 43; vicissitudes of 43, 47, 48
aggressive cathexes: at birth 65; omni-directional 176
aggressive instinctual drives: at birth 65, 66–7; dynamics of 96; homeostasis and 66; in psycho-oral area 65; temporal primacy viii
aggressive energy 6, 35; ego and 60; internal administration 60; inward discharge 6, 7, 9, 35, 37, 38, 41–2; and libidinal energy 7, 42–3, 44–5; and oral libido 40; outward discharge 6, 7, 35, 37, 38, 44–5; requirements of 40, 41; source 35;

unpleasure and 39
agoraphobia 12; and learning to walk 133; and parents' real personalities 80
amoeba, image of 63, 64
anaclitic relationship 24
analytic relationship 10; non-integration in 12, 135; see also therapeutic relationship
anorexia 12, 136, 175
anxiety: basic 7; evolutionary process 116; instinctual 11, 85, 117; of integration 13, 147; of non-integration 13, 146–8; reduction, transitional object in 76–7; and self-loss 85; see also loss-of-self anxiety 'as if' identifications 24–5
assimilation 129, 135; primitive imitation in 136
asthma 3–4, 12, 132–3
atopical dermatitis, see skin disorders
autarky: basis 193; pre-separation 172
autistic psychosis, object relationship of 31–2
autoeroticism 55
autoplastic duplication 25, 27

baby–mother sphere 62, 109, 110, 111
basic mental organization (BMO) ix, 14, 17, 164; aim 166, 176; conservative 166; contact and

212

feeding 171; creation 129; dating 173; dual organization 67; elementary functional modalities 166; formation 166; fragmentary 14, 168–70, 172–3; integration 14–15; loss-of-self anxiety and 169–70; and mental image of bodily self 165; and needs 172; and psychosensory area 165, 166–7
'being without' and primitive mental functioning 129
belief, capacities for 174
biological functional models, mental reproduction 109
biology and psychoanalytic theory 2–3, 16
birth: aggressive cathexes at 65; libidinal cathexes at 65
BMO, *see* basic mental organization
body: child's drawing of 140–1; discovery and recognition 140; elementary image 15, 140–1, 143, 180–1; functions, development 1; recognition by mind 12, 130
body–mind continuum ix, 178
body–mind–body circuit 13, 142–3, 145, 150
borderline forms 199, 200, 201
boundary: reinforcement 156; self as 112–13
breast: instinctual charges 13; as self 61
breathing: speaking and walking, relationship 133–4; while suckling 133
bulimia 12, 136, 175

catastrophe 130, 135, 139, 140; as past event 140; survival 173; uncertainty of 173–4
catastrophic anxiety 169
character disorders 20, 195, 196, 201
child analysis 6, 9, 49, 93, 195
child, drawing of self 15, 116, 140–1, 143, 180–1
child–mother relationship 62

circle: as first graphic symbol 180–1; image in dreams 183–4; as origin of creative expression of self 15, 180; symbolism 181–2; Winnicott's use 17
clinical data, theory and 90
combined parent figure 8, 72
compensation mechanism 7, 41–2, 43, 73–4; pathological form 74; and primal-scene process 73–4
conflicts in object relationship 23
contact: as defensive fantasy 148–9; and feeding, distinction 171; importance 148; need for 171; organs 14, 167; *see also* touch
counter-transference 95–6, 102, 196
crowd identity 174, 191, 193

dark, fear of 75
death instinct 46, 60, 92–3, 94, 96; in id 59; as instinct of aggression 7, 49
defences 48; pathological 74, 78; positive 140; primitive 62; and psycho-oral mental activity 72–3
denial of primal-scene process 86–7
depression, prototype 174
depressive position 5
dermatitis, *see* skin disorders
detachment: appropriate 134; and awareness of objects 6; ignoring 135–6; process 12; and psychophysical illness 131–2; as self-loss 130; sudden 131, 134
disintegration: anxiety 101; and integration 17; and non-integration 144–5
distance, in therapy 170–1
dream consciousness: as bridge 15, 177, 183; tasks 183
dreams: fantasy and 142; first mental image of body in 151–3; latent 15, 177; loss-of-self anxiety in 150, 151, 163, 183–4; male figures in 80; manifest 15, 177; as mask 15; origin 16; as psychosensory activity 65; as rich psychology 26–8; round